QUEER POPULAR CULTURE

Queer Popular Culture

Literature, Media, Film, and Television

Edited by
Thomas Peele

LIST OF FIGURES

LIST OF CONTRIBUTORS

Kendra Birnley received her master's in English and graduate certificate in Women's Studies from Northern Arizona University in Spring 2004. In addition to teaching several different rhetoric and composition classes, she has also taught Women's Studies courses and team-taught an online humanities course about ethics and technology. Kendra's research interests include gender violence, technology and pedagogy, and the presence of women in the rhetorical tradition. Kendra's article "Embodiment, Emotion, and Gender in the Developmental Writing Classroom" appeared on McGraw-Hill's Teaching Basic Writing Listserv in May of 2004.

Daniel Mudie Cunningham is an academic specializing in contemporary art, design, and cinema. Based in the Blue Mountains, Australia, Daniel completed his Ph.D. on "white trash" film cultures at the University of Western Sydney in 2004. Since 1997, Daniel has lectured across the Design and Art History programs at the University of Western Sydney. Daniel has chapters in *Everyday eBay: Culture, Collecting and Desire* (Routledge, 2006) and *The Bent Lens* (Allen and Unwin, 2003). A widely published arts writer, Daniel has also written articles that can be found online at *PopMatters, Senses of Cinema, The Film Journal, Refractory*, among many Australian print publications. Daniel is also an independent curator, having staged over ten art exhibitions in Australian galleries since 1994.

Aviva Dove-Viebahn is currently a Ph.D. Student in the Program in Visual and Cultural Studies at the University of Rochester. She also has an M.A. in Art History from the University of Virginia and is currently coeditor of the online academic journal *Invisible Culture*. Her interests include feminist and queer theory, television studies, psychoanalysis, spectatorship, and the exploration of pleasure in visual culture.

Jill Ehnenn is Associate Professor of English at Appalachian State University where she teaches Victorian Studies and LGBT Studies/Queer Theory. She is the author of *Women's Literary Collaboration, Queerness, and Late-Victorian Culture* (Ashgate, 2008), and several articles, including one on the lesbian romance novel. Her current projects include a book on sexuality and disability in Victorian Britain and another on anti-feminist and homophobic responses to contemporary American culture, from the Religious Right.

John P. Elia, a Ph.D. from the University of California at Davis, is associate professor and associate chair in the Department of Health Education at San Francisco State University. He has published a number coedited books, articles, and book reviews in the areas of GLBT studies, queer studies, and sexuality studies. He is currently at work coediting a volume (with Dr. Gust A. Yep) entitled *Sexuality, Education and Power: Intervening in Schools and Communities.* He continues to serve on the editorial boards of the *Journal of Popular Culture, The Educational Forum,* and *Journal of Gay and Lesbian Issues in Education.* Additionally, he is the associate editor and book review editor of the *Journal of Homosexuality.*

Laura Gray-Rosendale is associate professor of English and director of the S.T.A.R. (Successful Transition and Academic Retention) Summer Writing Bridge program at Northern Arizona University. Gray-Rosendale has published *Rethinking Basic Writing: Exploring Identity, Politics, and Community in Interaction* (Erlbaum, 2000), *Alternative Rhetorics: Challenges to the Rhetorical Tradition* (State University of New York Press, 2001) with Sibylle Gruber, *Fractured Feminisms: Rhetoric, Context, and Contestation* (State University of New York Press, 2003) with Gil Harootunian, and *Radical Relevance: Toward a Scholarship of the "Whole Left"* (State University of New York Press, 2004) with Steven Rosendale. Her most recent book, *Pop Perspectives: Readings to Critique Contemporary Culture,* forthcoming from McGraw-Hill in 2007.

Terri He is currently a Ph.D. candidate in Centre for Women's Studies, University of York, United Kingdom. Terri has an M.A. in Science, Technology and Society from Linköping Universitet, Sweden, and an M.A. in Foreign Languages and Literature from National Sun Yat-sen University, Taiwan. Her research interests include gender, sexuality, globalization, post-colonial studies, and queer theory. Her "Cyberqueer in Taiwan: An Attempt at Locating Histories of the Margins" in *International Journal of Women's Studies,* and "Hybridity Online: Observing and Representing the Cybercommunity of Spiteful Tots" in *Internationalising Internet Studies* are forthcoming from Routledge in 2008.

Wendy Hsu is a graduate student in the Critical and Comparative Studies program in the Department of Music at the University of Virginia. She currently researches Asian American identities and popular music and culture in contemporary United States. Her article "Between Narrative and Expressive, Fantasy and Melodrama in Bombay Film" was published in the *Virginia Review of Asian Studies* 5 (2003). She enjoys making noisy music whenever she has the time.

Cathy Leaker is an assistant professor of Cultural Studies at Empire State College, a leader in nontraditional education for adults. After having earned her Ph.D. in Victorian Literature from the University of Rochester, she expanded her research and teaching interests to include literature, composition, drama, film, popular culture, and the politics of higher education. Her work consistently emphasizes the importance of analyzing and rendering explicit the ambiguous ideological work of cultural texts.

Christopher Le Coney is a research fellow at Harvard University who hails from "the queer frontier," having grown up in Fort Worth, Texas. He has published several articles on queer history, literature, and pop culture and is currently working on a book tracing twentieth-century cultural representations of the queer frontier.

Sheila Liming is a graduate of the College of Wooster, where she conducted research on lesbian readership in fulfillment of her Independent Study requirement. For her work, she was awarded the Waldo H. Dunn Prize for Criticism. Her graduate work at Carnegie Mellon University continues to probe themes of lesbian literature and lesbian readership with connections to popular culture.

Mark McHarry is an independent scholar. In addition to following contemporary Japanese culture, his interests include the works of Colombian author Fernando Vallejo and modern Latin American literature. He has contributed to the *Encyclopedia of Erotic Literature, Journal of Homosexuality, Z Magazine, Alternative Press Review*, and *Gay Community News*. His translations from Spanish for *ZNet* include essays and articles by Gabriel García Márquez and Ignacio Ramonet. He is currently researching the life of author-inventor Hiraga Gennai and his place in the ukiyo (floating world) of Japan's Edo period.

Sharif Mowlabocus is a D.Phil. candidate based in the department of Media and Film Studies at the University of Sussex, United Kingdom, where he currently teaches Media Studies and Popular Culture. His research interests focus on gay male cybercultures, contemporary queer subcultures, and the representation of gay masculinities in film and popular culture.

Giovanni Porfido is a lecturer in Sociology in the School of Applied Social Sciences at Durham University. He recently completed his Ph.D. in Sociology at the London School of Economics, exploring questions of homosexual visibility and visual justice in late-capitalist societies. His research interests are in the area of sexuality, social exclusion/inclusion, justice, multiculturalism, identity politics, queer theory, and visual sociology. He is currently working on the visibility of queer teens in popular and visual culture.

Jennifer Reed received her Ph.D. in Comparative Culture from UC Irvine. She is an assistant professor of Women's Studies at California State University Long Beach. She writes on sexuality and representation in popular culture and has published several essays on the work of Ellen DeGeneres.

Zoe Trodd is a member of the Tutorial Board in History and Literature at Harvard University, where she lectures on American protest literature. Her books include *Meteor of War: The John Brown Story* (Brandywine Press, 2004), *American Protest Literature* (Harvard University Press, 2006), and the forthcoming *To Plead Our Own Cause: New Slave Narratives in the Global Economy* (Cornell University Press, 2007). She has published numerous articles on American history, literature, and visual culture.

Gust A. Yep, a Ph.D. from the University of Southern California, is Professor of Speech and Communication Studies and Human Sexuality Studies at San Francisco State University. His work has been published in numerous interdisciplinary journals and anthologies. He is the lead editor of *Queer Theory and Communication: From Disciplining Queers to Queering the Discipline(s)* (Harrington Park Press, 2003) and coeditor of the upcoming anthologies, *The Contested Terrain of Lesbian, Gay, Bisexual, and Transgender Studies and Queer Theory* and *Sexualities and Power in Education: Intervening in Schools and Communities*. He also coauthored *Privacy and Disclosure of HIV in Interpersonal Relationships* (Erlbaum, 2003), which was nominated for the 2004 International Communication Association "Book of the Year" Award. Dr. Yep is currently serving as the editor of the Non-Serial Publications (Book) Series of the National Communication Association.

Amalia Ziv, a Ph.D. from Tel Aviv University, is a lecturer at the Department of Literature and the Program for Women and Gender Studies, Tel Aviv University. She is coeditor of *Beyond Sexuality: Selected Papers in Lesbian and Gay Studies and Queer Theory* (Hakibbutz Hameuchad, 2003) and has published several articles in Hebrew on queer theory and culture, and on pornography. Among her publications are "Toward a History of Bars in Israel," in *Sappho in the Holy Land: Lesbian Existence and Dilemmas in Contemporary Israel*, ed. Chava Frankfurt-Nachmias and Erella Shadmi (New York: State University of New York Press, 2004) and "Shameful Fantasies: Cross Gender Queer Sex in Lesbian Erotic Fiction," in *Gay Shame*, ed. David Halperin and Valerie Traub (University of Chicago Press, forthcoming).

ACKNOWLEDGMENTS

MANY THANKS TO THE ASSISTANT EDITORS OF THIS COLLECTION: Mary Andrew, Andrea Ascuena, Amy Garrett-Brown, Patri Thompson, and Sarah Olson, who together tracked down hundreds of sources to check the citations in this collection. Their work was invaluable, and very much appreciated. Thanks also to the Office of the Dean of the College of Arts and Sciences at Boise State University; their award to me of the Faculty Research Associates Program grant allowed me the time I needed to complete this work. Thanks also to Professor Carol Martin of Boise State University, who helped me to navigate administrative requirements. I am extremely grateful to my editors at Palgrave, Farideh Koohi-Kamali and Brigitte Shull, for their support, perseverance, and generosity.

Introduction: Popular Culture, Queer Culture

Thomas Peele

THE TITLE OF RICHARD GREENBERG'S PLAY *Take Me Out*, winner of multiple Tony awards, works on many levels. In its most obvious sense, the title refers to the subject of the play: baseball. Next, as an imperative, the title functions as the main character's demand that he be taken out of sexuality's notorious closet; the play begins with its leading character, Darren Lemming, a baseball superstar, announcing matter-of-factly at a press conference that he is gay. Finally, and most ambiguously, the title reverses the direction of the phrase "take you out" and suggests (inadvertently?) that Lemming, in coming out, is simultaneously asking to be taken out, to be murdered.

The tension in *Take Me Out* results from deception. In an act of multicultural acceptance (with social class as the marker of cultural difference), Kippy Sunderstrom, Darren Lemming's best friend and teammate, tells a lie. Sunderstrom writes a letter of apology to Lemming and attributes that letter to another teammate, Shane Mungitt. The reason for the apology is that Mungitt, at a press conference, refers to Lemming as a "faggot." Sunderstrom writes the letter and says that Mungitt did, because he cannot believe that Mungitt actually feels that way. Sunderstrom believes that Mungitt only used the word as a result of his cultural difference, a cultural difference that Sunderstrom attributes to a lack of exposure to more contemporary ideas. The lie that Sunderstrom tells, though, backfires; rather than working to change Mungitt's views about gay men and others whom he perceives as different from himself, it only puts Mungitt in a position to accomplish greater violence.

Sunderstrom relies on the assumption that Mungitt's hatred of gay men and others is, to paraphrase Stanley Fish, a simple hatred, easily overcome through explanation. What Mungitt demonstrates is that his hatred is deep-rooted and complex, not at all responsive to Sunderstrom's persuasion.

Queer representations in popular culture often rely on this formula. The narratives are constructed around the assumption that once people know better, they will change their views. It is important to consider this representation in popular culture since popular culture both reflects current values and teaches them to us.

As Jennifer Reed argues in her essay in this collection on Ellen DeGeneres's movement from queer, to gay, to postgay, television teaches us about identity. Among other things, television, movies, the Internet, music, and fashion provide various normative discourses that simultaneously teach us and reinforce the division between the acceptable and the unacceptable. And, as Michael Warner points out, "educational practices that rely on the tolerant—in this case, the heterosexual—to accept what might be to them intolerable—in this case, the queer—necessarily overlook the desirability of queer culture" (xxi). Such representations are reductive because they cannot think of queer culture as desirable, but only as acceptable. Representations that ask for acceptance only make the claim that there is nothing really wrong with queer culture, but they have nothing to say about the ways in which queer culture might offer powerful models of community.

In addition, as Deborah Britzman writes, "curricula that purport to be inclusive may actually work to produce new forms of exclusivity *if* the only subject positions offered are the tolerant normal and the tolerated subaltern" (160). Because the texts of popular culture frequently represent lesbian and gay people as being in need of acceptance by straight people, just as Kippy Sunderstrom represents Darren Lemming, these texts construct a heterosexual audience that is in a position to be tolerant. The construction of this subject position, in turn, reproduces the very marginalization of lesbians and gay men that the text might be trying to undermine, since this construction more or less permanently isolates queer culture. And, as Britzman suggests, a model of acceptance that relies on tolerance might require some subjectivities to remain intolerable.

The now discontinued but for ten years hugely popular sitcom *Friends* demonstrates this ideological stance. As I have written elsewhere, the show frequently toys with the theme of homoerotic desire, yet that desire is never allowed a serious moment (Peele). Instead, the specter of same-sex desire, especially between the male regulars on the show, is suggested, but the markers of that desire are frequently connotative and thus ambiguous. Same-sex desire between the men is regularly invoked to propel the action of the series, but it is never allowed to achieve sexual expression. Queer desire is tolerated and made use of, but it is never presented as a desirable state, at least among the men of the series. In this series, queer female desire gets slightly more respect, as there is a regularly appearing female couple, one of whom is the former wife of one of the male regulars. In general, however, these two are trotted out in much the same way as the specter of male same-sex desire. The characters are regular but marginal; they are in no way central to plot. They are used to propel the action of the show but either both of them are almost always simultaneously required to provide erotic fantasy material for the representatives of heteromasculinity, or one of them is required to behave in an aggressive and confrontational manner (suggesting the concept of the mythic-mannish lesbian, as Aviva Dove-Viebahn discusses it in this collection). Finally, the ex-wife of one of the main cast members is often invoked by that cast member as a marker of his own sexual insufficiency; the implication is that her lesbian desire is exclusively the result of his failed heteromasculinity. The women rarely get beyond their subordinate role; they are tolerated so long as they can provide erotic fantasy material or evidence of male sexual insufficiency, but they rarely emerge as more or less complete individuals whose life might in some way provide a desirable model of identity.

This is not to say that there are not more nuanced and complex queer representations on television. As Cathy Leaker points out in this collection, daytime soaps have some surprisingly queercentric moments. Cable networks such as HBO and Showtime, relying less on the commercial dollar, have been remarkably uncompromising in some of their queer representations. The series *Six Feet Under* included an interracial gay male couple that was integral to the show's plot from the beginning of its five-year run. A cable network production, therefore reaching a significantly smaller audience, and, unlike *Friends*, a drama, the show nevertheless explored the pleasures and perils of contemporary queer identity, including the repeated problem of being merely tolerated, a problem that resulted not only from queer identity but also from racial identity and the intersections of the two. The intersection of queer and racial identities is explored in this collection by Gust Yep and John Elia in their analysis of another cable series, *Noah's Arc*. HBO's series, *Sex and the City*, included two gay men in roles that were essential to the plot line. One of these men achieves a state of partnered bliss long before any of the female stars, and thus becomes a source of advice and inspiration for the women. The other gay man, though a stark manifestation of a bitchy, controlling queen, is more than that: at odd moments, he is vulnerable. What is more, his bitch queer persona is not the source of shame, but rather a source of pride. The character, Anthony, is at the top of his game, an enviable force of nature. In addition to gay and lesbian representations, transgender subjects are also making their way onto the small screen, notably with prominent actors Tom Wilkinson and Jessica Lange appearing in *Normal*.

Probably cable television's biggest hit ever, *The Sopranos* in 2006 had a gay character. As Sharif Mowlabocus argues in this collection, queer presence in gangster films, especially in the United Kingdom, is not as uncommon as one might think. The development of this character, in addition to serving as a recuperation of queer identity in gangster stories, suggests the spectacularization of queer identity, as Giovanni Porfido discusses with regard to the British version of *Queer as Folk*. The actor who plays the character on *The Sopranos*, Joseph Gannascoli, explicitly requested that the producers of the show make his character gay so that he could expand the character's presence: "I thought that was a way of separating myself from the other actors, because I would have been in the background most of the time. You know, line here, line there, and nothing really substantial" (Rowe). Queer identity, then, is now specifically appropriated to exploit market forces.

As Suzanna Walters writes, "The complexity and diversity of the gay and lesbian community needs to be *represented*, not promoted as simply heterosexuality with a twist" (24). Whether or not this representation has been accomplished, or is even achievable, remains an open question. The authors in this collection analyze current and historical queer representations, both those thought to be queer unfriendly as well as queer friendly. Sheila Liming examines the reading practices of young women attempting to learn about lesbian identity; Terri He maps the movement of the term queer as it travels from the United States and Europe across Taiwan; Mark McHarry, in a similar kind of mapping, describes how young male characters in Japanese comics have been homoerotically reinscribed, crossing gender and national boundaries, in a form called yaoi. Daniel Cunningham looks at how the concepts of maps and the road function in new queer cinema. Wendy Hsu examines how *Hedwig and the Angry Inch* works to subvert the gender binary as presented in Plato, while Laura Gray-Rosendale and Kendra Birnley describe their work with queer identities and popular culture in the writing classroom. Finally, Jill Ehnenn examines how responses to the *Harry Potter* series from queer and proto-queer-identified youth, queer adults, and those on the religious and political far-right might intersect, especially regarding the issues of difference and Otherness. Collectively, they seek to look at how these texts of popular culture both replay mainstream representations and undermine them; to examine intersections of queer and ethnic identities; to study the commercialization of queer identities; to recuperate queer identities from texts where those identities are thought not to exist; to examine readers' constructions of queer identities; to examine queer work in global contexts; to map the production of queer identities; and to examine queer moments in the classroom.

These chapters broaden both the kinds of texts we look at and how we look at them; they employ a queercentric textual analysis, historical research, and the analysis of aspects of popular culture with which students are familiar but about which they are unlikely to have spent much time thinking. As Nikki Sullivan, in *A Critical Introduction to Queer Theory*, writes, "there is no single correct way to queer popular culture. . . . the queering of popular culture has taken multifarious forms, has focused on different issues, and has drawn on a range of theoretical positions" (189). Such is the nature of this interdisciplinary collection. The writers, in women's studies, comparative culture, languages and literature, media and film studies, history, sociology, speech and communication, and rhetoric and composition, all share an interest in the study of popular culture with a specific emphasis on queer culture. The collection does not adhere to a particular set of analytical methods; each writer brings her or his own disciplinary methods to their subject.

The essays in this collection represent a historical moment in queer representation, as many of them address some of the artifacts of popular culture, especially television shows and movies, that will be significantly less available in the next ten years. Both *Friends* and *Will and Grace* are already on air only as reruns, their cultural contexts and significance already obscure. And, since the texts present lively readings of these artifacts, we hope that they can be used to engage students in discussions of queer representation in popular culture. The historical perspective offered in these essays can be compared with the current era's landscape of queer representations—in 2010, *Modern Family* and *Glee*. The essays in this collection also examine the current wide visibility of queer life in some parts of the world.[1] Richard Hatch, an openly gay man and vicious competitor, was the first survivor of the *Survivor* reality show. Gay men have had their own reality show, *Boy Meets Boy*, in which straight men have to play gay. Michael Cunningham, gay author of *The Hours*, won the Pulitzer prize in fiction for that novel, in which the primary characters are lesbian or gay.

This volume aims to examine and complicate that visibility. After all, while we do have *Glee* and *Modern Family* do we really have anything more than amplified stereotypes of gay men and lesbians? Do our students who view this program think about the implications of having a straight man play a gay man? To what extent do queer representations undermine the gender hierarchy? How does the commodification of queer culture affect that culture? How is it that while we have television programs such as this, we continue to have extreme violence against gay men and lesbians? In 2006, transgender performer Kevin Aviance was attacked in New York; his jaw was broken (Fahim); the mayor of Moscow condoned state violence against gay and lesbian activists who attempted to stage a peaceful parade and lay flowers on the Tomb of the Unknown Soldier ("Gay"); in Iran, gay teenagers have been publicly executed ("Iran").

Proliferating queer representations in popular culture, however various and diverse, have not eliminated the problem of heteronormativity or antiqueer violence. Furthermore, as Eric Clarke points out, while "enthusiastic narratives about lesbian and gay inclusion seem at first glance to be warranted, they fail to ask how this inclusion is defined, and on what terms it is granted" (1). Clarke's argument addresses the inclusion of queers in the public sphere; he questions "how far the inclusive mechanisms of the public sphere can go in overcoming their historical limitations and admitting excluded groups, particularly when the very nature of such groups challenges the proprietary codes that (inappropriately) shape publicity practices" (5). Clarke's perspective on queer representation suggests that the excitement surrounding the 2006 Oscar nominations might not be warranted. Three of the biggest queer contestants were *Brokeback Mountain*, nominated for best actor, best film, and best supporting actor, among others; *TransAmerica*, nominated for best actress; and *Capote*, nominated for (and winning) best actor. Even though each of these films presents queer content in a very public forum, each film successfully places its protagonist firmly within the cultural space inhabited by unhappiness, murder, despair, freakishness, and invisibility, a cultural space long-familiar to queers. When Ennis and Jack come down from Brokeback, their lives are consumed by anger, misery, and death. As Christopher Le Coney and Zoe Trodd point out in this volume, the final scene from the film leaves Ennis alone while his daughter drives off into the sunset of heterosexual bliss. As presented in *Capote*, the eponymous character has perhaps not one redeeming social characteristic. His writing, though celebrated, is the result of the manipulation of people whose lives are at stake. Otherwise, he is self-absorbed, emotionally remote, and cruel. Finally, *TransAmerica*'s Bree Osbourne, hypercultivated well beyond the point of camp, routinely drops French phrases into conversations with her recently discovered, teenage, prostitute, drug-addict son; she seems to have modeled herself entirely on Michael from *The Boys in the Band*. More tragically, however, is that it is her failure to completely pass as woman, her failure to erase her transgender, that results in a rupture between her and her son. Passing as a woman is indeed her all consuming passion, a passion, as Amalia Ziv notes in this collection, that is not shared by all transgender women. As Clarke, quoting Amy Gluckman and Betsy Reed, writes, "What good does liberation do a queen if his [*sic*] rights depend on no longer being a queen?" (10). Does Bree Osbourne's transgender liberation depend entirely on the erasure of her transgender status?

Clarke's concerns about the sanitizing of queer life are inescapable; do positive representation and queer equality spell the end of queer culture? Is acceptance based on homogeneity rather than difference? Can the public sphere adjust to accommodate a difference that has historically been used to define the public sphere? Do the many current representations redefine queer subjectivity or merely reinforce hegemonic constructions? The answers to these questions are contextual; they shift as the contexts shift.

As David Halperin argues,

> The last thing we should want to do, then, is to devise and distribute a kind of
> cultural resistance meter, a test to determine how radically transformative, or
> *truly queer*, one practice or another *really* is. . . . Without advancing a notion of
> political ascesis so minimal and empty that it might include shopping for the
> right outfit, in other words, what we really need to do is to avoid formulating
> a set of criteria for resistance so rigorous and systematic that they would
> absolutely exclude the possibility that resistance could *ever* take the form of
> shopping for the right outfit. (115)

In this work, Halperin notes that "queer culture is likely to suffer, on a larger
political scale, the normalizing vicissitudes already undergone by so-called
queer theory" (113). Yet his analysis holds out the possibility that queer
representation in popular culture might to some extent function to reshape
hegemonic cultural narratives about nonnormative sexuality. Since identity is
the product of a relation of power, queer identity and queer culture must
necessarily change as the unacceptable becomes acceptable, however transi-
tory that acceptability might be. The essays in this text are not radical;
none of them claim that hegemonic narratives about nonnormative sexuality
have been completely undermined. Instead, the essays examine the ways that
popular culture destabilizes and decenters queer subjectivity. They chart
queer representations as they exist in word and image and provide insightful
readings of how and to what extent those representations might challenge or
confirm hegemonic narratives.

NOTE

1. Though this collection contains only one essay that was presented at the
   American Culture Association/Popular Culture Association International
   Conference in the spring of 2003, it is nevertheless the result of the out-
   standing conference presentations on queer subjects at that conference. That
   year in particular, the papers were extremely rich and varied in their approaches
   to queer subjects. More people had more to say about more subjects—the
   number of overtly queer representation on television, in films, and on the
   Internet seemed to be drawing more people into discussion and analysis of
   these representations.

WORKS CITED

Boy Meets Boy. Bravo. 29 July–2 Sept. 2003.
The Boys in the Band. Dir. William Friedkin. National General Pictures, 1970.
Britzman, Deborah P. "Is There a Queer Pedagogy? Or, Stop Reading Straight."
   Educational Theory 45 (1995): 151–65.

Brokeback Mountain. Dir. Ang Lee. Focus, 2005.

Capote. Dir. Bennett Miller. United Artists, 2006.

Clarke, Eric O. *Virtuous Vice: Homoeroticism and the Public Sphere*. Raleigh, NC: Duke UP, 2000.

Cunningham, Michael. *The Hours*. New York: Picador, 2002.

Fahim, Kareem. "Three Arrested in Attack on Singer on East Side." *The New York Times* 11 June 2006, late ed.: A40.

Fish, Stanley. "Boutique Multiculturalism, or Why Liberals Are Incapable of Thinking about Hate Speech." *Critical Inquiry* 23 (1997): 378–95.

Friends. NBC. 22 Sept. 1994–6 May 2004.

"Gay Activists Beaten by Extremists, Jailed by Police." *Los Angeles Times* 28 May 2006, home ed.: A38.

Greenberg, Richard. *Take Me Out*. New York: Dramatist's Play Service, 2004.

Halperin, David. *St. Foucault: Towards a Gay Hagiography*. New York: Oxford UP, 1995.

Happy, Texas. Dir. Mark Illsley. Perf. Steve Zahn. Miramax, 1999.

Hedwig and the Angry Inch. Dir. John Cameron Mitchell. New Line Home Entertainment, 2001.

"Iran Executes Two Gay Teens in Public Hangings." *UKGaynews.org.UK* 21 July 2005. 15 June 2006 <http://www.ukgaynews.org.uk/Archive/2005july/2101.htm>.

Noah's Arc. LOGO. 19 Oct. 2005–Present.

Normal. Dir. Jane Anderson. HBO. 2003.

"The One with Phoebe's Husband." *Friends*. NBC 12 Oct. 1995.

Peele, Thomas. "Composition, Popular Culture, and Heteronormativity." *Computers and Composition Online*. 2004. 15 June 2006 <http://www.bgsu.edu/cconline/home.htm>.

Queer as Folk. Channel 4. 23 Feb. 1999–22 Feb. 2000.

Road Trip. Dir. Todd Phillips. Perf. Steve Zahn. Dreamworks SKG, 2000.

Rowe, Douglas J. "Gay '*Sopranos*' Mobster Glad for Exposure." Interview with Joseph Gannascoli. Gay.com. 15 June 2006 <http://www.gay.com/entertainment/news/?sernum=1232>.

Sex and the City. HBO. 6 June 1998–22 Feb. 2004.

Six Feet Under. HBO. 3 June 2001–21 Aug. 2005.

The Sopranos. HBO. 10 Jan. 1999–Present.

Sullivan, Nikki. *A Critical Introduction to Queer Theory*. New York: New York UP, 2003.

Survivor. CBS. Perf. Richard Hatch. 31 May–23 Aug. 2000.

TransAmerica. Dir. Duncan Tucker. IFC Films, 2005.

Walters, Suzanna Danuta. *All the Rage: The Story of Gay Visibility in America*. Chicago: U of Chicago P, 2001.

Warner, Michael. Introduction. *Fear of a Queer Planet: Queer Politics and Social Theory*. Ed. Michael Warner. Minneapolis: U of Minnesota P, 1994. vii–x.

Will and Grace. NBC. 21 Sept. 1998–18 May 2006.

CHAPTER 1

THE THREE PHASES OF ELLEN: FROM QUEER TO GAY TO POSTGAY

JENNIFER REED

Abstract: *This chapter explores the representational politics of Ellen DeGeneres' two sitcoms, Ellen (ABC 1993–98) and* The Ellen Show *(CBS, 2001). In particular, I look at her character's evolution from a queer character as she flirted with coming out, to a lesbian after she famously came out, to a postgay character in her second sitcom. These three characterizations represent three distinct positions in queer, gay, lesbian politics, and thus offer not only three perspectives on queer identity, but also the explicit example of the creation and re-creation of those identities.*

IT IS NOT NEWS AT THIS POINT TO SAY THAT ELLEN DEGENERES made television history in 1997 when she came out as a lesbian—in both her incarnations as a public person and as the character Ellen Morgan on *Ellen*. Not the first lesbian on television, the history-making was in the creation of a life for a lesbian as the star of the show. Although the series was cancelled after only one season of Ellen as a lesbian, it was indeed a significant cultural moment for many viewers, for many reasons.

By the time Ellen came out, the show was at the end of its fourth season. It had been a show adrift for much of its run, largely because the lead character, Ellen, did not have a sexual identity. This was clear to the producers of the show for some time. In an interview with *The Boston Globe*, one of the show's producers, Mark Driscoll, makes the point, "Everyone knew the series was missing something at its core . . . The problem was not that the writers weren't writing good scripts, it's that there was no center to the show. . . . Ellen whose character is 35 was an asexual character who hung out with friends, really exhibiting behavior more suited to 20-somethings" (Biddle D1).

Throughout the fourth season, the show began dropping hints that Ellen may be gay. (And "gay" is the word Ellen eventually used most often to describe her own sexuality.) With the hints on the show, there was plenty of speculation in the press. It was an open secret that depended not so much on whether Ellen really was gay, but when she would come out. According to DeGeneres, the plan was to come out much earlier in the season, but it was delayed until ABC gave the nod to do it. DeGeneres explains in a May 12, 1998 interview with Larry King:

> Well, the teasing was not supposed to go on that long. The teasing was supposed to be just a few episodes and then I thought the coming out episode was to air maybe episode 10, something like that. It just—we never got the OK. It just kept getting pushed back, and the story leaked out way in advance before anybody—we didn't want it to leak—we wanted the teases to make the audience look every week and wonder if we were going in the direction it seemed it was going.

This was not about a single television series. It was more of an epic drama. It was an intertextual media event. Whatever happened, or what was going to happen on the television show was commented upon or speculated about in other media: news articles in magazines and newspapers, including polls asking what people thought of her coming out, talk shows with Ellen DeGeneres doing the talking, talk shows with semiserious news figures such as Charlie Rose and Larry King interviewing experts about the possibilities of Ellen coming out, and entertainment shows creating a buzz about Ellen and then reporting on the buzz. Certainly, the implications of Ellen's saga of coming out and creating a lesbian life, the series getting cancelled, and then starting another series three years later, were all formed at least as much in the mass media's discussion about it as in the actual series itself. And in this case there was yet another layer of mass media reporting and speculation about DeGeneres' personal love life with Anne Heche and their subsequent breakup. Taken together, this was a particularly public time for lesbian identity in the person of Ellen DeGeneres.

The unfolding of this epic in mass media, of course, made it an important participant in the movement of gay and lesbian representational politics, performance, and identity and also perhaps pointed to both the possibilities and limits of liberal pluralist acceptance among those viewers for whom gay and lesbian people are others. Mass media is where public life happens at this point in Western history. And television in particular can be seen as the most productive place to play out this drama if we see it as a place where viewers learn about others. According to John Hartley in *Uses of Television*,

television is a "teacher in the best sense," through its use of cross-demographic communication, or "teaching people from 'they' communities how to operate successfully in institutions, from school to 'life,' not of their own making" (32, 31).

For Hartley, television teaches in the "anthropological," not "schooling" (45) sense of the word, as it can explore "the way in which different populations with no necessary mutual affinity do produce and maintain knowledge about each other, communicate with each other, stay in touch" (32). In fact, the teaching that happens on television is the most influential teaching that allows us to cohere as a society. For Hartley, television "teaches the formation of identity and citizenship in a society characterized by the unknowability of its nevertheless sovereign populations" (46). It is the primary way we understand the differences between us. And more importantly, it is the place we learn how to behave toward each other as fellow citizens. Again in Hartley's words, "cross demographic communication is more important than identity, although the effort to communicate respectfully and equitably is a recognition of identity and difference" (32). The point here is that the actual differences that are represented are less important than learning to deal with difference "respectfully and equitably."

In fact, for Hartley, television is actually a teacher of citizenship, two new kinds made possible, in part, because of mass media: what he calls cultural citizenship and do-it-yourself (DIY) citizenship (155). In Hartley's view, citizenship "needs to be seen in historical rather than categorical terms; it is an evolving and cumulative concept adapting to changes in western development" (157). Citizenship has developed since the Enlightenment period from civil citizenship, involving individual freedoms, through political citizenship that centered especially on voting rights, to social citizenship issues such as rights to social welfare (162–63). Cultural citizenship is the fourth step in this process and is dependent on mass media (163–64). It also applies mostly to "the disenfranchised or unenfranchised so-called 'minorities' " (163) and is the citizenship that recognizes distinct identities. He writes:

> Oddly enough, these great unknowable masses that have stalked the pages of social and media theory, government legislation and cultural criticism since the nineteenth century have themselves been the locus of the development of the form of citizenship based not on sameness (undifferentiated mass), but on difference. The so-called masses . . . are historically the site whence the fourth type of citizenship has arisen, taking *difference* to the point where it can be claimed, and increasingly recognized, as a human right. (164)

As a right, we come to expect it, and that happens through the mass media, the massest of which, by far, is television. It has created a cultural citizenship among the marginalized, including gays and lesbians, along with many others—a citizenship that "allowed such communities among the 'masses' both to participate freely as audience along with all the other people in the mediasphere, and to observe an official culture that was not comfortable with their presence" (170).

Some of my questions about the series *Ellen* and later *The Ellen Show* (which debuted on CBS in the fall of 2001 and ended the same season) are about how they communicated difference "respectfully and equitably," how they constructed a lesbian character, for what kinds of viewers, and what that taught us, each in our own unknowable, sovereign populations. And how did these series "take difference to the point where it can be claimed, and increasingly recognized as a human right?" In other words, what do these series teach, and to whom? And is it possible to see them as part of a discourse creating new kinds of citizenship?

This chapter will explore those questions by looking at three seasons of Ellen DeGeneres' lesbian persona on her sitcoms, each one corresponding to a distinct set of terms and strategies in the socioperformative politics of same-sex desire. If that sounds a little vague, it is because the use of any label grounds the politics in a particular place. That is, each term (gay, lesbian, queer, homosexual) carries with it the histories and politics of meanings. And my contention here is that each season of *Ellen/The Ellen Show* speaks most closely to the discourses, histories, and goals of separate, identifiable moments in the politics of the creation and assertion of spaces in the dominant culture for identities constructed around same-sex desire.

ELLEN'S QUEER YEAR

Back to where Ellen's public lesbian presence began: at the beginning of the fourth season of *Ellen*, the show began to drop hints that Ellen may be a lesbian. This was immediately followed by speculation in entertainment news about the possibility of Ellen Morgan, the character played by Ellen DeGeneres, coming out. This was very exciting news for this lesbian, and for many of my queer friends. The hints and rumors worked very well to get us to watch for what would come next. The excitement was inseparable from our unconfirmed knowledge, our assumption that Ellen DeGeneres was herself a lesbian. Taken together, this created a very queer atmosphere. It was based mostly on the open secret, the wink, the anticipation—and it played itself out both on the show and in the media about the show.

Ellen went on the talk show circuit to promote her CD, *Taste This*, released right at the time the rumors were in full swing. She did interviews on *Good Morning America, Late Show with David Letterman, The Rosie O'Donnell Show*, and others in which she was asked about her character coming out. In all of those interviews she played with the interviewer and the audience, but she would not answer directly. The interviews with David Letterman and Rosie O'Donnell made for great television. She is a comedic match for both of them, and the banter back and forth was not only very funny, it added to the queer mystique. She never uttered the word lesbian but did say that her character might reveal herself to be Lebanese later in the season with hints along the way: "You've seen her eating baba ghanoush, hummus. . . . She's got Casey Kasem posters on her wall." The exchange with Rosie O'Donnell was particularly queerly productive, since O'Donnell too at that time was widely believed to be a lesbian and has of course since publicly come out. At the time though, they were two not-quite-all-the-way-out nationally famous lesbian comics, discussing being out on a national daytime talk show, without saying the word. Rosie replied to Ellen, "you know, I think I might be Lebanese too," and Ellen agreed that she did seem kind of Lebanese to her (DeGeneres, *Rosie*).

Operating in the liminal spaces of straight society this way created a "queer discourse" that allowed for a "queer reading," as defined by Alexander Doty in *Making Things Perfectly Queer: Interpreting Mass Culture*. His succinct definition of queerness "is a quality related to any expression that can be marked as contra-, non-, or anti-straight" (xv). Doty, like other queer theorists, emphasizes the idea of queerness not being any particular category. It is, in his words "an open and flexible space" (xv), marked only by "a range of nonstraight expression in, or in response to, mass culture. This range includes specifically gay, lesbian, and bisexual expressions; but it also includes all other potential (and potentially unclassifiable) nonstraight positions" (xvi).

Ellen opened up nonstraight positions during this year, and the positions from which she operated were unclassifiable. She was not straight and she was not lesbian. By refusing any particular category, and in so doing, by foregrounding heterosexuality as a social institution, DeGeneres was able to do the most queerly productive work of her career thus far. The hints on the show that started very early in the season—along with the narrative changes that occurred, and the rumors that saturated all of the national entertainment news that year—combined to make it impossible to not know that something queer was going on here, and not just for queer readers.

The hints made their way onto almost every episode. One of the first was when she was sitting on the H of the Hollywood Sign mourning her parents' breakup. They find her there and try to explain what has happened, and she says, "What if I told you something about me that just shocked you? Like what if I told you I was lllleeeft-handed?" ("Splitsville, Man"). Another occurred in "Give Me Equity or Give Me Death," when she was looking at a house to buy and came walking out of the closet. Her real estate person says, "Oh, you were in the closet." And Ellen replies, "Yeah, I wouldn't want to spend too much time in there." There are well-placed pictures of k.d. lang above her bed, and there is a moment when Paige holds up boxer shorts in a pile of laundry, thinking they are Ellen's male roommate's, but Ellen grabs them, indicating that they are hers. These kinds of hints happened all season long and proved to be the cleverest jokes of the entire run of the show. They were knowing, pointed, and, ironically enough, the creation of such liminality gave the show some focus.

The narrative structure also became more focused, even as Ellen clearly had no solid place to be in the social milieu in which she existed. Many of the plots for each episode developed around the fact that Ellen just did not fit. For example in "The Pregnancy Test," which aired in November 1996, Ellen and her friends Paige and Audrey get together for a girls' night at Ellen's apartment. Paige brings pregnancy tests because she thinks she might be pregnant. The jokes in the scene revolve around the fact that Ellen is not really one of the girls. For instance, Audrey has a new boyfriend about whom everyone but Ellen knows. Ellen is hurt that Audrey did not tell her about the new boyfriend; and Audrey explains that she did not want to make Ellen feel bad because she is alone. Audrey suggests that they all take the pregnancy tests in support of Paige who is afraid about finding out if she is pregnant. The ensuing jokes center on the impossibility of Ellen's "circle turning blue," or of her being pregnant. It is clear that it is not just that Ellen does not have a boyfriend at the moment that is funny (which is not really that funny), but that she is just not part of the economy in which pregnancy occurs. Ellen is excluded from the fundamental elements of their lifestyles as straight women. In fact Paige and Audrey bond over the possibilities of being pregnant, discussing how it would change their lives and identities. This is noteworthy because they are not friends. They have nothing in common except that they are both friends with Ellen. They usually do not engage with each other at all. This scenario, impending, unplanned pregnancy brings them together over what they do have in common: straight womanhood. Throughout their exchange, Ellen performs her increasing hurt and frustration at her increasing invisibility. Ellen tries to take part in the conversation but she is pointedly ignored and talked over. It is a very effective comedic bit and ideologically even more significant.

Paige and Audrey perform normative heterosexuality and, in so doing, point to Ellen's outsider status. One of the most significant things this did is foreground what materialist feminist Monique Wittig calls the "heterosexual contract."[1] For Wittig the social contract itself is the heterosexual contract. In her essay "On the Social Contract," she writes: "For to live in society is to live in heterosexuality. In fact, in my mind social contract and heterosexuality are two super-imposable notions" (40). The power of heterosexuality lies in its complete and mostly unquestioned normativity. Wittig explains, "Because even if they, if we, do not consent, we cannot think outside the mental categories of heterosexuality. Heterosexuality is always already there within all mental categories" (43). It just is. Thus, it is invisible. Ellen's performance of her outsider status, though, made it visible as the normative, dominating institution that it is simply by not being a part of it. This denaturalizing of heterosexuality is part of what queered Ellen that season.

She queered herself in a slightly different way with her overperformance of woman in one episode called "Not-So-Great Expectations," which also aired in November 1996. This episode finds her at a dating service with her mother. Through a series of sitcom-type events, Ellen is forced into making a video to try to get a man. Ellen ends up in full feminine regalia with big hair, full makeup, and plunging neckline that can barely hold her voluptuous bosom. As she is unveiled to the audience, there is immediate laughter simply at the sight of her. In fact, she used that image of herself in a promo of her show saying, "This is what I meant by coming out." With some coaching from Paige, she works at heterosexual feminine sexuality, and it is hilarious to watch because it is so obviously a performance. She is clearly in drag here. This foregrounded performance of woman points to the performance of heterogender[2] itself and is thus another move toward the denaturalizing of heterosexuality.[3]

Later in that episode, Ellen shows up at a country/Western bar dressed as a cowboy, looking, incidentally, for her mother to save her from a man whom she sees as being lecherous. Ellen is all boy here, right down to her chaps. Moving from femme to butch in the same episode, again, denaturalizes heterogender and provides a queer discourse to be read by those who can read that queerly. Ellen takes herself out of the heterosexual economy also by not playing by the rules.

Taken together, these strategies worked to denaturalize heterosexuality and create a queer text that was hard to miss by any reader, but was especially savored by queer readers. By placing Ellen outside the norms of heterosexuality, but not placing her in any other sexual category, the show was able to mine the political potential of queer. The foregrounding of heterosexuality not as a natural state of being but as a social institution is a radical move in mainstream media. Further, to queer a character for an entire season allows us to conceptualize "outside the relatively clear-cut and essentializing categories of sexual identity under which most people function" (Doty 15). This also allows us out of the confines of realism imposed by most sitcoms. Queer readings do not have to correspond precisely to lived identity. This is part of its liberatory potential. As Doty states, queer "positions, readings, and pleasures also suggest that what happens in cultural reception goes beyond the traditional opposition of homo and hetero, as queer reception is often a place beyond the audience's 'real-life' definition of their sexual identities and cultural positions—often, but not always, beyond such sexual identities and identity politics, that is" (15).

16 JENNIFER REED

The season allowed much of that shifting in identification, and slipping of categories. We could not stay there long, however. *Ellen* was a sitcom created within the terms of realism. Alas, Ellen finally came out. On April 30, 1997, the historic episode was shown to parties and gatherings all over the country. It truly was a culturally historic moment for many queers, lesbians, gay men, straight allies, and right-wing heterosexuals committed to the unquestioned righteousness of their own lifestyle. It was a momentous occasion. But then the show had to deal with Ellen as a lesbian.

ELLEN BECOMES A LESBIAN

Ellen marking herself as gay was productive in new ways because it made her sexuality visible, but it was for the same reason difficult to represent on network television. Coming out, claiming the so-long (and still) shamed gay or lesbian identity has been a cornerstone of gay and lesbian politics since Stonewall. Simply by adopting the label and the identity, one is taking a stand against the hegemony of heterosexuality, and the shame used to maintain its hegemonic power. This action alone claims not only some level of dignity for the one coming out but, more importantly, has also worked collectively to create gay and lesbian subject positions in the public sphere. Gay Pride—one of the most important slogans of the gay and lesbian political movement since the early 1970s—has been a direct challenge to the shame of same-sex desire. Not until the moment that Ellen came out had the gay and lesbian movement experienced such a public and well-publicized coming out.

But it was happening on prime-time. As a network television sitcom, *Ellen* was defined by the terms of realism. And as a realist text, it is trapped in the terms of heterosexuality. Jill Dolan, materialist feminist performance theorist, makes this point succinctly: "The heterosexual assumption of realism also marginalizes lesbians and gay men, since it presupposes a traditional nuclear family arrangement" (139). Dolan elaborates on the possibilities for lesbians caught in realist texts:

> The only viable positions for lesbian characters within realism appear to be as heterosexuals-in-transition, as they are in coming-out stories. . . . The personal, local conditions of their concerns somehow mire them in the domestic drama of heterosexuality. The lesbian is posed as singular, alone on the margins of what is really a heterosexual drama. Her community, which might allow her to *act* . . . is absent, repressed by the exigencies of the realist text. (137)

Ellen's journey as a lesbian certainly was defined by the coming out experience, as a heterosexual-in-transition, for all the world to witness. It, by definition, marginalized her, made her the other on her own show. As understanding, sympathetic, tolerant, and accepting as the other characters were, they were the reference point for normal. And as such, they were the representatives for most of the audience. And like any good teacher, television cannot afford to alienate its audience. If we think of television as a teacher, the question becomes who was being taught and what?

The obvious tension that *Ellen* had to negotiate this season was how to represent a lesbian character to a heterosexist society. The address could not be a gay/lesbian/queer literate audience *only*, because, to revisit Hartley's ideas, television "is teaching audiences about cultural distinction, the expansion of difference," and gay/lesbian/queer is the difference to be learned about here (45). If coming out is an othering process, the challenge for Ellen was how to create a lesbian life that did not keep her in that othered position. It was, after all, her show. Or was it? Ellen struggled against alienating her heterosexist audience; at the same time she tried to create a subject position for a lesbian character. She was up against the straight mind. The straight mind is another term coined and described by Wittig in her essay of the same name. Here is one partial description: "The discourses which particularly oppress all of us, lesbians, women, and homosexual men, are those which take for granted that what founds society, any society, is heterosexuality" (24). She adds: "The consequence of this tendency toward universality is that the straight mind cannot conceive of a culture, a society where heterosexuality would not order not only all human relationships but also its very production of concepts and all the processes which escape consciousness, as well" (28).

Given the enormity of the project of challenging consciousness itself, Ellen had to define her character as a lesbian, or as a gay person, in her words. This public and unitary subject position corresponded to gay/lesbian identity and politics. Again, the emphasis here is on claiming the identity, not hiding or passing as heterosexual, since to be anything but heterosexual, one must explicitly claim it. This puts a sitcom on network television in an awkward ideological position. To claim the identity is to confront the heterosexual imperative and hegemony in the society, and that is to confront the normative structure of the society itself.

Ellen spent the season moving through the developmental stages of creating a lesbian identity. The episodes alternated between dealing fairly directly with her newly developing self, and the old Ellen when she was anywoman, dealing with some situations having little to do with sexual identity in an explicit way. The tone was not stuck in getting a straight audience to accept gayness; it assumed that the audience at the very least was not hostile to the idea. It assumed a liberal acceptance. So other than having to confront the heterosexual imperative, the show was not explicitly confrontational.

In fact, the first show of the new season, titled "Guys or Dolls," which aired in September 1997, has Ellen kissing a man, something she had not done in previous seasons as a straight or queer character. The show opens with her on a double-date with her friend Paige and her boyfriend Spence, and the woman that Paige has set Ellen up with. Ellen's date is a conventionally beautiful, but very dumb and a very self-absorbed stand-in in the film industry. Ellen's witty remarks get right by her. When the date gets up to use the restroom, Paige says to Ellen, "Just give this one a shot, OK? I am running out of lesbians." Ellen, frustrated, says, "Yeah, we're not reproducing like we used to." As it turns out, a man she used to date works at the restaurant, and the rest of the show is about her exploring whether maybe she is still attracted to him and wants to date him again; the show culminates in a kiss. Granted, she realizes from the kiss that there is no attraction there, but this show must have been to reassure straight audiences that we would ease into this gently. It also can be seen to fit into the coming out narrative of many gay and lesbian people, that last bit of wondering if it is really true, and trying to date someone of the opposite sex just to make doubly sure. From this perspective, this is part of the development of Ellen into a lesbian person.

Ellen moved along quickly in the season from trying to date her spinning class instructor by going on a rock climbing trip with her, only to find out the instructor had a girlfriend, to learning how to cruise in a grocery store and dealing with the discomfort of her best friend Paige, to finally meeting Ms. Right (Laurie, another tall, thin, white, middle-class conventionally attractive woman to match Ellen very well). The shows that developed Ellen's relationship with Laurie took us out of the relatively easy jokes about gay and lesbian culture to actually representing lesbian desire and intimacy.

Their relationship moves from a confused first date, to a kiss, to meeting Laurie's daughter, to the first time they sleep together. In "Like a Virgin," which aired in November 1997, we see Ellen dealing with her fear about sleeping with a woman for the first time. It is a particularly poignant episode that has Ellen making excuses to leave Laurie's apartment on the night that Laurie has planned a romantic evening and invited Ellen to spend the night. Ellen does leave abruptly, but then through the counsel of her gay friend Peter, she realizes that she needs to go back and fix the mess she has made. By the end of the episode, in a gallant gesture, Ellen is luring Laurie into the bedroom by dropping the petals of a plant saying, "she loves me, she loves me not." There is nothing explicit shown, but it is a very sexy scene that ends with Ellen grabbing Laurie's hand as they disappear into the bedroom.

Ellen and Laurie become a couple quickly—following lesbian tradition— and deal with some typical couple issues. In a particularly lesbian situation, Laurie mistakenly thinks that Ellen is asking her to move in—on their one month anniversary in "The Break Up." When Ellen clears up the misunderstanding, Laurie breaks up with her, afraid she does not want a real commitment. Ellen is devastated, and they eventually get back together, to go on to a few more adventures together, before ABC interrupted the show for six weeks to give the mid-season replacement *Two Guys, a Girl, and A Pizza Place* a try, in a gesture that made it clear to all that *Ellen's* days were numbered.

Ellen was cancelled at the end of the first full season that Ellen was an out lesbian. ABC blamed a decline in ratings due to a decline in quality. Given the political project of this show, its awkward moments were inevitable. Even so, the awkward moments of the season were matched by decidedly funny scenes, snappy jokes, and witty dialog. In terms of quality TV, it was as good a show as it ever was, and often better than it had been

ELLEN MOVES BEYOND GAY

When DeGeneres did return to prime time, it was not as a queer, nor was she a lesbian in the context of lesbian and gay politics. Her character was gay and out, but in a postgay kind of way. That is, in a way that said, "I'm gay, but it doesn't matter." *The Ellen Show* debuted on CBS in the fall of 2001 and did not last an entire season. Just like on *Ellen*, DeGeneres was both star and executive producer. The lead character was named Ellen, but this time her last name was Richmond.

The premise of the show is that the character, Ellen Richmond, is a big dotcom mogul in Los Angeles. The first show opens with Ellen leading a meeting, acting the insensitive and self-important boss with her staff ("Pilot"). She then returns home to a little town called Clark (in a nonidentified state) to receive the Spread Your Wings award, given to successful Clarkians. While there, her company folds and she goes bankrupt. She decides then to simplify her life and move back to Clark. This lays the foundation of the show for the rest of its short season. It becomes about Ellen fitting into life in the small, quaint, slow-paced, decidedly uncool town of Clark. The appeal of Clark to Ellen is that it is all those things. She is burned out on big city living. It is too fast-paced, too stressful, too much (too gay?).

Certainly, the trajectory of the show implies just that. She moves in with her mother and her single, younger, heterosexual sister. She goes back to her old room, left intact from her teenage years. She gets a job as a guidance counselor at her old high school. Her life becomes peopled by wacky, simple, earnest, small-town straight folks. And most of her life in Clark becomes defined by the tension between its charms and its irritations.

Ellen is introduced immediately as a lesbian on the show. In fact the first episode does a few funny scenes with her sexuality. In her aforementioned old bedroom, she walks in with her mother to posters of Wonder Woman and Charlie's Angels on the walls and says, "Didn't have a clue, huh, Ma?"

There is mention of her last girlfriend, and there is a promising scene in which Ellen meets the high school gym teacher, the other lesbian on the show. Unfortunately, these scenes serve only to introduce her as a lesbian and then the plot line is dropped.

In a real retreat from the cultural work DeGeneres was able to do with her coming out seasons on *Ellen, The Ellen Show* backed off from that mission entirely. In this new incarnation, DeGeneres so desexualized herself, so depoliticized herself that she evacuated the cultural space she created with *Ellen. The Ellen Show* brings the lesbian home and puts her right back in her place. In fact, the concept of place is used as a displacement to move sitcom's most famous lesbian back to where she belongs.

Ellen DeGeneres' explicitly stated intent was to abandon any kind of politicized identity. One can hardly blame her. She took a beating in the press in the year that her character tried to develop a lesbian identity. As she did the press for her new show she seemed almost on the verge of apology for her last show when to a roomful of TV critics (quoted in the *Dallas Morning News*) she said:

> I think what happened with the last show is it got to be too issue-oriented, and I take responsibility for that . . . That was something that I felt I needed to do. I did a show for four years, and then suddenly I did something that kind of overshadowed everything else. So now I just want to be funny again. I think people want to sit at home and turn on their TV and just laugh. That's all they want to do. And I understand that now. (Bark)

In this press conference, she actually says she is playing a character who "just happens to be gay." DeGeneres says repeatedly in interviews that she just wants to be funny again, presumably in a way that does not challenge any of the dominant culture's ideologies. It seems that to be gay is ok on television at this point, in part because of the work her earlier show did, and others (e.g., *Will and Grace*) have continued to do. But she does not want to emulate that show. Indeed it is too gay for her. In an interview in *The New York Times* discussing her new show she says, that *Will and Grace* is just "gay, gay, gay all the time. . . . I like that show, but in my daily life I very rarely talk that way. I don't go to the gas station and say, 'fill it up with unleaded, and I'm gay' " (Green 30). She sees herself more in the tradition of Bob Newhart. At the same press conference with the TV critics, but reported by the *Knoxville News-Sentinel*, she goes on to say, "Now I think life can be funny without talking about sexuality. On Bob Newhart's show, he was married, but the show was not about him being married. It was just observations about his life. That's what I want to do" (Morrow 2). This is a classic assimilationist move and reminds us that indeed the social contract is the heterosexual contract.

Bob Newhart's marriage was not an issue because it was simply life, and all of his observations about his life are inextricably intertwined with the very *naturalness* of his marriage.

A lesbian cannot be represented as just making observations about her life without either challenging the heterosexual (and thus social) contract, or blending in, assimilating using the strategy of *The Ellen Show*. This is the strategy of what Richard Goldstein in his book *The Attack Queers: Liberal Society and the Gay Right* calls the "homocon." Homocons, according to Goldstein, "claim to represent a 'new gay mainstream,' and armed with that contention they've ensconced themselves in the liberal media" (x).

> Their claim to fame is dissing gay types that threaten straights, such as sissies, sluts, tribal dykes, and the ultimate sexual outlaws, trannies. Under the banner of "common sense" they mock anyone who lives outside the orbit of respectability. If there's a motive for this assault, it has less to do with gay rights than with assimilation. Job number one for homocons is promoting the entrance of gay people into liberal society. (6)

I am not here accusing Ellen DeGeneres of being a homocon, or of intentionally promoting that ideology. I think *The Ellen Show* coincides very well, though, with the ideology of the homocon. Not only did the activity of the homocon, or the gay right, allow the show a cultural space, the show had to also support the ideology. It fit very well with the goal of making gay people indistinguishable from straight people. The overriding goal of the gay right ideology is to make gay people seem normal, or just like straight people. Ellen, on this show, achieved that very well. Again, her difference was marked only by place. DeGeneres was fairly straightforward about replacing sexuality with place—urban versus small town—as the marker of difference. As reported in *The Record*, asked whether the character will have a love life, DeGeneres says, "I don't think it's necessary. There are so many stories that don't involve dating. Maybe—if it's going to be funny. But when you look at the shows I grew up watching—I'm thinking of Andy Griffith—'it's just the town' " (Rohan).

This convenient shift then allows the show to sidestep the challenge that lesbian subjectivity makes to the heterosexual contract. She is a lesbian without being lesbian, or a postgay lesbian. One more materialist feminist, Kate Davy, makes the point: as "we describe lesbian resistance, the multiple and heterogeneous possibilities her narrative spaces, positionalities, and subjectivities present, it is imperative to inscribe the ways in which these possibilities are enacted or performed so as to retain the specificity of . . . if not lesbian desire, then lesbians desiring; if not lesbian sexuality, then lesbians as sexual" (63). In other words, without lesbian desire, there is no lesbian. Under the all-encompassing force of the heterosexual contract, the lesbian is lost, devoured into its terms if she does not perform her own desire. And this is the end point of liberal tolerance, fed by the gay right: gay difference is swallowed into the norm. These are the terms that *The Ellen Show* set up.

The displacement of Ellen's difference residing in her urban style and sensibilities, and now living in a provincial small town among small town people, is made the most clear in the episode when her stuff finally arrives at her mother's house ("The Move"). Two things go on in this episode. One is the actual stuff. It is the stuff that young urban professionals use. She has a high-tech chair that her mother cannot even identify as a chair. All the jokes involve Ellen's mother and sister making fun of the expensive, useless, pretentious stuff that Ellen seems to need. This concretizes the difference between her and them. And that difference shows as urban versus small town. It is worldly versus provincial. It is ambitious professional versus no-ambition-small-town-job.

This is related to the other plot line in this episode. Ellen feels left out. Her mom and sister have a comfortable, settled-in kind of relationship in this episode, and Ellen feels outside of it. They have their routines, their TV shows, and a shared set of references they understand. Ellen wants to be part of that. She wants to feel a part of them. She spends this episode trying to create a family that all three of them can participate in. She tries to join them, changing the routine a bit, but basically just trying to fit in to what they have. Ellen is going home again. In Ellen's case, this is particularly disturbing, since it clearly means becoming one of them. To be there, she has to be recuperated back into the family. For Ellen to be absorbed back into the family is to give up her real difference, her sexuality. And she does.

At least the show does acknowledge, at times, that Ellen must be lonely. In the next episode, Ellen starts complaining that there is no nightlife in this town ("Just the Duck"). She decides that she would like to go to the "fancy French restaurant" in town. She cannot find anyone to go with her. Everyone she asks says that they cannot go because it is a place for couples.

Ellen decides that she will just have to go alone. In this episode, there are a couple of references to sexuality. There is the Lebanese joke, and some reference to her not being in a relationship. At least it is a reference to her lack. And then as she is being seated, there is a funny bit. The hostess asks where "he" is. Ellen says, "There is no he. I'm one." The hostess replies, "I hear there is a teacher at the high school who is a one too."

So Ellen finally sits and there are plenty of jokes playing on the fact that she is alone. But then she sees her sister and her best friend from school, Rusty, sitting at a table on a date. They have been sneaking around and have now been caught. The three of them have a great time together, and they all start going out together all the time. It becomes Ellen dating Rusty and Katherine. Ellen is very enthusiastic about it. But after a time, Rusty and

Katherine want to end their relationship. Ellen is devastated, as if she were being dumped. They try to comfort her by saying, "you'll meet other couples." Ellen is again completely desexualized here. She occupies no space that allows her to be a sexual adult. She is existing through their lives.

These are a few of the many possible examples from the run of the show. There are a few promising jokes that gesture toward the enactment of her sexual difference throughout the season. But they are not enough to create an actual space for that difference. The very structure of the show absorbs those references into the dominant form of reference: heterosexuality. The assimilation strategy here erases the lesbian and allows the heterosexual contract to remain undisturbed. This is precisely the homocon strategy. She can be gay, but being gay cannot infringe on heterosexual life.

This is the perfect gay person for straight liberal America. It is worth quoting Goldstein here at length:

> They [the gay right] speak directly to the contradictory climate of our time. Theirs is a conservative philosophy that appeals to liberals. It may reject the concept that gays are a people, but it advocates their integration into civic society. This is a deal liberals have always offered the other. It summons up the Enlightenment and it doesn't frighten the horses. As agents of this accommodation, homocons carry the imprimatur of liberal society. That is their special strength—Liberals are no less fearful than conservatives when it comes to homosexuality, but they see us in a different light. The right regards gay people as emblems of sinful culture that is undermining the nation and the family. Liberals don't feel unduly threatened in that respect; indeed they are willing to welcome us into full citizenship, as they have other pariah groups. For them, the issue isn't our sexuality but our sensibility and the distinctiveness it generates. Liberals fear for their place in the world true pluralism would create. And so, the bargain they set requires us to deny our difference, thereby affirming the bedrock principle of liberalism: that all people are fundamentally the same. (29)

By watching the Ellen on *The Ellen Show*, it is possible that a liberal straight audience gets the satisfaction of knowing that they are open minded and accepting of lesbians, at the same time that they do not have to be bothered with any of the real differences that lesbian identity can present, or with their own homophobia. And if the difference that is being offered is one of such banal significance as small town versus urban as code for more important social differences as embodied in sexual differences, then we come to the limits of television's role as the teacher of cultural citizenship.

Back to our question of who is teaching what to whom.

Even when television has not represented particular identities, or represented those identities particularly well, by making some differences visible, it has created the recognition of those different from oneself, and what we learn is that differences exist in a pluralistic society, and we even get some sense of what those differences are. Hartley discusses the example of representing women's issues on television in ways that have been less than satisfying for feminists. His ideas can easily be applied to the work Ellen has done on television for gay and lesbian representation. He writes: "what I'm suggesting is that TV made visible the 'culture' and condition of women to *others*, including those who didn't want to know, and this made certain kinds of assertions, assumptions and abjection simply unspeakable. Television . . . made women visible, their issues and 'culture' normal; brought them into everyday conversations of the whole nation-audience-public" (181). For Hartley, this works to create "social cohesion based not on sameness but on difference, identity not shared with the whole population but nevertheless shown to them" (181).

It is easy to see the cultural work that both *Ellen* and *The Ellen Show* did to create the visibility of lesbians, especially for "those who didn't want to know." The coming out saga and the season of Ellen as an out lesbian on *Ellen* was especially productive for audiences who thought they did not know any lesbians, or for those who held varying versions of homophobic ideas. The creation of lesbian subjective space on television was a public service in this regard. It was part of a discourse that insists on making lesbian or gay identity a human right, in the tradition of cultural citizenship.

It also pushed past that public service into Hartley's fifth version of citizenship, DIY citizenship. This is the postmodern version of selves, "the practice of putting together an identity from the available choices, patterns and opportunities on offer in the semiosphere and mediasphere. . . . How do you learn this difficult trick of 'suiting yourself' as it were, while remaining locked in to various actual and virtual, social and semiotic communities? Television audienceship provides the training ground" (178). As Hartley makes the point about DIY citizenship, "Now we are moving rapidly past 'identity' politics towards something new; citizenship based not on an authenticist notion of cultural identity, but on a radically decontextualized network of meanings which locate identity in the mediasphere, not the public sphere" (179).

The *Ellen* and *The Ellen Show* trajectory, the very shifts those shows made each season, were an example of DIY citizenship in action. Ellen recreated herself in the mediasphere three times, calling out and using three different political and cultural contexts in which to create her self. Even for queers who have political problems with any of the incarnations that Ellen created (and there are many to be had), the creations themselves are active; they are self-determining. As Hartley makes the point, "DIY citizenship is a choice people can make for themselves. Further, they can change a given identity, or move into or out of a repertoire of identities" (178). Ellen DeGeneres, in her movement between different ways of defining her sexuality, provided one example of some of the cultural shifts possible. Perhaps what television is teaching here is not the correct way to be a gay person, but that one can define that for oneself. It does suggest, though, the conservative impulse of television, as Ellen's re-creation of her sexuality ultimately takes her from queer to gay to postlesbian.

NOTES

1. The "heterosexual contract" is a concept that Wittig develops in several chapters in her book, *The Straight Mind*. Those essays are, "One is Not Born a Woman" (9–20), "The Straight Mind" (21–32), and "On the Social Contract" (33–45).
2. For a more detailed discussion of the term "heterogender" see Harris 257–76.
3. I have discussed this season using many of the same episodes in a review; see Reed.

WORKS CITED

Bark, Ed. "Ellen Returns to Humor Home Base." *Dallas Morning News* 1 Aug. 2001: F6+.

"The Break-Up." *Ellen.* 17 Dec. 1997.

Biddle, Frederic M. "Ellen's Coming Out, The Inside Story: A Q and A with the Show's Producer on the Season's Most Controversial Half Hour." *The Boston Globe.* 23 Apr. 1997, D1+.

Davy, Kate. "From Lady Dick to Ladylike: The Work of Holy Hughes." Hart and Phelan, 55–83.

Degeneres, Ellen. Interview with Rosie O'Donnell. *The Rosie O'Donnell Show.* "Show No. 65." NBC. 25 Sept. 1996.

———. Interview with Larry King. *Larry King Live.* CNN. 7 Sept. 2004.

———. *Taste This.* Atlantic, 1996.

Dolan, Jill. *Presence and Desire: Essays on Gender, Sexuality, Performance.* Ann Arbor: Michigan UP, 1993.

Doty, Alexander. *Making Things Perfectly Queer: Interpreting Mass Culture.* Minneapolis: Minnesota UP, 1993.

Ellen. By Ellen DeGeneres. Prod. Ellen DeGeneres. Perf. Ellen DeGeneres, 109 episodes. ABC. 29 Mar. 1994–22 July 1998.

The Ellen Show. By Ellen DeGeneres. Prod. Ellen DeGeneres. Perf. Ellen DeGeneres. 18 episodes. CBS. 24 Sept. 2001–11 Jan. 2002.

"Give Me Equity or Give Me Death." *Ellen.* 18 Sept. 1996.

Goldstein, Richard. *The Attack Queers: Liberal Society and the Gay Right.* New York: Verso, 2002.

Good Morning America. ABC. 3 Nov. 1975–Present. Oct. 1996.

Green, Jesse. "Come Out. Come Down. Come Back. Being Ellen." *The New York Times* 19 Aug. 2001, sec. 6: 28 +.

"Guys or Dolls." *Ellen*. 24 Sept. 1997.

Harris, Hilary. "Toward a Lesbian Theory of Performance: Refunctioning Gender." Hart and Phelan, 257–76.

Hart, Lynda, and Peggy Phelan, eds. *Acting Out: Feminist Performances*. Ann Arbor: Michigan UP, 1993.

Hartley, John. *Uses of Television*. New York: Routledge, 1999.

"Just the Duck." *The Ellen Show*. 11 Jan. 2002.

Late Show with David Letterman. CBS. 30 Aug. 1993–Present.

"Like a Virgin." *Ellen*. 26 Nov. 1997.

Morrow, Terry. "DeGeneres: Yep, I'm More Than Just Gay." *Knoxville News-Sentinel*. 16 Sept. 2001: G1+.

"The Move." *The Ellen Show*. 19 Oct. 2001.

"Not-So-Great-Expectations." *Ellen*. 13 Nov. 1996.

"Pilot." *The Ellen Show*. 24 Sept. 2001.

"The Pregnancy Test." *Ellen*. 20 Nov. 1996.

Reed, Jennifer. "Yep, They Won: *The Ellen Show* and the Loss of Cultural Space." *Iowa Journal of Cultural Studies* 1 (2002): 78–83.

Rohan, Virginia. "Her Work, Not Her Life." *The Record*. 10 Sept. 2001. F6+. 1 July 2002 <http://web.lexis-nexis.com>.

The Rosie O'Donnell Show. NBC. 10 June 1996–15 May 2002.

"Splitsville, Man." *Ellen*. 2 Oct. 2002.

Two Guys, a Girl, and a Pizza Place. ABC. Premiered 10 Mar. 1998.

Will and Grace. NBC. 21 Sept. 1998–May 2006.

Wittig, Monique. *The Straight Mind and Other Essays*. Boston: Beacon, 1992.

CHAPTER 2

QUEERING/QUARING BLACKNESS IN NOAH'S ARC

GUST A. YEP AND JOHN P. ELIA

Abstract: *This chapter provides a description and critical analysis of* Noah's Arc, *a Logo cable television series featuring a predominantly African American gay male cast. Queer theory and quare studies are used as theoretical tools to examine the conceptions of blackness in general, as well as representations of blackness in* Noah's Arc. *Thereafter this chapter turns to an analysis of the representations in this series to illustrate how* Noah's Arc *not only queers and quares notions of authentic blackness but also serves to expand various notions of blackness. Finally, this chapter provides a treatment of how whiteness and heteronormativity are implicated in this recent iteration of a racialized queer visibility in popular culture.*

[T]he commodification of blackness and its global circulation via commercial mass media continues to pose especially vexing questions. For those liberal left critics who are most skeptical of the purportedly negative influence of the market on moral values, market commodification is the obstacle that prevents black collective mobilization. For others, cultural traditionalists, who are most invested in nationalist discourses of authenticity and the central role of culture in the discursive constitution of the black nation, the rapid global circulation and commodification of blackness weakens traditions, historical forms of association and community, identity, and nation. (Gray, *Cultural Moves* 30)

[The] jargon of racial authenticity insists, in the words of gansta-rapper Ice Cube, that "true niggers ain't gay." (Thomas 330)

WHILE AMERICAN TELEVISION HAS INCLUDED A FEW SERIES on queer life in general, only recently has there been a television series devoted exclusively to black gay men. Dubbed as the black *Queer as Folk*, and the black gay *Sex and the City*, *Noah's Arc* debuted nationally on October 19, 2005. Despite some controversy involving the Nation of Islam during its filming, this series was produced and aired on Logo, a new cable television network for lesbian, gay, bisexual, transgender, and queer (LGBTQ) audiences (Cannick). Focusing on the lives of four African American gay men and rated as one of *Advocate* magazine's "top 10" television shows of 2005 ("Top 10"), this unprecedented television series offers a unique black gay voice in a sea of (mostly white) LGBTQ programming targeting mainstream audiences.

The current television landscape offers viewers, both African American and non–African American, a limited and skewed view of black identity, subjectivity, and experience. How do the representations in *Noah's Arc* interplay and collide with current conceptions of blackness? This chapter, using queer theory/quare studies as its framework, examines the representations of blackness in *Noah's Arc*. To accomplish this, we first provide an overview of the series. Next, we look at the process of the queering and quaring and discuss various conceptions of blackness. Third, we examine how the representations in this series queer/quare notions of authentic blackness. We conclude by exploring how *Noah's Arc* broadens current conceptions of blackness and how whiteness and heteronormativity are implicated in this new form of racialized queer visibility in popular culture.

NOAH'S ARC: THE LOGO SERIES

Noah's Arc is a unique and groundbreaking nine-episode television series that provides an in-depth and complex exploration of the lives of three African American gay men and one Latino gay man—who are best friends—residing in the Los Angeles area. This series was conceptualized, directed, and produced by Patrik-Ian Polk. While it resembles some aspects of *Queer as Folk*, *Noah's Arc* offers viewers a completely new focus on gay men of color. For the first time in television history this series focuses exclusively on the intimate, sexual, and professional lives of black gay men and a Latino gay man; furthermore, they all play major rather than minor roles. This is precedent-setting for television programming.

The main character in *Noah's Arc* is Noah (Darryl Stephens), a struggling screenwriter, who has tight-knit friendships with Alex (Rodney Chester), an HIV counselor; Chance (Doug Spearman), a university economics professor; and Ricky (Christian Vincent), a fashion boutique owner on Melrose Place in Los Angeles. All of these men's lives are intertwined, and they share their romantic, sexual, and professional intrigues with one another, which often involves offering and receiving advice and support.

The first episode, "My One Temptation (Part 1)," begins with Noah, Alex, Chance, and Ricky strolling down a walking path of a southern California beach while visiting with one another. As they share the intimate details of each others' lives, one of Noah's new acquaintances—a hypermasculine African American hunk—Wade, approaches the group and chats briefly with Noah about meeting him later. This interaction creates a buzz among the group about the nature of Noah's relationship with his newfound friend, Wade. This first episode and subsequent ones deal almost entirely with the relationships and sexual escapades of Noah and his three friends.

In episode two, "My One Temptation (Part 2)," the opening scene includes all four major characters in a nightclub. The focus is on the nascent romance between Noah and Wade, and as the scene progresses, heavy flirtation between the two ensues. The two men negotiate and navigate their budding sexual relationship, and Wade's complex sexuality is unveiled. Next, in episode three, "Don't Mess with My Man," Noah, Wade, Alex, Chance, and Ricky exchange campy quips, and in the process, Wade becomes jealous of Ricky's playful flirtation with Noah. Then, the episode turns to a crisis in Chance and Eddie's relationship when Chance confronts Eddie's infidelity. Episode four, "Don't Make Me Over," begins with a scene in a drag club, and the focus is on how Chance, still hurting from Eddie's infidelity, meets an alluring homo thug, T Money, in the restroom. Chance and T Money embark on an interesting relationship. The episode also depicts Noah and Wade's deepening but complicated relationship, Alex's participation in a drag show, and Chance's receiving homo thug lessons from T Money. Episode five, "Nothin' Goin on But the Rent," involves a complex set of events when Noah and Wade are forced to deal with financial problems and Alex opens his own HIV testing center for African Americans and Latinos.

Episode six, "Writing to Reach You," shows the complexity of Noah and Wade's sexual life. Ricky begins to fall in love, and the issue of HIV emerges. In episode seven, "Love is a Battlefield," Ricky ends up in the hospital, and his boyfriend, Junito, a medical doctor, becomes his primary caregiver. In the meantime, Eddie proposes marriage to Chance and he accepts. Alex suspects that his boyfriend, Trey, might be unfaithful, which results in a crisis. Episode eight, "I'm with Stupid," devotes a lot of attention to Chance and Eddie's impending marriage in a Baptist Church, and the prejudice they face from the church board. The series concludes with Noah and Wade's apartment hunting, and Wade reveals by his actions that he continues to be uncomfortable with his (homo)sexuality ("Got til It's Gone"). Ultimately, the episode and the series conclude with a scene at Chance and Eddie's wedding ceremony where major drama between all the major characters and their partners unfolds.

QUEERING/QUARING BLACKNESS

To queer is to "complete the Foucauldian move from human being to human doing" (Jakobsen 516). Consistent with queer theory, using queer as a verb is to move away from identity positions to focus on actions that resist norms, normativity, and the normal (Halperin). The process of queering attempts to make the familiar into something unfamiliar and strange so that analysis can reveal underlying relations of power. More recently, E. Patrick Johnson, calling our attention to the whiteness in queer theory and its lack of attention to race and class, proposes " 'quare' studies as a vernacular rearticulation and deployment of queer theory to accommodate racialized sexual knowledges," to analyze the discursive and material effects of sexuality and its relationship to race, class, gender, and the body ("Quare" 1). We use queer and quare as verbs to suggest a deconstructive practice that is not taken on by an essential and coherent subject and does not, in the process, endow this subject with a particular identity. What is queering/quaring blackness? In this section, we examine the context for the emergence of blackness, the nature of blackness as a cultural signifier, the deployment of the trope of authenticity and the boundaries of dominant conceptions of blackness, and the possibilities of queering/quaring hegemonic constructions of black authenticity.

Blackness emerged in a historical context of white racism and white supremacy. According to Cornel West, the current obsession with sex and the U.S. American fear of black sexuality have had profound effects on interracial relations and black individuals' perceptions of their own bodies. Fueled by sexual myths of black women and men, this fear distorts, dehumanizes, and pathologizes black bodies and desires (Rose; West). The fear has also created and perpetuated much black self-hatred, self-disgust, and self-contempt. In an ongoing struggle to affirm black humanity, preserve black sanity, maintain black hope, and defend against white racism, black institutions focused on black survival (West). To survive means accommodation with, adjustment to, and acceptance from white America. This process requires avoidance of anything deemed fearful, subversive, and transgressive by white Americans. Consequently, dominant black institutions, such as the church and the family, stayed away from substantive engagements with black sexuality (Collins; West). It is in this context that a particular type of blackness emerged.

What is blackness? According to Herman Gray, blackness refers "to the constellation of productions, histories, images, representations, and meanings associated with black presence in the United States" (*Watching* 12). As such, it is a cultural production in the creation of which U.S. Americans—black, white, and others—participate, and these constructions do not contain essential qualities (Johnson, *Appropriating*). Although blackness is an elusive and slippery cultural signifier that is, in Gray's words, "open to multiple and competing claims," there have been numerous attempts to fix, pin down, and foreclose its meaning (*Watching* 12). One such attempt invokes the trope of authenticity.

A particular form of blackness, created and sustained by the trope of authenticity, has become hegemonic in current U.S. society. In its current form, authentic blackness "has increasingly become linked to masculinity in its most patriarchal significations . . . this particular brand of masculinity epitomizes the imperialism of heterosexism, sexism and homophobia" (Johnson, "Specter" 218). The consequences of this construction are obvious. Although it is harmful to all African Americans—women and men, gay, lesbian, bisexual, and heterosexual, gender conforming and nonconforming—the effects on their lives are different. Gender ideologies subjugate black heterosexual women and limit the range of relational expressions and possibilities of black heterosexual men (Collins). Black gay men and lesbians are silenced and made invisible (Cohen). Black gay men, according to this trope, are then viewed as inauthentic because of their presumably "underdeveloped" masculinity (Harper; Johnson *Appropriating*). The current hegemonic blackness provides men, performing black heteropatriarchal masculinity, with the "authority and legitimacy to speak for the race as representational subjects" (McBride 225).

With the popularity of *Noah's Arc* and the presence of out African American gay men on prime time television, the authenticity of blackness as heteropatriarchal, sexist, and homophobic is called into question. This version of blackness has reached a state of crisis as different racialized performances of gender and sexuality take hold in the popular imagination. The portrayal of African American male gay life in this series opens up the discursive field to new horizons and possibilities for imagining, embodying, performing, renegotiating, and unfixing hegemonic blackness, or to put it differently, *Noah's Arc* is queering/quaring authentic blackness. For example, in television shows that have mostly all-black casts, such as *The Cosby Show, Good Times, The Jeffersons*, and *Sanford and Son*, (male) homosexuality is rarely if ever broached—and on the few occasions when it has been portrayed, it was through the usual heteropatriarchal, sexist, and homophobic lens. Although not entirely unproblematic, *Noah's Arc* challenges authentic blackness at multiple levels.

QUEERING/QUARING BLACK AUTHENTICITY

The storylines and the characters in *Noah's Arc* provide, in Johnson's words, the "occasions when those excluded from the parameters of blackness [such as effeminate and out gay men] invent their own" (*Appropriating* 2). As new parameters of blackness are envisioned and created, the current dominant

feminine such as the communication and sharing of feelings. Johnson further points out that "although silence as a sign of masculinity is a trope that circulates in the broader U.S. cultural context, within raced communities, and especially among black men, silence often sustains a dysfunctional denial of sexual difference and the imperialism of patriarchy" (*Appropriating* 31–32). To put it differently, authentic blackness forces men to perform black machismo to uphold heteropatriarchal authority.

Gender performance related to black authenticity is shown quite clearly in episode five, "Nothin' Goin but the Rent," in the relationship between Noah and Wade. Noah is portrayed as effeminate throughout the series, while Wade is pictured as hypermasculinized. In the scene where Noah is in the process of leaving his apartment to go on a date with Wade, he discovers an eviction notice on the front door of his apartment. When the two have an opportunity to discuss Noah's notice, Wade responds by saying "don't worry. I am your man," implying that he will pay Noah's back rent. Wade then proceeds to inform Noah that he will "hook him up" with Brandy, a Hollywood executive who will help Noah launch his career as a screenwriter. Wade then tells Noah that he needs to be self-sufficient, so Noah responds by selling his convertible car to pay his bills. Wade is portrayed throughout this scene as being fully in control and offering directives to solve Noah's financial difficulties: a markedly masculine way of showing power and problem solving. Wade ends up buying back Noah's car and giving it to him as a birthday gift; he also connects Noah with Brandy so he can have access to the screenwriting business.

Noah is effeminate, and Wade is portrayed as the real man, who, in this instance of Noah's need, becomes the savior. His hypermasculine persona keeps him in control. It is even a way that he maintains control within his sexual relationship with Noah. In part, some black men have adopted patriarchal values to create and maintain black gender roles to maintain control as a demonstration of authentic blackness. Macho tactics are used to achieve such an end (Julien and Mercer). This certainly seems to be the case in this interaction between Noah and Wade. However, in the same episode, Noah discovers that Wade is struggling financially as he finds a number of Wade's unpaid bills. When Noah shows concern and asks if he can be of help, Wade declines Noah's offer. It is clear from this scene that Wade does not want to talk about his financial troubles and even makes light of the issue as a strategy to preclude a discussion. Wade remains silent about his feelings and is unable to be vulnerable with Noah. This is certainly a display of hegemonic masculinity.

Another scene between Noah and Wade that illustrates the connection between real blackness and black masculinity is when Noah is becoming intimate with Wade. Wade is relaxing while lying on his stomach, and Noah is touching and kissing him. Wade seems to be relishing this experience and appears sexually excited until Noah pulls out a bottle of lube and begins putting some on his fingers as if he is going to use the lube to fuck Wade. At this point, the scene moves from being erotic, playful, and enjoyable to ending abruptly when Wade declares vociferously that he is not into "that kind of thing," that is, being anally penetrated. Even though Noah and Wade are clearly in a sexual relationship, Wade does not really discuss this with Noah. It is apparent that Wade is calling the shots in the relationship, and this is negotiated, in part, by being silent on key issues. As one can see, Wade is a man of few words—another masculine signifier—when it comes to financial issues and certain sexual topics.

QUARING SEXUALITY

In terms of sexuality, authentic blackness is profoundly homophobic (Johnson, *Appropriating*; McBride). Black homosexuality is viewed as a white disease and a threat to the essence of black heteronormative masculinity. Because homosexuality is believed to be a threat to hegemonic black masculinity, it is often dismissed, laughed at, and violently rejected. However, this virulent and ongoing attempt to get rid of homosexuality "might reveal the slippage between the mask of black masculinity as always already heterosexual and melancholic desire for the homosexual Other" (Johnson, "Specter" 218).

Sexuality in general is played out to reinforce authentic blackness in the final two episodes of this series. Following Chance and Eddie's initial relationship difficulties, Eddie proposes to marry Chance. When Chance agrees to Eddie's proposal, Chance wants to be married in his Baptist church. This is extremely important to him because of his history of growing up in the church and how important this would have been to his parents. In the scene where Chance and Eddie visit the minister in his chambers, Chance informs Reverend Allen that he is going to get married. The reverend congratulates him, and then assumes Eddie is accompanying Chance as his best man, and then the reverend proceeds to ask Chance about who his bride will be. At that point Eddie blurts out that he is going to marry Chance. The emotional tenor drastically changes in the room. Reverend Allen's facial expression looks pained and he takes a serious tone with both men and indicates that while he is supportive of such unions, the church board would not take kindly to such a request, and that it would most likely be denied. Chance asks for "his day in court" to present his case to the church board so he could get married in the church. The episode turns to a heated discussion between Chance, Eddie, their supporters, and the church board, and it is clear that this religious body is vehemently opposed to allowing Chance and Eddie the opportunity to have their ceremony in the church. During one exchange, a church member makes a comment about how Chance's mother would have been ashamed of him. At the conclusion of the meeting, members of church board ask Chance and Eddie and their supporters to leave the room so they can deliberate and reach a decision. Chance and Eddie and their friends leave the room and are called back fairly quickly to find out that while the church board agreed to allow them to have their commitment ceremony, it could only happen in the church's reception room and not in the church itself.

What this scene indicates is that members of the church want to esteem those who embody authentic blackness in terms of sexual expression. Authentic black sexuality makes little room for openly gay black men. While the black church has served as a social and political institution that has fought "for the racial freedom of its constituents, it has also, to a large extent, occluded sexual freedom for many of its practitioners, namely gays and lesbians" (Johnson, "Quare" 15). Although the African American church has been a very liberating and important institution in African American communities, this is clearly not the case for gay and lesbian constituents (Cohen). Chance's insistence that he be married in the church exemplifies his life-long connection to his religion and that particular church. Yet, as an out black gay man, he is given the status of a second-class citizen. His sexuality—not being authentically black—precludes him from being a fully accepted and respected member of the congregation. Even though the marriage ceremony takes place, Chance and Eddie face some serious challenges at the ceremony in terms of it being poorly attended, and a fight breaking out between several guests, which concludes with Eddie being badly injured to the extent of being hospitalized. The final scenes from this episode spell out quite clearly that transgressing authentic blackness comes at quite a cost. Not only is Chance and Eddie's fight to be married in the church a traumatic event in and of itself, but the wedding day too is calamitous for them. The message is quite clear.

QUARING CLASS, GENDER, AND SEXUALITY

Although we teased apart how authentic blackness is expressed in *Noah's Arc* in terms of class, gender, and sexuality, and we commented on each separately, they are integral to one another and inseparable in many ways, for example, Noah, the title character of the show, is presented in nonverbal (his manner of talking and acting, clothing style) and verbal ways (how he talks about himself and others, how his friends refer to him) as an effeminate African American man. This gender performance is read in sexual terms: He is a gay man. As an effeminate gay man, he is also attributed a certain class status based on his ways of acting and speaking (he is educated), profession (he is a Hollywood screenwriter), material possessions (he has a nice apartment and drives a convertible), and personal style (he wears flamboyant designer clothes). Operating in seemingly simultaneous and mutually constitutive ways, these signifiers produce a racialized gender, sexual, and class subjectivity that challenge prevailing conceptions of blackness.

Wade, on the other hand, is presented as a hypermasculine African American man who can be read as straight. Throughout the show, he is certainly "straight acting." In the scene when Wade is on his stomach being touched and kissed by Noah, everything is fine until Noah nonverbally expresses an interest in fucking Wade. When the lube becomes part of the scene, Wade protests, asserting that he does not engage in that kind of sexual behavior. Wade's resistance can be read intersectionally: As a black man who has had sexual experiences with both women and men, he retains his status of a real man as long as he penetrates—both women and men—but is never penetrated. A penetrable body is a vulnerable and feminized one in contemporary Western cultures, including African American communities (Bersani).

Chance's experiences with his church serve as another illustration of intersectionality. Although he is with his partner Eddie, Chance is read as a heterosexual black man and is granted heterosexual privilege (Carbado, "Straight"). As long as Chance maintains this presumption, his upcoming marriage is a source of collective pride, joy, and celebration in his church community, which might be understood as the benefits of authentic blackness. This currency is quickly lost when Chance reveals his sexual difference by refusing to conform to the gender and sexual ideologies associated with hegemonic blackness.

Race, class, gender, and sexuality are always operating simultaneously. As Dwight A. McBride accurately points out, "if I am thinking about race, I should already be thinking about gender, class, and sexuality" (224). He is quick to add, "race is already more than just race" (224). For example, Lindon Barrett suggests that race is associated with value: Blackness becomes the signifier for the valueless and whiteness the signifier for the valuable as contemporary U.S. culture presents binarisms such as "alliterate," "singing," and "street" for blackness and "literate," "signing," and "academy" for whiteness (4). McBride concludes, "race is always already everything that it ever was, though some of its constitutive aspects may have been repressed for various nefarious purposes or for other strategic ones" (224). The trope of authentic blackness is one such move.

IMPLICATIONS AND CONCLUSIONS

In this chapter, we focused on a popular cultural artifact, *Noah's Arc*, a new and groundbreaking television series depicting the lives of a small group of gay African American men living in South Central, a primarily African American

hooks, bell. *Outlaw Culture: Resisting Representations.* New York: Routledge, 1994.

"I'm with Stupid." *Noah's Arc* 7 Dec. 2005.

Jakobsen, Janet R. Queer is? Queer does?: Normativity and the Problem of Resistance. *GLQ: A Journal of Gay and Lesbian Studies* 4 (1998): 511–36.

The Jeffersons. CBS. 18 Jan. 1975–1 May 1983.

Johnson, E. Patrick. *Appropriating Blackness: Performance and the Politics of Authenticity.* Durham, NC: Duke UP, 2003.

———. " 'Quare' Studies, or (Almost) Everything I Know About Queer Studies I Learned from My Grandmother." *Text and Performance Quarterly* 21.1 (2001): 1–25.

———. "The Specter of the Black Fag: Parody, Blackness, and the Hetero/ Homosexual B(r)others." *From Disciplining Queers to Queering the Discipline(s).* Ed. Gust A. Yep, Karen E. Lovaas, and John P. Elia. Binghampton, NY: Harrington Park-Haworth, 2003. 217–34.

Julien, Isaac, and Kobena Mercer. "True Confessions: A Discourse on Images of Black Male Sexuality." *Brother to Brother: New Writings by Black Gay Men.* Ed. Essex Hemphill. Boston: Alyson, 1991. 167–73.

"Love is a Battlefield." *Noah's Arc* 30 Nov. 2005.

McBride, Dwight A. *Why I Hate Abercrombie and Fitch: Essays on Race and Sexuality.* New York: New York UP, 2005.

"My One Temptation (Part 1)." *Noah's Arc* 19 Oct. 2005.

"My One Temptation (Part 2)." *Noah's Arc* 19 Oct. 2005.

Neal, Mark Anthony. *New Black Man.* New York: Routledge, 2005.

Noah's Arc. Perf: Jensen Atwood, Jeremy Batiste, Rodney Chester, Jonathan Julian, Gregory Keith, Douglas Spearman, Darryl Stephens, and Christian Vincent. LOGO. 19 Oct. 2005–Present.

"Nothin' Goin on but the Rent." *Noah's Arc* 9 Nov. 2005.

Queer as Folk. Showtime. 1 Dec. 2000–7 Aug. 2005.

Riggs, Marlon. "Black Macho Revisited: Reflections of a Snap! Queen." Carbado. 306–11.

Rose, Tricia. *Longing to Tell: Black Women Talk About Sexuality and Intimacy.* New York: Farrar, 2003.

Sanford and Son. NBC. 14 Jan. 1972–25 Mar. 1977.

Sex and the City. HBO. 6 June 1998–22 Feb. 2004.

Shapiro, Greg. "Interview with *Noah's Arc* Creator Patrik-Ian Polk." *After Elton.com.* 25 Oct. 2005. 25 Nov. 2005. <http://www.afterelton.com/TV/2005/10/polk.html>.

Smith, Valerie. *Not Just Race, Not Just Gender: Black Feminist Readings.* New York: Routledge, 1998.

Thomas, Kendall. " 'Ain't Nothin' Like the Real Thing': Black Masculinity, Gay Sexuality, and the Jargon of Authenticity." Byrd and Guy-Sheftall 327–41.

"Top 10: Television." *Advocate* 17 Jan. 2006: 70.

West, Cornel. "Black Sexuality: The Taboo Subject." Byrd and Guy-Sheftall, 301–07.

"Writing to Reach You." *Noah's Arc* 16 Nov. 2005.

Chapter 3

All My (Queer) Children: Disrupting Daytime Desire in Pine Valley

Cathy Leaker

Abstract: *In this chapter, I assess the fraught cultural messages embedded in the trials and tribulations of daytime TV's only leading gay character, Bianca Montgomery of* All My Children *(AMC). While I touch upon the responses of soap fans to the Bianca story line, I rely largely on narrative analysis. Such an analysis indicates that the investments and meanings generated by this experiment were uneven, ambiguous, and contradictory. The most intriguing aspect of that unevenness is that while Bianca's sexuality was emphatically lesbian, her story lines were irredeemably and necessarily queer. Indeed I hypothesize that it is Bianca's queer unmanageability within the conventions of serial narrative, rather than her sexuality per se, that led AMC's producers to write the surprisingly popular Bianca out of the show in the spring of 2005.*

ON FEBRUARY 24, 2005—with her newly restored baby daughter, Miranda, and her newly renewed sort of gal pal, Maggie, in tow—Bianca Montgomery, longsuffering daughter of Erica Kane and daytime's only leading lesbian, left the fictional town of Pine Valley. Her departure marked the end of *AMC's* bold, and necessarily fraught, five-year experiment: its attempt to make lesbian sexuality visible and viable within the circulating and circuitous heterosexualist desires of soap opera narrative. This attempt also marked the only period in which a sustained and familiar "face of queerness," to use Richard Dyer's phrase, was available to American network television audiences on a daily basis (11). That the investments and meanings generated by this experiment were uneven, ambiguous, and contradictory—given the historical context and the marginal cultural space in which they were played out—is hardly surprising. Still, its relatively abrupt termination (coincidentally, but not incidentally, following close upon the heels of PBS's decision, under pressure from the Bush administration, not to air an episode of "Postcards from Buster" featuring a Vermont two-mommy family) marked an unambiguous loss for queer cultural politics ("Sugartime"). For in absenting Bianca from Pine Valley, the writers, and producers of *AMC* foreclosed the radicalizing gaps, proliferations, and resistances, as well as the particularized compromises, circumlocutions, and silences made possible by her insistent narrative presence.

If it is naive to claim that The Bianca Chronicles signaled a radical sea change in cultural representations of homosexuality, it is also churlish to simply chart their failure to live up to some presumed radical agenda. Thus my own project analyzes how the discontinuities and gaps in her stories uncover the performative possibilities and expose the narrative limits of same-sex representation within a particular, and particularly stigmatized, popular cultural form. My analysis plots both potential and limitation in the following formulation: while Bianca's sexuality was emphatically, insistently (white, upper-class, neoliberal) lesbian, and while her story lines often emerged from the most conservative impulses of the soap genre, her effect, if not her affect, was irredeemably and radically queer. This is so much the case that I suspect it was Bianca's queer unmanageability within the conventions of serial drama, rather than her sexuality per se, that ultimately sent her packing to Paris.

The queer effects of Bianca's often tepid story lines need to be understood in the context of the contained radicalism of American soap opera. Both Joy Fuqua and Tania Modleski (15) have argued that soaps are structurally resistant to homosexuality because its representation creates a "generic pressure upon the most elemental of the soap opera codes," that is to say, heterosexual romance (Fuqua 204). Similarly, C. Lee Harrington notes soap opera's historic treatment of "homosexuality . . . as a form of 'radical excess' " ("Homosexuality" 220). In making her claim, Harrington references the work of Australian media critics Ien Ang and Jon Stratton, who define radical excess as "that which is, excessive to, and therefore generally excluded from, the prevailing moral order of soap opera" (123). Yet both the inherent conservatism and the stability of the "prevailing moral order of soap opera" are easily overstated. Thus, for example, Ang and Stratton stress the "significance of soap opera as a site for the naturalization of the central value system of capitalist modernity" (124). Their view problematically relies upon a functionalist conception of culture in which its products become unmediated transmitters of ideology. Michel Foucault, among others, cautions against assuming that "capitalist modernity" reproduces itself through such univocal mechanisms, and indeed there is reason to argue that soaps articulate a contemporary "discourse of sexuality," in Foucault's sense of the term, quite as much as they collude in a monolithic effort to "give absolute status to a . . . moral repertoire which articulates bourgeois ideology" (Ang and Stratton 125). Thus, soaps can best be understood as participating "in a complex and unstable process" that "transmits and produces power," simultaneously upholding it, undermining it, and making it "possible to thwart it" (Foucault 101).

To say this is to challenge the dominant assumption that soap operas reproduce bourgeois ideology largely because they are "predicated on the celebration of heterosexual courtship, romance and family life" (Harrington, "Homosexuality" 216). But the admittedly problematic history of homosexual representation on soaps, up to and including Bianca's sojourn in Pine Valley, is both complicated and illuminated if soaps are understood to operate in and as narrative networks that produce and determine what Foucault called the "sexual mosaic," linked to, but not delimited by, the nuclear family and the heterosexual couple (47). Foucault's famous rejection of the "repressive hypothesis" offers an alternative understanding of how soap operas articulate the relationship between heterosexual romance and family, on the one hand, and desire and pleasure, on the other. Foucault questioned the commonplace premise that "modern society has attempted to reduce sexuality to the couple—the heterosexual and insofar as possible, legitimate couple," suggesting instead that "there are equal grounds for saying that it has, if not created, at least outfitted and made to proliferate groups with multiple elements and a circulating sexuality" (45). In addition, he distinguished between a premodern regulation of sexuality based on alliance (or family) and a modern strategy based on sexuality, saying that the former "is attuned to a homeostasis of the social body, which it has the function of maintaining" while the latter was deployed not for the sake of reproduction, but for the purpose of "proliferating, innovating, annexing, creating and penetrating bodies in an increasingly detailed way and in controlling populations in an increasingly detailed way" (107). Admittedly, Foucault was not analyzing American soap operas when he made these claims, but his ideas may be usefully applied to them; thus for example, Merri Lisa Johnson's claim that Showtime's *The L Word* dramatizes the tensions between "the slut utopia of promiscuity and the domestic utopia of nesting" arguably speaks less to the political and economic pressures on television's first serial drama about lesbians than it does to the narrative pressures of serial drama as a popular form (132). And any even casual watcher of soaps knows, despite the familiar (and familial) set speeches asserting family über alles, which utopias yields the better story lines. Indeed, soaps construct stable family life as so bereft of (melo)drama that not only, as

from That Lesbian On Daytime into " 'just plain gay folk,' " struggling for love and happiness [and, it's worth adding, circulating and proliferating] alongside everyone else in Pine Valley" ("Homosexuality" 232–33).

Since Harrington's detailed analyses (focusing on Bianca's coming out story and the industry/fan response to it) went to press, Bianca's continuing adventures in life and love validated the widespread assumption that a gay core character would have a more profound, and possibly proliferating, effect on the genre than an issue-laden marginal figure. In particular, Harrington's prediction that Bianca would become a folksy gay mainstay of Pine Valley society was borne out as was her concomitant claim that such centrality would ultimately dictate that she be given a love interest.

A brief summary of Bianca's romantic history is in order here. After her initial love interest departs for Paris (apparently the soap safe haven for lesbians), Bianca develops a crush on a straight friend who succumbed to heart disease. When her next attachment to bisexual Frankie ends with Frankie's brutal murder, Bianca pines away for Maggie, Frankie's twin sister. Maggie finally realizes that though she loves Bianca, she was "into guys," leaving Bianca free to fall for Polish seductress and industrial spy, Lena. Lena not only reciprocates her love but does so with daytime's first ever same-sex kiss that aired to much publicity and fanfare on April 23, 2003. Soon after Bianca is raped by Lena's former lover, Michael, and becomes pregnant with his child and delivers a baby, Miranda, who, in the infamous baby-switching plot, is presumed dead but is in fact alive and well, living with the prominent, if troubled, heterosexual newlyweds JR and Babe Chandler. Bianca's grief leaves her little time to worry about Lena's departure for Poland to tend to her suddenly ill mother. After a fall (viewers had reason to suspect she was pushed) from a balcony lands her in a coma, Bianca awakens to find the Chandler baby's identity discovered and baby Miranda cooing in her arms. Before she meets or loses anyone else, Bianca decides that she needs a fresh start and leaves for Paris. Best friend Maggie, to whom Bianca had once again declared her love, decides at the last minute to accompany her. In the last episode in which Bianca appears, the two deliberately leave the status of their relationship unresolved, significantly agreeing that baby Miranda is "Priority Number One."

At first glance, there is little reason to interpret these events as queer. Indeed they are in some ways hardly lesbian. Fuqua argued that soaps typically incorporate "taboo social issues" only if they can credibly develop ways to "detach" or "disembody" that issue from the particular characters with whom they were associated; for her, this precludes the representation of homosexuality, since "the problem of gay sexuality can never be disembodied from that . . . character" (201). The series of narrative choices *AMC* made regarding Bianca, however, would seem to belie this assumption. For example,

Harrington attributed the success (that is widespread industry praise and generalized audience acceptance) of the early Bianca story lines to the normalization of gay identity: the producers' clear decision to characterize Bianca as what Harrington, following Dow, calls "a user friendly lesbian," that is to say "gentle, sensitive, soft-hearted, soft-spoken, absolutely non-butch, stereotypically feminine" ("Lesbians" 215–16). This normalizing pattern continued, in almost exponential fashion, throughout Bianca's tenure on the show, generating a series of compromises that seemed to offer *AMC* a retreat from the more radical narrative and political possibilities of Bianca's sexuality. The cumulative effect of such compromises delimited the "available face of queerness" (at least insofar as Bianca WAS that face) and erased much of the gay in just "plain gay folk." Bianca's highly touted popularity with audiences (typified by GLADD executive director Joan Garry's props to *AMC* for developing Bianca as "the lesbian that many American television viewers want to spend time with") must be interpreted within this context (qtd. in Healy).

Moreover, while it is true that *AMC* explored Bianca's lesbianism through her romances more explicitly than had previously been seen on daytime, the show also went to almost Herculean lengths to ensure that those relationships never progressed beyond a certain point. As early as January 2003, former editor of *Soap Opera Digest* and online columnist for *Soapnet* Mimi Torchin blasted *AMC* for "their major bungling of the Bianca/Maggie relationship" and dubbed them "the most blatantly chicken and intimidated show on the air" ("One"). Even the much ballyhooed same-sex kiss between Bianca and Lena, promoted by the network as "a moment of truth and true love" failed to carry either its truth or its true love to the bedroom (qtd. in "Lesbian Kiss"). To the extent they addressed it at all, *AMC* represented their evolving physical relationship in what Olga Sosnovska (the actress who played Lena) described as a "kind of ostentatiously reserved" style (qtd. in Yimm). *AMC* persisted in their discretion even after Lena and Bianca were actually voted "Hottest Couple" by the readers of *Soap Opera Weekly* in October 2003 and were as a result the first same-sex couple gracing the magazine's centerfold.

Yet, as if haunted by the (im)possibility of a disembodied "hot" lesbian, however ostentatiously reserved, *AMC* worked to further detach Bianca from her sexuality by putting her on a treadmill of trauma that, while ostentatious, was anything but reserved. Serial catastrophe is hardly unusual in soap opera, but so over the top was Bianca's sustained suffering that the irrepressible Torchin quipped in an online chat that "it's a good thing the Titanic already sunk or [headwriter] Megan McTavish would have Bianca taking a cruise on it" ("Soapnet"). Bianca was most infamously shipwrecked in the summer of 2003, when she was raped by bisexual Lena's former lover. She was then simultaneously burdened with, and redeemed by, the narrative effects of that rape, namely her pregnancy and (endlessly deferred) motherhood. These events combined to construct a fundamentally sexless martyrdom that contributed to Bianca's neuter-alization. In her early analysis of the problematic history of rape narratives in soap operas, Mary Buhl Dutta highlighted their tendency to reinforce a paradigm wherein "rape is reinterpreted . . . as character formation; exploitation is purification" (3).

While Bianca's story departed in important ways from the paradigm Dutta identified, her rape did function to reform her character and purify her sexuality. To begin, Bianca's initial response was to retreat from intimacy of all kinds, but particularly from her lover, marking the beginning of the end of her relationship with Lena. When she finally did tell her story, Bianca confided first in omnipresent best friend Maggie, then in her mother, her sister, a physician friend of the family and the list went on. Lena, the other half of this once hottest couple, was quite literally the last to know, so much so that Torchin joked that even "the 7–11 clerk up the street" knew before she did ("Smiley"). As Bianca made the transition from rape victim to rape survivor, Lena's unaccountable exclusion from the process fueled the perception that Bianca's emotional, even moral, health could not only be detached from her sexuality but was in fact contingent upon its erasure.

Equally problematic was the fact that Bianca's emotional well-being was secured by her decision to bear the child of the rape. Right after the rape scene aired, Torchin speculated—in a too perspicuous prophecy—about the possibility of a pregnancy, suggesting "a child is a perfect desexualizing element forever!" ("Rape"). As it turns out, a kidnapped but presumed dead child proves even more desexualizing. Bianca's absent child easily replaces her too often absent lover as the prime object of her desire, her affections and erotic cathexis to Miranda prove so strong that when Lena (whose mother conveniently contracted a fatal illness) asks her to move with her to Poland, Bianca refuses, claiming her need to stay connected to the memory of her child. Predictably, the fan response to this emotional shift from lover to (not so dead) child, and hence from lesbian to falsely grieving mother, was represented as a triumph of tolerance, teaching and storytelling. Straight identifying actress Eden Riegal, who played Bianca for the five years the character was on the show, remarked on the spectacle of fans testifying to their "personal connection, which was unexpected and overwhelming, to this woman who was a mother, lost her baby and happened to be gay" (qtd. in Healy). The depoliticizing effects of that "happened to be gay" were signaled in the lead to the *New York Times* article in which Reigal was quoted: "Last fall, as Americans were choosing sides over gay marriage . . . there was one concern quietly uniting people across the ideological spectrum: Bianca Montgomery deserved to get her baby back" (Healy).

It would seem, then, that the acceptance—on the part of soap opera's combined constituencies of fans, advertisers, and network executives—of Bianca as daytime's (barely) available face of queerness came at the expense of her complexity as a woman and her visibility as a lesbian. Yet because the soap genre demands continuous, serial, and "proliferating" romance premised upon circulating sexualities, and because soap romance is inseparable from the secret surrounding who is (and is not) having sex with whom, Bianca's displaced sexual orientation could not be so easily put back in the closet. The dilemma was neatly articulated in Harrington's interview with *TV Guide's* Michael Logan:

> A new hot chick comes on to *The Young and the Restless* and she could be with Victor, she could be with Jack, she could be with Joe and Schmo. There are any number of potential possibilities. . . . But you don't have that kind of thing going on with a gay character because there just aren't any other gay characters on that canvas for that character to match up with. [A newly introduced gay character would obviously be] for the gay character that we [already] have on the canvas, so the mystery of who so-and-so's going to hook up with . . . the romantic triangles . . . all the building blocks of soaps get tossed out. (qtd. in "Homosexuality" 221)

If this dilemma resulted in politically regressive choices on one level, it simultaneously opened a potentially explosive narrative space through which the writers would (wittingly or otherwise) articulate a more radical vision of sexuality. Ironically because (rather than in spite of) there "just weren't any other gay characters on the horizon," as long as Bianca remained, even in name only, a lesbian, the logic of soap opera narrative ensured that her presence subverted and annexed the heteronormative paradigm her victimization was designed to reinforce. Far from reassuring her fellow Pine Valleyians that they were not gay, then, Bianca continually raised the possibility that they might be.

Writing about the dependent relationship of queer to straight culture, Richard Dyer argues that while "straight culture [is] indelibly structured by queer," straight retains "the prestige of normative sexuality, its felt centrality and taken for grantedness" (10). Yet on *AMC*, Bianca's lesbianism, and the political investments of her multiple constituents, not only made unusually visible the often elided relationship between queer and straight, it also reversed Dyer's paradigm, giving Bianca the prestige of a taken-for-granted, central sexuality that suddenly did not apply to Pine Valley's heterosexuals. Having assimilated Bianca into Pine Valley, the writers needed to keep her within the community's romantic circuit in a way that would generate suspense, hint at possibilities, and maintain the narrative's liberal credentials.

and the famed homosexual kiss, Maggie and Bianca—through dialogue crafted in innuendo—slowly built a relationship that was arguably more tender and more teasing, and no less physical (if considerably less publicized), than either of these heavily promoted "soap opera firsts."

The interstitial development of the Bianca/Maggie romance suggests that Bianca's queer effect was most resonant when she was *not* coming out, *not* being kissed, *not* being raped, and (*not* incidentally), *not* being featured in *The Advocate* or honored by GLAAD. While this claim may seem counterintuitive, the fortunes of gay and lesbian characters in other television formats, as Stacey D'Erasmo (writing about *The L Word*) and Anna McCarthy (writing about *Ellen*) argue, indicate that queer-inflected television is most radical when it moves away from the shock and awe of the media event and tends to the perhaps oxymoronic demands of representing the queer mundane. As McCarthy puts it:

> [ABC's] fear of a quotidian, ongoing lesbian life on television suggests that, although the network could support queer television as a spectacular media event, it could not sanction a lesbian invasion of serial television's more modest form of history making, the regularly scheduled weeks of televisual flow. Queer TV in short could make history as event television but not as what we might call "uneventful" television. (597)

Thus however much the eventful kiss prompted the hysterical headlines "Daytime Goes Gaytime" and "Disney Continues its Gay Habits" from Concerned Women for America (Kleder) and American Family Association respectively, *AMC*'s faltering efforts to represent—and ultimately discontinue—an uneventful lesbian relationship suggest that daytime could truly go gaytime only if and when "gay habits" became routine.

Yet it is important to distinguish here between the routine, the uneventful, and the habitual. For beyond its inclusive value, the low-key Bianca/Maggie narrative emphasized, as it might not have been able to had it been aired under the burden of representing "a moment of truth and of true love," that "gay habits" are not as definitive or as visible as the American Family Association would have its audiences believe. Heteroflexible Maggie made it uncomfortably clear that desire is not habitual, not simply gay or straight, noble or tragic, proud or hidden, hot or romantic, but complex and fluid. Ultimately, then, Maggie is only the most resonant example of an outfitted and proliferated sexual identity, one that provocatively blurred any fixed boundaries between sexuality as narrative, sexuality as performance, sexuality as choice, and sexuality as ordinance. In outfitting her this way, *AMC* simultaneously offered a potentially powerful solution to the dilemma of how to represent same-sex relationships serially and produced a proliferating vision of sexuality that escaped the managerial implications of Foucault's sexual mosaic, a structure that, after all, controlled the desiring body through the discursive acts of naming and delimiting. Maggie's representation suggested that rather than mainstreaming a definitively gay (or even bisexual) character into a heteronormative community to serve as obligatory love interest for a gay lead, soaps could produce and determine, in the words of D'erasmo, "a world of an advanced state of sexual identity blur" (2) in which desire, love, and sexuality are unresolved and thus fraught with tension, indeterminacy, and, not inconsequentially, romance.

It is too much to interpret the Bianca/Maggie relationship scenes as designedly transgressive, and *afterellen.com*'s Sarah Warn was no doubt right to argue that "Maggie's long-running confusion over her sexuality didn't seem to represent a deliberate attempt by the writers to explore sexual confusion or bisexuality as much as it did the writers' indecision over what to do with her." However, while Warn sees political weakness in the writer's failure to establish narrative control over Maggie's sexuality, her very ability to elude narrative control might also be construed as a potential site of resistance. As D'Erasmo noted in her review of *The L Word*, "When the subject has anything to do with sex and love, television has always herded like with like," and thus *The L Word*'s understated commitment to challenging the herding instinct is more radical than its louder "libidinous drumbeat" (26). AMC writers/producers seemed to nervously share D'Erasmo's insight into the "axis shifting" potential of uncertain orientation. While they lacked the decisiveness to offer Bianca a more recognizable "lesbian happily ever after," they were also, it seems, uncomfortable with sexual ambiguity, so much so that they twice short-circuited Bianca and Maggie's tentative efforts to define their relationship with references to shopping. Bianca's bizarre effort to woo Maggie to Paris with the promise "Nous pouvons acheter beaucoup de vetements!" (We can buy a lot of clothes) can be read as a sign of the desperation with which *AMC* writers sought a more decisive, less heteroflexible, signifier of girl/girl bonding. When all else, including fixed orientation, fails, let them buy clothes.

In her assessment of the "end of a lesbian era," Sarah Warn claimed that *AMC*'s "disappointing but not surprising" refusal to resolve Bianca and Maggie's relationship one way or the other was emblematic of their timid treatment of lesbianism throughout Bianca's tenure on the show. Expressing appreciation for "what we had for four years on *All My Children*: a prominent lesbian character who was likeable, complex, and not ashamed of her sexual orientation," Warn nonetheless wondered "what might have been, had the story line and the characters been allowed to realize their full potential." Yet, while she is surely right to highlight the mixed legacy of the Bianca years, Warn perhaps misreads the arc of their "unrealized full potential" by locating that potential in a declarative affirmation of the characters' core sexuality.

My own analysis suggests that in representing queer sexuality as forever unrealized and unrealizable, *AMC* productively, if unwittingly, deferred narrative closure not just in terms of a single relationship (or two or three), but also in terms of sexual identity and sexual desire more broadly. That deference in turn produced an anomalous queer subject who challenged heteronormativity far more radically than the likeable lesbian "many American viewers want to spend time with." As such, the value of gay soap characters for queer politics, may lie in their serving less as icons of pride (though in an era when even Buster Bunny can be censored, gay icons can hardly be sneezed at) than as forces of instability that outfit, proliferate, and annex—without ever fixing—sexual subjectivities. Further exploration of this thesis, however, will have to be suspended until Bianca returns to Pine Valley, or until soaps (such as *General Hospital* or *As the World Turns*) currently toying with gay characters make those characters mainstays of the community. Until then, we can only imagine Paris.

WORKS CITED

ABC Soaps in Depth. 31 Aug. 2004.

All My Children. ABC. 5 Jan. 1970–Present.

American Family Association. "Disney Continues Its Gay TV Habits." *American Family Association Journal* (June 2003). 15 June 2006 <http://afajournal.org/2003/june/603_noi_dw.html>.

Ang, Ien, and Jon Stratton. "The End of Civilization as We Knew It: *Chances* and the Postrealist Soap Opera." *To Be Continued . . . Soap Operas around the World*. New York: Routledge, 1995. 122–44.

As the World Turns. CBS. 2 Apr. 1956–Present.

Behrens, Web. "Bianca Gets It On: All My Children's Lesbian Finally Gets Some Lovin'. But Will Girl-on-Girl Action Help or Hurt the Ratings-Plagued Soap?" *The Advocate* 888 (29 Apr. 2003): 58–59.

D'Erasmo, Stacey. "Lesbians on Television: It's Not Easy Being Seen." *The New York Times*. Section 2. 11 Jan. 2004. 1, 26.

Dutta, Mary Buhl. "Taming the Victim: Rape in Soap Opera." *Journal of Popular Film and Television* 27.1 (1999): 35–39.

Dyer, Richard. *Culture of Queers*. New York: Routledge, 2002.

Foucault, Michel. *The History of Sexuality*. Vol. 1. New York: Pantheon, 1978.

Fuqua, Joy. "There's a Queer in My Soap: The Homophobia/AIDS Storyline of *One Life to Live*." *To Be Continued . . . Soap Operas around the World*. Routledge, 1995. 199–212.

General Hospital. ABC. 1 Apr. 1963–Present.

Harrington, C. Lee. "Homosexuality on *All My Children*: Transforming the Daytime Landscape." *Journal of Broadcasting and Electronic Media* 47.2 (2003): 216–35.

———. "Lesbian(s) on Daytime: The Bianca Narrative on *All My Children*." *Feminist Media Studies* 3.2 (2003): 207–28.

Healy, Patrick. "After Coming Out, A Soap Opera Heroine Moves On." *The New York Times* 24 Feb. 2005, late ed. E3 +.

Johnson, Merri Lisa. "L is for 'Long Term': Compulsory Monogamy on *The L Word.*" *Reading The L Word: Outing Contemporary Television.* Ed. Kim Akass and Janet McCabe. New York: Palgrave, 2006. 115–37.

Kleder, Martha. "Daytime Goes Gaytime: *All My Children* Features Lesbian Affair." *Concerned Women for America.* 4 Apr. 2003. 15 June 2006 <http://www.cwfa.org/articles/3814/CFI/cfreport/index.htm>.

"Lesbian Kiss Coming to *All My Children.*" *Advocate.com.* 15 Apr. 2003. 15 June 2006 <http://www.advocate.com/print_article.asp?id=12411>.

McCarthy, Anna. "*Ellen*: Making Queer Television History." *GLQ: A Journal of Lesbian and Gay Studies* 7.4 (2001): 593–620.

Modleski, Tania. "The Search for Tomorrow in Today's Soap Operas: Notes on a Feminine Narrative Form." *Film Quarterly* 33.1 (1979): 12–21.

One Life to Live. ABC. 15 July 1968–Present.

Rapping, Elayne. "Daytime Utopias: If You Lived in Pine Valley, You'd Be Home." *Gender Studies* 1.3 (2004): 28–58.

Soap Opera Weekly. 7 Oct. 2003.

"Sugartime! (Hinesburg, Vermont)." *Postcards from Buster.* Writ. Cydne Clark. PBS.

Torchin, Mimi. "One Step Forward, Two Steps Back." *Soapnet.* 17 Jan. 2003. 10 Feb. 2006 <http://soapnet.go.com/onlinefeatures/mimi/news/2003/mimi_011703.html>.

———. "The Rape of Innocence." *Soapnet.* 25 July 2003. 10 Feb. 2006 <http://soapnet.go.com/onlinefeatures/mimi/news/2003/mimi_072503.html>.

———. "Soapnet Coulmnist Mimi Torchin." *Soapnet Star Chats.* 30 Sept. 2004. 15 Mar. 2006 <http://soapnet.go.com/community/twts/transcripts/twts_transcript_mimi_093004.html>.

———. "Smiley Faced Mimi" *Soapnet.* 22 Aug. 2003. 10 Feb. 2006 <http://soapnet.go.com/onlinefeatures/mimi/news/2003/mimi_082203.html>.

Warn, Sarah. "The End of a Lesbian Era on *All My Children.*" *AfterEllen.* 24 Feb. 2005. 10 Feb. 2006 <http://www.afterellen.com/TV/2005/2/amc.html>.

Yimm, Lisa. "Olga Sosnovska, *AMC's* Unlikely Lesbian Icon." *AfterEllen.* Apr. 2004. 10 Feb. 2006 <http://www.afterellen.com/TV/amc-olga.html>.

CHAPTER 4

QUEER AS FOLK AND THE SPECTACULARIZATION OF GAY IDENTITY

GIOVANNI PORFIDO

Abstract: *This chapter explores the problem of homosexual visual exclusion in mass-mediated societies. It examines the public debates on questions of gay visibility that followed the U.K. broadcast of* Queer as Folk: *the first gay TV drama in English and worldwide televisual history. It considers mainstream and gay press concerns about* Queer as Folk's *contribution to the visual commodification of homosexuality in the popular representational arena. In particular, it discuss the accusations that the program's glamorized portrait of gayness was a cynical commercial strategy to entice homosexual audiences in an overcompetitive visual market rather than a symptom of homosexual visual and social enfranchisement.*

COMING OUT OF THE TELEVISUAL CLOSET

IN 1999 AND 2000 CHANNEL 4 BROADCAST THE TWO SERIES of one of the most discussed and successful media events of the last few decades, that is, the gay TV drama *Queer as Folk*,[1] which was the first TV drama in English televisual history—and for that matter, in worldwide TV history—in which all the main characters and most of the supporting ones were gay and in which heterosexual characters were the guests of this happy and proud gay world. Set in present times, *Queer as Folk* is the explicit portrait of a group of white, male, and openly gay friends who live in Manchester and who spend most of their social life around Canal Street—the city's gay district.

Through Stuart, Vince, Nathan (the three main characters), and their friends, national TV viewers were given a straightforward introduction to the world of bars, discos, saunas, backrooms, threesomes, cyber sex, and intergenerational relationships that define the lives and loves of these proud-to-be-gay men. In *Queer as Folk*, homosexuality, rather than being a "drama" or tragedy, was just the starting point and the dramatic engine for telling the story of some queer folk. Stuart, Vince, and Nathan were not portrayed as tortured souls struggling to come to terms with the "problem" of being gay. *Queer as Folk* was taking for granted the normality of their homosexuality and was not trying to convince the mainstream audiences of the social worth of its characters by portraying them in a totally unrealistic positive light. Stuart, Vince, and Nathan were represented neither as heroes nor as villains. They were depicted as complex human beings, sometimes behaving nobly, sometimes badly, who happened to be gay and for whom homosexual desires and pleasures were just part of who they were. Indeed, *Queer as Folk* was "one of the first mainstream dramas to take the characters' sexuality as a given—the storylines do not revolve around 'coming out' to a straight world but instead are focused on the men's relationship with each other, as friends and lovers" (Thynne 209). Moreover, the sexuality of the characters was not merely hinted at or left to the viewers' imagination. This time, homosexual erotic and sensual fulfillment was graphically, explicitly, and joyously represented, rather than being left in the televisual closet. *Queer as Folk* was challenging the mainstream representational regime in which "gays are desexualized, denied the pleasure of the flesh" (Walters 121). In fact, Stuart, Vince, and Nathan "are not represented so much as stuck in an ur-moment of being gay—they are busy *doing* gay" (Munt 534).

The series elicited interest and suspicion well in advance of its actual broadcast. Its daring poster campaign dotted the cityscape with images of the three main characters hugging each other, followed by the line "How much fun can three lads have together?" Excited or enraged press previews also contributed to the national public's alarmed or thrilled expectations, and around 2.2 million viewers tuned in for the first episode. Despite the fact that a reported 750,000 viewers turned over or switched off before the end of the episode, and that the following ones were watched by fewer viewers, *Queer as Folk* still maintained impressive viewing rates as much as it elicited a strikingly high number of complaints.

Unsurprisingly, some segments of the national public hated *Queer as Folk*. They saw it as an obscene program that was visualizing matters that should be kept private. In Britain, in fact, the rationale behind decriminalization of homosexuality in 1967 had been based on the principle that the law did not have any right to interfere with the private life of citizens although it had to guard public order and decency. Homosexuals were granted a degree of negative freedom as long as they were going to pursue their dubious pleasures only in private, away from the public gaze. This confinement of homosexuality to the claustrophobic freedom of the closet and to a ghostly public existence was based on the assumption "that 'homosexual' acts in public might cause offence to others. By implication, public decency and public order . . . is identified with heterosexuality" (Richardson 33). Given this absolute hetero-normative appropriation of the very idea of publicness (Warner), as much as of notions of decency or public order, *Queer as Folk* was seen by conservative and homophobic viewers as a direct challenge to the heterovisual regime, and as an attack to the hitherto uncontested heterosexuality of the televisual representational arena. Traditionally, mainstream television has been struc-tured and articulated around family viewing, and it has often been the most unwelcoming place for visions and images of nonnormative, nonhegemonic identities, sexualities, and lifestyles (Gamson; Gross). If images of homosexu-ality had been barely tolerated, even in the more selective and elitist realm of art-house cinema, they were almost absent in the representational field provided by terrestrial TV broadcasting that remains a stronghold of hetero-sexual normativity (Walters). In fact, the bold and explicit portrayals of heterosexuality that relentlessly fill the national TV screens are never accused of being offensive or disruptive of public decency. Rather, they are seen as fulfilling the patriotic duty of producing and reproducing family values and heterosexuality. It is in this perspective, then that we must consider *Queer as Folk*'s review article by Lynda Lee-Potter, the homophobic columnist of the homophobic *Daily Mail*:

> *Queer as Folk*, with its lewd and coarse language and ceaseless copulation, goes out at 10.30 at night but it shouldn't be going out at all. More than anything it proves that we need censorship. Year by year the boundaries of what is deemed permissible are pushed wider and wider apart. Sadly there are far too many cynical people in powerful positions in television who lack any kind of common sense or antennae about what we ought to be free to see in our own homes. Certainly we shouldn't be at liberty to watch naked actors having relentless homosexual sex. Any nation which allows this without any voice raised in dissent is lacking in both wisdom and self-respect. It's hell-bent on destruction. (8)

While people such as Lee-Potter saw *Queer as Folk* as undermining the very notion of nationhood and as a form of visual and moral pollution, other seg-ments of the national audience welcomed it instead as an example of a more democratic widening of the representational arena, as a symptom of greater social inclusion and acceptance of gays in mainstream culture and society. *Queer as Folk* was seen as radically subverting the twin problems of underrep-resentation or misrepresentation that have usually haunted the homosexual presence in the national televisual arena (Dyer).

At a quantitative level, gay characters were hardly ever present in TV productions. If present at all, they were relegated to marginal and secondary supporting roles that were providing subplots for the main storyline. Their fictional existence was allowed in so far as it supported, underlined, and reinforced the heterosexuality of the leading characters. They were the gay brother, the gay neighbor, the gay son, the gay friend, or the gay colleague of the straight hero. They did not have a narrative life of their own and they were totally disconnected from the wider homosexual community. Gay characters in popular televisual culture were tokens in an otherwise totally heterosexual world.

On a qualitative level, their representations were characterized in a quite predictable, stiff, and stereotypical way. When TV viewers were exposed to images of homosexuality, they were usually proposed two main stereotypes. To the first belonged a plethora of introverted, lonely, criminal, suicidal, alcoholic, or terminally ill characters who were supposed to embody and visualize the intrinsically pathological and destructive nature of homosexuality. They were never represented as the positive characters: the winners or the heroes of the narrative. They had to be the villains or losers, the nasty or the evil ones. The alternatives to these doomed characters were the effeminate hairdressers or camp interior decorators whose iconographical excesses made them more acceptable simply because they look unthreatening and hopeless or comic and funny. All these grotesque stereotypes existed only as standardized pictures of a derogatory quality and were never allowed the textual freedom of becoming or developing through the narrative as complex characters with aspirations, dreams, and desires. Frozen in the stereotype, homosexual characters were condemned to be simply and only a caricature of gayness.

Queer as Folk's characters and storylines were a radical departure from these representational constraints. They visualized homosexuality in a realistic and much more textured way that also showed the extraordinary normality of gay lives as never seen before on TV.

> Whether you loved it or hated it, *Queer as Folk* certainly succeeded in portraying its trio of upfront gay men as being rather anti-climatically normal and predictable. Regardless of the circus of criticism and scandal that surrounded the series, its content proved that being young and openly gay was not fundamentally different from being young and openly heterosexual. The *Queer as Folk* characters are attractive and socially active gay men who just happen to lust after other men rather than women. (Williams 4)

The significance of *Queer as Folk*'s normalization of homosexual images within the mainstream visual arena should not be underestimated. This is because, as

Richard Dyer has forcefully argued, we should bear in mind that

> How a group is represented, presented over again in cultural forms, how an image of a member of a group is taken as representative of that group, how that group is represented in the sense of spoken for and on behalf of (whether they represent, speak for themselves or not), these all have to do with how members of groups see themselves and others like themselves, how they see their place in society. . . . Equally re-presentation, representativeness, representing have to do also with how others see members of a group and their place and rights, others who have the power to affect that place and those rights. How we are seen determines in part how we are treated; how we treat others is based on how we see them; such seeing comes from representation. (1)

Indeed, cultural representations do not simply mirror reality. They also construct and fabricate it. Homosexual discrimination and social exclusion is constantly produced, maintained, and shored up by the hegemonic culture and cultural apparatuses such as the mass media. Televisual representations cannot be read as "merely cultural" (Butler) and as detached from the material processes of social structuration and power negotiation. On the contrary, they need to be understood as one of the main channels through which het- erosexist and heteronormative values are diffused and homosexual invisibility and exclusion perpetuated and reinforced (Warner). Consequently, cultural invisibility, underrepresentation, and misrepresentation in mainstream culture are some of the major objectives that ought to be addressed in both gay polit- ical praxis and cultural intervention. In visually mass-mediated societies the lack of visual representation and/or misrepresentation of gays in mainstream and popular televisual culture are indeed a form of injustice that needs to be seriously addressed. Given the ubiquity of television in Western societies, it is paramount to reflect on the ways in which homosexual social exclusion and inclusion has been articulated in this particularly powerful medium. Likewise, it is important to appreciate *Queer as Folk*'s contribution in bringing images of gayness to the center of the public arena and its effort in promoting a more pluralistic and multivisual representational regime. But, if *Queer as Folk* represented the proudest British televisual coming out of images of gay male sexuality, its contribution to homosexual visual inclusion must be carefully evaluated in regard to its possible entanglements with the spectacular dynamics that characterize late-capitalist Western societies.

GAY VISUAL SPECTACULARIZATION

In his *Society of the Spectacle*, Guy Debord poignantly argues that "in societies where modern conditions of production prevail, all of life presents itself as an immense accumulation of spectacles. Everything that was directly lived has moved away into a representation" (par. 1). Expanding Marxist analyses of alienation, commodification, and fetishism, which were supposed to be at the core of capitalistic forms of production, he suggests that the spectacular and visual dimension of late capitalist societies is the final stage of capitalism's relentless colonization and reification of all recesses of human life.

> The first phase of the domination of the economy over social life brought into the definition of all human realization the obvious degradation of being into having. The present phase of total occupation of social life by the accumulated results of the economy leads to a generalized sliding of having into appearing, from which all actual "having" must draw its immediate prestige and its ultimate function. (par. 17)

As a consequence of the forces unleashed by industrialization and capitalism, all Western societies must be understood as spectacular societies or visually structured societies in so far as "the spectacle is capital to such a degree of accumulation that it becomes an image" (par. 34). Having said that, we should bear in mind how, in the visual regime of spectacular societies, images should not be understood merely as the still or kinetic visual representations of social life that, happening in the supposedly separated sphere of culture, simply mirror reality rather than produce it or intervene in it. It is paramount to emphasize that "the spectacle is not a collection of images, but a social relation among people, mediated by images" (par. 4). In spectacular societies, it is the entirety of human relations that have come to be articulated, structured, and mediated by images and representations. In fact, in his relentless analysis of the scopic alienation of the spectacle (Jay), Debord draws attention to the fact that "the spectacle cannot be understood as an abuse of the world vision, as a product of the techniques of mass dissemination of images. It is rather, a *Weltanschauung* which has become actual, materially translated. It is a world vision which has become objectified" (par. 5). In this way, he warns us not to mistake visual media, just because they are producers of images, for the spectacle as such. Cinema and television—or any image-based medium— are only the spectacle's "most glaring superficial manifestation" (par. 24). They are themselves the most spectacular manifestations of the spectacle, cogs of the total spectacularization of social life. Through the lenses of the spectacle, then, the visual field—instead of being understood and circumscribed solely to the space of the canvas, of cinema, or of the TV screen—is expanded to the entirety of society, which becomes an all-encompassing visual arena in which images and representations become political matters and the matter of politics.

    In this light, then, the visual exclusion of gay people from the visual arena of the spectacle should be seen as a clear symptom of their subaltern position in a heteronormative and homophobic society. If images represent and articulate social relations among people, homosexual misrecognition and underrecognition in the public visual arena are forms of structural subordination. *Queer as Folk* clearly readdressed these forms of symbolic and material injustice by bringing uncompromisingly realistic images of gay life to the center of the national televisual arena. But its undeniable contribution to visual pluralism and to homosexual visibility is not immune form potential political drawbacks. In fact, *Queer as Folk's* promotions of gay visibility could also be understood as a further step toward the spectacle's colonization of all recesses of human life. It could be seen as the ambivalent and dangerous entanglement of homosexual politics of visibility with contemporary processes of commodification of social identities and neoliberal forms of visual govermentality.

These kinds of suspicions were at the core of the public debates that followed the broadcast of the series. Critical voices on the mainstream press had argued that *Queer as Folk's* bold introduction of images of gay lives in the public representational field did not necessarily correspond to an authentic recognition of homosexual visual rights as citizens, national audiences, and TV license payers. Some gay commentators saw it in much more skeptical terms as the product of careful or canny economic considerations and spectacular marketing strategies. They argued that the program's normalizing representation of gay identity was just an expression of television broadcasters' "grab-that-niche-market" attitude toward gay visibility (Sawyer 10). They were suggesting that *Queer as Folk's* unproblematic portrait of proud and liberated Stuart, Vince, and Nathan was illusory and misleading. The program's glamorized postacceptance representation of gay male existence was accused of being part of a ruthless and cynical entrepreneurial race to entice and attract hitherto neglected segments of the national viewing constituencies in an overcompetitive visual market.

No longer content—and no longer able—to mass market in the hopes of touching all, marketing strategies have shifted to a more targeted approach. We see this most dramatically, of course, in television. If TV programming and its attendant advertising was originally organized around a sort of lowest common denominator mentality, the proliferation of cable and second-string networks . . . have forced into play a much different strategy. So now we have entire networks or segments of networks largely addressing a youth market . . . or a black market . . . or a women's market . . . The attempt to "reach everyone" through a sort of bland sameness (assuming a white and heterosexual viewing public) has given way to aggressive targeting of populations deemed golden either in terms of their spending patterns (youth) or untapped in terms of their spending potential and brand loyalty (blacks and gays). (Walters 236–37)

And indeed, *Queer as Folk*'s contribution to gay visibility could easily be seen as part of the processes of commodification or reification of gay identity, because as Peggy Phelan points out "[v]isibility politics are compatible with capitalism's relentless appetite for new markets . . . you are welcome here as long as you are productive. The production and reproduction of visibility are part of the labour of the reproduction of capitalism" (11). This problematic nexus between consumerism and gay visibility in late capitalist societies is further emphasized by Rosemary Hennessy when she argues that gay visibility has "to be considered critically in relation to capital's insidious and relentless expansion. Not only is much recent gay visibility aimed at producing new and potentially lucrative new markets, but as in most marketing strategies, money, not liberation is the bottom line" (143). In spectacular societies, gay visibility, then, may be actively produced in so far as gays are seen as conspicuous consumers of goods and images. Gay people are allowed to be visible because they are seen as a new and attractive market niche, ripe for being exploited.

Public debates on *Queer as Folk*'s explicit representation of sexuality must be contextualized within a broader dispute on the program's spectacularization of homosexuality. For example, Lee-Potter, the *Daily Mail*'s journalist had clearly expressed her opinion that TV bosses were using explicit images of sexuality to seduce and captivate audiences. In her view, it was only economic greed and the race toward profit that instigated such an irresponsible use of images of perverse sexuality that would have weakened the national moral fiber. But, although her concern was dictated by the homophobic belief in the unsuitability for the mainstream visual arena of any image of homosexuality— let alone of explicit gay sex—she was paradoxically also highlighting some of the potential ambiguities of contemporary gay visibility in a market-driven visual arena. In fact, as Beverley Skeggs argues, we should bear in mind that

> The search for new markets and the ability of capitalism to marketise its own contradictions has enabled the opening out of new markets for which new resources and new consumers need to be produced. It is in this search for new markets that what was once abject, legitimated through biology and science, is now being accessed and re-legitimated in order to produce the "new" and "exciting." Moral boundaries are being redrawn whereby what was once projected onto an "other" is now being drawn back into the mainstream. Yet this is not a wholesale incorporation of bodies that were once positioned at a distance. Rather, it is a re-valuation process, whereby prior immoral abject culture is being used to open up new markets. The expanse of sexuality . . . as a mechanism for selling goods is one obvious example. (63)

Indeed, even commentators from the gay press had been troubled by the frankness of Stuart and Nathan's lovemaking scenes that had some viewers wondering about their narrative necessity or purposes: "The man and his boyfriend had already discussed rimming, so did we really have to see tongue on bottom to get the idea? . . . but Channel 4 needs the rating, so the spunk had to be not just mentioned, but seen dripping from the actor's hand" (Sanderson 67).

Surely *Queer as Folk*'s candid and joyful images of sex and lust were a defiant challenge to a representational regime in which homosexual pleasures are either completely ignored or associated to disease, contagion, and death. Yet this visual celebration of embodied pride and sexual freedom may be seen as less challenging if we consider that spectacularization can be understood as a "kind of power of recuperation and absorption, a capacity to neutralize and assimilate acts of resistance by converting them into objects or images of consumption" (Crary 100). Thus, we must be aware that the visual liberation of images of gay sexuality in the omnivorous representational arena of spectacular societies could easily turn from a political project into a marketing strategy out of which *Queer as Folk*'s contribution to homosexual visual enfranchisement may emerge seriously impaired.

Queer as Folk's glamorous representation of Canal Street, the city's gay district, was also discussed in the gay press as highly suspicious. On the one hand, the program showed Manchester's gay district as a friendly and supportive space in which to safely and freely experience gay identity. On the other hand, it highlighted how freedom and visibility are often dangerously entangled with the ambiguous dynamics of commodification that seem to foster visibilities and identities as long as they generate revenue. What emerged from the series was the image of a gay space in which freedom seemed achievable only by means of conspicuous consumption. None of the characters seemed to have any problem in spending money to buy stylish clothes, to pay the entrance fee to clubs, to buy drinks, and so on. None of them seemed particularly troubled by the narrowness of this liberated space or by the idea of having to purchase freedom. Manchester's gay community was portrayed as a spending community whose freedom and integration within the wider city life was mediated and justified by its spending power. These concerns are clearly spelled out by Sally Munt when she says that

> Most of the action in *Queer as Folk* takes place in Manchester's postindustrial, cosmopolitan landscape of gentrified fetishism. Manchester city is marketed internationally as a gay mecca; gay tourism, endorsed by a historically left-wing council, creates an estimated wealth of £40 million per annum. Gayness has been formulaically rebranded as attractive and aspirational, it has acquired cultural and symbolic capital, it has, through commodification, become *respectable*. (538–39)

Thus, *Queer as Folk*'s upbeat representation of gay life on Canal Street also shows by default the limits and shortcomings of a freedom that is granted only as a form of productive spectacle; that is circumscribed to a few blocks; that beyond those boundaries is still haunted by the specter of homophobia.

At this point, having addressed some of the pitfalls of spectacular visibility, it is also important to question any self-evident negative relation between gay visibility and forms of spectacularization. As Dick Hebdige suggests, we should consider how "the relationship between the spectacular subculture and the various industries which service and exploit it is notoriously ambiguous" (94) and that it is problematic "to maintain any absolute distinction between commercial exploitation on the one hand and creativity/ originality on the other" (95). Indeed, we should not forget that it was also through the possibilities offered by the market and articulated through consumption that, from the late 1970s onward, the constitutions of a stronger, safer, and more politicized gay community or social network was made possible or at least greatly facilitated (Seidman). In this ambiguous relation with the spectacular forces of commerce, gay people had often managed to establish or articulate a troubled, unstable, but also resourceful alliance with the market. For example, *Queer as Folk* had clearly represented the sense of safety and empowerment that spaces of gay consumption, such as the gay bars of Canal Street, may offer to real-life Nathans, Stuarts, or Vinces, in spite of the potential exploitation the straight owners of the breweries may be subjecting them to (Skeggs et al.).

Moreover, the gay struggle for a democratization of the representational arena cannot be directly translated as a form of liberation from the supposedly evil forces of capitalism. Coming out and achieving social visibility has never been agreed upon within the multifaceted gay network as an exclusively anticapitalist project (Weeks). The radicalism and anticapitalism of some gay liberationist projects have often been perceived as highly particularistic and as sources of endless controversies in the wider gay population, given that some of its reformist objectives "could be attained within the framework of liberal bourgeois society" (Weeks 205). Not all homosexuals saw the Marxist socialist project as the indispensable prerequisite for homosexual enfranchisement. In fact, the commitment of socialist regimes, such as the Cuban or Chinese, to liberate their people from the unfreedom, slavery, or alienation produced by capitalist forms of production has done very little for the welfare of gay people and their struggle for social visibility. Additionally, gay invisibility is not exclusively a problem of homosexual employees but also of employers. The almost total absence of openly gay TV bosses (Gross) is an example of how gay invisibility affects all gay people involved in the spectacular production of social life: employers and employees alike. The fight against sexual discrimination surely intersects questions of political economy but it does not coincide exclusively with it. Thus, no matter how bourgeois and limiting this may sound, it is a democratic right of gays to demand the same opportunities of visual entertainment that heterosexual audiences have, to claim their right to be able to sit in front of the television and enjoy "the pleasure of spectacular public self-entitlement" as straight people always do (Berlant and Freeman).

Having said that, it is undeniable that gay visibility can be entangled with problems of economic disparities and unequal access to visual resources. Even the gay community is riddled with problems of exploitation or inequality not only vis-à-vis straight or heteronormative society but also between affluent gays and less economically empowered gays. Visibility, as everything else in the integrated dimension of contemporary spectacular relations (Debord, "Comments"), is a commodity not equally distributed or available to all. But this problem, which surely needs to be addressed, does not completely nullify the justice of striving for achieving visibility. *Queer as Folk* was indeed com-missioned and broadcast by a mainstream TV channel with gay audiences in mind as potential consumers of spectacular images of gayness. The program's contribution to gay visibility was indeed part of consumerism and commerce. However, it also represented an attempt to equally redistribute visual shares and a way to queer the phantasmagoria of the spectacle. In its ambiguities, this was one of the possible forms of *Queer as Folk*'s contribution to the democra-tization of the representational public arena. The program's introduction into the mainstream visual arena of explicit images of homosexuality offered the unprecedented opportunity for a greater equalization of the dynamics of consumption and spectacular participation. In fact, traditionally visual consumption has exclusively addressed heterosexual audiences, designing, producing, and reproducing endless images of hegemonic heterosexuality.

> As a specific target group, gays have long been ignored by corporate interests. Seen as either too invisible (how do you market to the closet?), too despised, or too depressed within the general population, gays have largely escaped the direct onslaught of advertising. Companies have long been wary to advertise to a population so demonised, for fear of backlash and possible boycotts. Surely, this fear still exists and we should in no way underestimate the way in which "fear of association" still governs decision-making at the profit-centered corpo-rate level. Moves are still tentative and still one-way, with gays consuming "straight" images and products and straights immersed in a world in which their centrality is taken for granted. (Walters 235–36)

This time, with the public broadcast of *Queer as Folk*, it was homosexual audiences that were addressed as visual constituencies and/or visual con-sumers. In this light, then, it is a form of possible justice to be able to enjoy the intoxicating pleasures of consumption as much as heterosexuals do. *Queer as Folk* represented a form of redistribution of images-objects, of visual goods that, either fetishized or not, had always been denied to homosexuals in the mainstream visual arena. It was a form of justice for gays to be recognized as a rightful segment of the national audience, a segment whose representational needs should be considered and addressed, and this was an interesting challenge to the hegemonic grip of heteronormativity over images and practices of the market. Moreover, we should bear in mind that at the same time in which *Queer as Folk* was exposing gay identity to the danger of visual commodification, it was also opening up the possibility of a critical debate on homosexuality and spectacularization. But most importantly, it was opening up the unprecedented possibility of articulating in the wider public arena, and not merely in the claustrophobic space of the closet, the crucial debate on the visual exclusion of homosexuals. By doing so, it was generating a much needed public awareness about homosexuals' visual rights as national audiences and about their entitlement to a more democratic and multivisual society.

NOTE

1. In this chapter, I will only survey the public debate triggered in the United Kingdom by the British version of the program and I will not discuss reactions to the American version of it. The differences between the two series and, crucially, between British and American society are far too big for any sweeping generalizations. For example, whereas the British series was broadcasted on a national terrestrial channel and was bringing images of homosexuality in all national households, the American one was viewed on a private channel and so its social and cultural impact was less public. Although my considerations are bound to a particular social and cultural context, I also believe they will highlight crucial similarities in transatlantic patterns of homosexual visual exclusion and spectacularization.

WORKS CITED

Berlant, Lauren, and Elizabeth Freeman. "Queer Nationality." Warner, 193–229.
Butler, Judith. "Merely Cultural." *New Left Review* 227 (1998): 33–44.
Crary, Jonathan. "Spectacle, Attention, Counter-Memory." *October* 50 (1989): 97–107.
Debord, Guy. *Society of the Spectacle*. Detroit: Black and Red, 1983.
———. *Comments on the Society of the Spectacle*. London: Verso, 1998.
Dyer, Richard. *The Matter of Images: Essays on Representation*. London: Routledge, 2002.
Gamson, Joshua. *Freaks that Talk Back: Tabloid Talk Shows and Sexual Nonconformity*. Chicago: U of Chicago P, 1998.
Gross, Larry. *Up from Invisibility: Lesbians, Gay Men, and the Media in America*. New York: Columbia UP, 2001.
Hebdige, Dick. *Subculture: The Meaning of Style*. London: Methuen, 1979.

Hennessy, Rosemary. "Queer Visibility in Commodity Culture." *Social Postmodernism: Beyond Identity Politics*. Ed. Linda Nicholson and Steven Seidman. Cambridge: Cambridge UP, 1995. 142–83.

Jay, Martin. *Downcast Eyes: The Denigration of Vision in Twentieth-Century French Thought*. Berkeley: U of California P, 1993.

Lee-Potter, Lynda. "Why There's Nowt So Queer as TV Bosses." *Daily Mail* 23 Feb. 1999: 8.

Munt, Sally R. "Shame/Pride Dichotomies in *Queer as Folk*." *Textual Practices* 14.3 (2000): 531–46.

Phelan, Peggy. *Unmarked: The Politics of Performance*. London: Routledge, 2001.

Queer as Folk. Channel 4. 23 Feb. 1999–22 Feb. 2000.

Richardson, Diane. *Rethinking Sexuality*. London: Sage, 2000.

Sanderson, Terry. "Mediawatch." *Gay Times* Apr. 1999: 64.

Sawyer, Toby. "This Is the Gayest Television Show I've Ever Seen." *Pink Paper*. 26 Feb. 1999: 10.

Seidman, Steven. "Identity and Politics in a 'Postmodern' Gay Culture: Some Historical and Conceptual Notes." Warner, 105–42.

Skeggs, Beverley. "The Re-Branding of Class: Propertising Culture." *Rethinking Class: Culture, Identities and Lifestyles*. Ed. Fiona Devine, Mike Savage, John Scott and Rosemary Crompton. Basingstoke: Palgrave, 2005. 46–68.

Skeggs, Beverley, Leslie Moran, Paul Tyrer, and Jon Binnie. "*Queer as Folk*: Producing the Real of Urban Space." *Urban Studies* 41.9 (2004): 1839–56.

Thynne, Lizzie. "Being Seen: 'The lesbian' in British Television Drama." *Territories of Desire in Queer Culture: Reconfiguring Contemporary Boundaries*. Ed. David Alderson and Linda Anderson. Manchester: Manchester UP, 2000. 202–12.

Walters, Suzanna Danuta. *All the Rage: The Story of Gay Visibility in America*. Chicago: U of Chicago P, 2001.

Warner, Michael, ed. *Fear of a Queer Planet: Queer Politics and Social Theory*. Minneapolis: U of Minnesota P, 1993.

Weeks, Jeffrey. *Coming Out: Homosexual Politics in Britain*. London: Quartet, 1977.

Williams, Precious. "Mum, I've Something to Tell You . . . : *Queer as Folk* May Have Attracted Thousands of Complaints—But It Also Helped Change Lives." *The Independent*. 23 Jan. 2000: 4.

CHAPTER 5

FASHIONABLY FEMME: LESBIAN VISIBILITY, STYLE, AND POLITICS IN *THE L WORD*

AVIVA DOVE-VIEBAHN

Abstract: *Lesbian politics have long been underscored by a discourse of fashion and visibility. However, the very feminine fashions portrayed by characters in* The L Word—*the first mainstream television drama about lesbians and bisexual women—has attracted criticism of appropriating heterosexual conventions. Is such a highly stylized version of lesbian visibility still politically potent or is* The L-Word *simply catering to a popular demand for images of beautiful people? This chapter considers the ramifications of this affirmation of the fem(me)inine, while, in turn, exploring whether overtly feminine stylistic trends can sustain the queer and feminist political potency implied by lesbian visibility.*

ON THE SMALL SCREEN, FOUR IMPECCABLY DRESSED WOMEN stealthily infiltrate a country club—complete with a Bondesque soundtrack, surreptitious text messaging, subtle hand signals, and the obligatory regrouping in the restroom—and I wonder, for a moment, if I accidentally changed the channel and happened across a rerun of *Charlie's Angels*. However, despite the spy-movie overtones (not at all common for the show as a whole), I am still watching a pivotal scene from the second episode (entitled "Let's Do It") of the first season of Showtime's hit series *The L Word*. Furthermore, while Bette, Tina, Alice, and Shane are not international spies, in this scene they *are* playing fashion detectives, and the heartstrings of their friend Dana are at stake. The women's mission is classic, at least in the realm of lesbian politics: Is Lara, Dana's love interest and the sous-chef at the club, a lesbian or not? In the end, the ladies are flummoxed, unable to glean even the least bit of information from Lara's fashion choices, and send in Shane—as the irresistible heartthrob of the group—as a last resort. Lara's disinterest in Shane's flirtations leaves the ladies with little choice but to abort their mission, and they leave the club bewildered and apologetic. When Dana asks hopefully "Maybe she's a different kind of lesbian?" her friend Alice quips succinctly, "Yeah, like the straight kind," suggesting that having failed both the fashion and flirtation tests, the possibility that Lara's proclivities are in Dana's favor is slim to none.

Of course, Dana eventually discovers that Lara is, in fact, "a different kind of lesbian," proving once again the old adage that you cannot judge a book by its cover. On the one hand, the bafflement of Dana and her friends is not wholly unfounded, as fashion and its cohort visibility have driven the politics of the lesbian community from its inception through the present day, from ideas about butch and femme to notions of lesbian feminist androgyny. On the other hand, this game of fashion detective reads as somewhat ironic, since *The L Word*'s relationship to this political fashion discourse is tenuous at best. All the characters are relatively young, pretty, and decked out in a range of LA high fashion, attracting criticism that they carry no visible markers of lesbianism and are indistinguishable from, and can therefore be conflated with, the heterosexual norm. While butchness is one of the most conventional markers of lesbian fashion, *The L Word*'s plethora of feminine lesbians and bisexuals complicates this basic understanding of lesbian visibility. Simultaneously, it generates a whole new set of questions about the potential mainstreaming of sexual minorities and queer representation in popular media. To wit, is this new, highly stylized version of lesbian visibility still politically potent, or is *The L Word* simply catering to a popular demand for beautiful people? How do the qualifiers "beautiful" and "fashionable" function alongside taxonomic designations such as race, class, sexuality, and gender? What are the ramifications of the popular representation and reification of the fem(me)inine, and how do they affect lesbian aesthetics and political power?

When Dana hedges that Lara is "a different *kind* of lesbian," she underscores that there is a commonly understood notion of lesbian visibility even within the lesbian community; Lara's failure to fall within the conventional registers of this visibility heightens the ambiguity of style as a political tool for the other characters as well. Moreover, there are at least two perspectives to consider: the mainstream (heterosexual) imagining of the visible (or perhaps stereotypical) lesbian, and the queer viewer's understanding of what lesbian visibility is supposed to look like. In this chapter, I will approach both of these perspectives as alternate sides of the same coin. Through an examination of its premise and some early episodes, I will elucidate some of the more explicit ways *The L Word* renders lesbian visibility—the "politics of looking like what you are" (Walker 866)—anew, both despite and because of its femmecentric cast. On the surface, the show seems to offer a queer utopia in which lesbian identity can function both within a community and without the need for a conventionally recognized gender system (that is butch/femme or masculine/feminine). However, the characters' inherent complicity in mainstream notions of class, race, and gender also reveals the conundrum of lesbian visibility from a lesbian perspective, suggesting ways in which *The L Word*'s apparent flaws can be understood subversively as a critique of the lesbian community's own version of style-driven prejudice.

LESBIAN LOOKS: THE VISUAL POLITICS OF FASHION

> If femme reads as lesbian only in the presence of a butch partner, then femme becomes a wholly dependent category, borrowing an aura of authenticity from the masculine woman. In turn, the masculinity of the butch can become a trap for lesbian imaging because it depends on stereotypical homophobic constructions of what Esther Newton has called "the mythic mannish lesbian."
>
> —Judith Halberstam, *Female Masculinity* (176)

The unease borne out of the overwhelming femininity of the lesbians in *The L Word* originates from the extraordinary emphasis placed within the lesbian community on a style that often runs counter to mainstream notions of women's fashion. Politics are inextricably bound to lesbian fashion, largely due to an emphasis on visibility, and lesbian style has historically functioned as an outward sign of a person's subjugation under or liberation from patriarchal conformity, heteronormativity, and/or the binds of a masculine/feminine binary (Walker 868). Broadly speaking, the narrative of this lesbian fashion discourse marks important territory that significantly influences our contemporary understanding of style and its role in the lesbian community.

In the early twentieth century, it would seem that the predecessors to the modern butch—mostly women who dressed in men's clothing, often termed sexual inverts—were the only lesbians around (or, more correctly, the only lesbians who could be distinguished visibly from heterosexual women). However, as the twentieth century progressed, butch-*femme* couples were to be found more frequently, and by the 1950s, a working-class lesbian bar subculture had become more pronounced in the United States. The narrative of this subculture has been recounted time and again in a variety of sources, most of which outline both its liberatory quality—for the first time lesbians could be part of a community—and its divisive nature. In these bars, the butch-femme divide was often very strictly controlled by its members. It was not unusual for women who did not easily fit into the category of either butch or femme to be threatened, mocked, or accused of not being real lesbians (Faderman 168).

In this extreme example of the distinction between butch and femme, it is easy to see why lesbian feminists of the 1960s and 1970s so fervently rejected the butch-femme model, as it seemed to mimic the male/female binary too closely and too strictly for feminist comfort. However, this interest in *feminist* solidarity also created a restrictive environment for some women who felt pressured to conform to a politically correct feminist style of androgyny lest they be mistaken as unpolitical, antifeminist, naive, or hopelessly mired in the masculine-feminine binary (Everett). Clearly, an analysis of the 1970s lesbian-feminist fashion as androgynous, characterized by comfortable and loose-fitting clothing, is reductive, and yet an understanding of the effects this stereotype had on the movement's participants—fueling the pigeonholing of feminists as ball-busting and mannish (read: not bound to socially accepted symbols of femininity such as skirts and heels)—provides a valuable insight into how strongly fashion can affect societal outlooks and community formation.

On the other hand, as many scholars have noted, when butch-femme pairings became prominent again in the 1980s, they were theorized as occupying a different and more revolutionary space. In fact, to a certain degree, butchness was seen as a "refusal to play a part in the heterosexist binary," and the resurgence of butch-femme binary was marked primarily by a playful reassertion of sexual freedom through gender switching, cross-dressing, and gendered role-play (Solomon 264). For example, in her documentary *Framing Lesbian Fashion*, Karen Everett describes lipstick lesbians as tongue-in-cheek, irreverent enactors of femininity, indicating that a woman needs to feel safe enough in the lesbian community and secure enough in her lesbianism to play the femme. She cautions, however, that there is always still the danger of lesbian fem(me)ininity becoming too favorable to the mainstream and too bound to a rigid and heterosexual notion of femininity, stressing that both butches and femmes have to maintain a certain degree of criticality in order to avoid being subsumed by the heteronormative mainstream.

I am particularly drawn to this notion of criticality—mentioned time and again in texts on butch/femme and lesbian visibility—because it succinctly and unconditionally renders those women apolitical who do not consciously acknowledge their fashion or lifestyle identity as a role. For example, if a woman dresses in feminine clothing and is a lesbian (or bisexual, an even more fraught identity position) but does not identify, critically or otherwise, as femme, where is her political potency? Furthermore, in the eyes of the beholder, is a femme without a butch, or at least without a female partner to validate her as a lesbian, merely feminine and no longer lesbian? If she cannot be visibly identified as a lesbian, what good is she to lesbian politics?

Some accounts, such as Alison Eves's "Queer Theory, Butch/Femme Identities and Lesbian Space," glorify the femme coming-out narrative as a crucially subversive act: because she supposedly appears heterosexual, her self-identification as lesbian is even more powerful than it would be for a woman who could be visibly identified as a lesbian. However, even this narrative continues to discuss femme identity as performative, explaining how femme lesbians can be recognized as such either in the company of a butch woman or within the confines of lesbian space (490–91). At the extreme, scholars such as Lisa Pottie discount femme identity as wholly apolitical, regardless of any supposed subversive effect. In her essay "Hierarchies of Otherness: The Politics of Lesbian Styles in the 1990s, or, What to Wear?" Pottie laments that the "lesbian community has . . . adopted feminine style as the standard" and stresses that "Femmes may argue that they are more liberated, because they don't have to look like 'dykes,' and can be even more effective when they come out to straight people. But if one looks feminine, then one is less likely to be challenged by heterosexuals, and may consequently find less need to be out" (49–50). Despite her dishearteningly vehement stance, Pottie succinctly describes one of the many criticisms of feminine dress in the spectrum of lesbian politics. If you do not look like a lesbian—whatever that means under the circumstances—you do not count as a lesbian in the realm of political visibility and awareness. Ironically, what this indictment suggests is that looking like a lesbian is more important in determining a woman's status within the lesbian community than whether or not she actually sleeps with other women.

The discourse on lesbian chic, a phenomenon of 1990s fashion advertising, clothing trends, and media representation, is an even more trenchant example—ingrained, as it is, in popular expression and consumption—of the debates surrounding the women of *The L Word*. On the one hand, Laura Cottingham's 1996 essay-book *Lesbians Are So Chic . . . That We're Not Really Lesbians at All* recounts a tale of lesbian commodification wherein "many of the representations literally act out a simple disappearance ritual whereby a 'lesbian' is presented and then eliminated: that is, made into a heterosexual female and/or otherwise expunged" (3). Cottingham, an outspoken feminist art critic, is almost dogmatic about her definition of lesbian identity. While her analysis of how lesbian chic is used to sell products and liven up television shows—by employing token lesbian characters who appear and disappear with little preamble and are often used as mere plot devices—is largely accurate, Cottingham still betrays a rigid view of lesbian sexuality that privileges visibility and politics over many other factors. Furthermore, even though I am not sure it is feasible to demand that all lesbians on television be *played* by lesbian actors (24), I will certainly grant that lesbian chic does not necessarily dominate the lesbian community. As Cottingham explains, "one of the features of contemporary 'lesbian chic' is to keep the lesbian exclusively fictionalized; that is, to disallow any steady appearance of actual lesbians, of lesbianism as self-contained, stable, steadily lived and culturally incorporate" (19). In Cottingham's critique, real lesbians are overshadowed by the media phenomenon of "lesbian chic," which amounts to commercial use and commodity presentation of—often token—representations of lesbian characters or lesbianism on television and in magazines.

On the other hand, in her article "The Straight Goods: Lesbian Chic and Identity Capital on a Not-so-Queer Planet," Linda Dittmar is less concerned with the *misrepresentation* of lesbianism in the popular media than with how lesbian chic is used simply and solely as a style, divorced from its ties to politics and erasing lesbian sexuality and identity completely. For Dittmar, lesbian chic is often employed by fashion magazines and stylists to neutralize the image of the powerful woman (320); for example, the use of men's clothing— ties, pants, vests—as a subversive appropriation of patriarchal signifiers is rendered ineffectual because it is deemed merely stylish. Furthermore, she argues that lesbian chic allowed heterosexual women to play with lesbian desire as an unthreatening and affected fashion choice, while it simultaneously opened up "a hospitable new space for self-definition [for lesbian and bisexual women] whose 'safety' was predicated on wealth as well as gay/straight indeterminacy" (320). Dittmar's emphasis on wealth is crucial, and she further explicates how middle- and upper-class fashion was able to subsume lesbianism so that even butch dress was rendered feminine:

> Aiming to have it both ways, [the media] at once banked on the fact that femmes and "lipstick dykes" can be misrecognized as straight and found ways to absorb butches into normative female dress and lifestyle. That smart, coordinated look called "chic" is a concept defined by class, not sexual orientation. Its main task is to encode power and give women a commanding presence at the crossroads of femininity and wealth. (323)

Through lesbian chic, a fashionable alternative that rendered common markers of a minority identity mainstream, lesbians are cunningly redefined to fit the parameters of a suburban, middle-class ideal of normalcy and decency (333).

While normal is neither an ideal nor a politically viable category, it is a bit rash to dismiss the normalizing tendency of lesbian chic and popular media representation of lesbians so readily. Both Cottingham and Dittmar wrote in the years before *The L Word*'s inception, and even though the show does not escape the mainstreaming impulse of popular television—it is still mired, for example, in a very white, upper-middle class notion of fashion and lifestyle—its unapologetic and affirmative portrayal of a community of lesbian and bisexual women is nevertheless a groundbreaking innovation in media representation of sexual minorities. This alternative—and more optimistic—viewpoint is supported by queer theorist Eve Kosofsky Sedgwick, whose article "*The L Word*: Novelty in Normalcy" advocates the idea that *The L Word* is daring precisely because of its relative normalcy and is appealing because the show foregrounds a community of women and an assemblage of interweaving, dynamic narratives instead of one or two token lesbian characters. She maintains that despite the show's racial and generational blind-spots, "A visible world in which lesbians exist, go on existing, exist in forms beyond the solitary and the couple, sustain and develop relations among themselves of difference and commonality . . . seems, in a way, such an obvious and modest representational need that it should not be a novelty when it is met" (B11). There may still be detractors who claim the show is just soft-core lesbian porn with "better hair and shorter nails," as Kate Nielsen puts it in her review in the gay news magazine *The Advocate*, but, in the long run, "Humanizing [lesbians] can only help disarm prejudice" (9). Furthermore, the advantage of normalcy is the ability to insert lesbianism into mainstream culture without supporting widespread misrepresentations and prejudices that it is monstrous, perverse, or abnormal, or any number of other homophobic epithets that could possibly be leveled at an edgier depiction of lesbian life.

On the other hand, while normalcy has its merits and the wholehearted representation of lesbianism in *The L Word* is laudable merely for its existence, the classification of lesbian chic along with the problematic rendering of upper-middle-class white femininity as lesbian norm cannot just be ignored. The idea of butch-femme as a necessary lesbian pairing is certainly eschewed by the show, but the women are still rendered as femme/feminine characters uncritical of their overt femininity. However, rather than suggest that the feminine and highly fashionable dress of the women negates their political potency, in the following section I will consider ways in which this femmeness both complicates a popular rendering of lesbian visibility and nuances the way lesbian fashion is articulated within the lesbian community itself.

LESBIANS LOOKING: COMMUNITY, GENDER, AND SUBVERSIVE SPECTATORSHIP

We've arrived. The postmodern lesbian: not totally butch and not totally lipstick chic but definitely demographically desirable—and Showtime's banking on it, big time. It's called *The L-Word*. That's right, folks, L for lesbian—say it loud, say it proud. We're about to become as common as that household phrase *Queer Eye for the Straight Guy*.

—Kate Nielsen, *The Advocate*

The L Word is a forty-five-minute drama produced by the exclusive pay-cable channel Showtime. Its largely romantic and dramatic plots—with comedic moments and varyingly explicit sex scenes liberally interspersed throughout—feature an ensemble of lesbian, straight, and bisexual women (and a few men), their day-to-day lives, relationships, and emotional struggles in a friendly, upper-middle-class neighborhood of Los Angeles. The first season core cast is relatively multiethnic, heralding the biracial Bette (played by Jennifer Beals of *Flashdance* fame); her African American half-sister, Kit (Pam Grier); and the olive-skinned Italian café owner, Marina (Karina Lombard), who leaves after the first season and is replaced in the second and third season by Carmen (Sarah Shahi), an Hispanic hipster DJ. Except for the former sex worker/drug addict turned hairdresser Shane (Katherine Moennig) and, perhaps, Jenny (Mia Kirshner), the sensitive, sexually confused writer, all of the core cast are middle- or upper-middle-class in terms of their lifestyle. Tina (Laurel Holloman) can afford to give up her job and allow her partner Bette to support her as they attempt to start a family, Dana (Erin Daniels) is a star tennis pro, Alice (played by Leisha Hailey, the only "out" lesbian actor in the cast) supports herself with a steady flow of chichi articles for *LA Magazine* and, later, as a radio talk show host. Many of the second and third season characters, such as the independently wealthy Helena (Rachel Shelley), also fall into the class bracket set up at the beginning of the series. While the women all have uniquely varied wardrobes, their individual looks are mostly feminine and almost wholly fashionable. As Neilsen suggests, none of the characters are really butch or entirely femme (in the intentionally performative sense), but they all fall into conventional registers of beauty and (feminine) attractiveness. To further this conceit of wholesale trendiness, the official *L Word* Web page comes complete with a style guide, with fashion items—available for purchase—sorted by episode and character. Nevertheless, while fashion is an integral and crucial part of the show, it is not in any way *The L Word*'s subject matter but functions instead in its usual supporting role as a sign of identity, difference, and communion between the women.

The overall stylishness of the women clearly indicates a class privilege, perhaps placing more emphasis on conventional notions of beauty than on the political potency of visually presenting oneself as a lesbian. While the show offers this surface projection of heteronormative femininity, the characters themselves—their lives, their romantic entanglements, and their community engagement and involvement—offer a distinctly more complex version of lesbian identity and lesbian visibility than this initially perceived mainstreaming. There is also a sense in which the women's apparent distance from the discourse of lesbian fashion and its attendant politics is liberating; they are not concerned with trying to look like lesbians and, instead, are able to embody their own personal style. The aforementioned situation with Lara brings to light another constructive aspect of this apolitical fashion: when the more obvious, visual clues for revealing a woman's sexuality are removed, viewers are forced to look beyond outward appearances. Not only does this emphasize the ways in which queerness can be rendered through nonvisual (or not solely visual) means, but it also points to the potential failure of fashion as a marker of lesbian identity in contemporary culture. Therefore, lesbian visibility in the *The L Word* is rendered potent and political through the ways in which the characters succeed in constructing a cohesive and diverse community of powerful, self-assured gay women *as well as* in the startling ways in which the structure of the show calls attention to their failures at wholehearted diversity and acceptance.

In the first season episode "Looking Back," Alice, Dana, Tina, and Jenny embark on a weekend trip to Palm Springs during the LPGA's Dinah Shore golf tournament, which Alice cites as a veritable haven for lesbians. This episode is full of varying representations of lesbian bodies, dress, and styles, and the profusion of women during the weekend sparks an actual dialogue between the characters about butchness and lesbian visibility. Sitting by the pool watching women walk by, Alice points to a stocky, short-haired woman and proclaims, simply, that she is "a hundred-footer." When Jenny asks her what she means, Alice succinctly explains that anyone could tell that the woman is a lesbian from one hundred feet away. "Is it her hair? Is it her jog bra? Is it her mandles [a slang, masculine rendering of sandals]?" Alice queries the group rhetorically and with a smile, suggesting that a combination of athletic gear (the sports bra) and masculine fashion choices (short hair, men's shoes) circumscribe the stranger as a highly visible and recognizable butch/ lesbian subject.

Alternatively, when Jenny asks her friends to classify her they are unable to do so, and Alice suggests that Jenny needs a man or a woman with her to help her visibly shift into either a straight or lesbian register.

This reliance on visible and gendered fashion clues, and the idea that feminine women need to be accompanied by other women to recognizably express their lesbianism, may seem a frustrating implication—that any attempt made to affirm nonbutch visibility or to applaud the political viability of feminine lesbians ultimately circles back on itself. *The L Word*, however, continually renders its characters as visible lesbians in spite of their fashionably feminine and, therefore, culturally ambiguous attire. The show positions *all* the characters—lesbian or straight, male or female—in a heterogeneous lesbian community, one in which *most* differences are accepted and sexual/gender diversity is acknowledged (if not always fully or supportively appreciated).

At the beginning of the series, Alice creates a colossal grid, one that she refers to as The Chart, on a public Web site that maps lesbian relationships across the city—women can enter themselves and their partners into this network, with its six-degrees-of-separation schema, and appreciate the complexity of multivalent sexual ties between women in the community. Alice's grid, initially designed for a magazine article she never finishes, takes on a life of its own during the course of the first, second, and third season and is used to evoke the connectedness and visibility of the lesbian community as a whole, demonstrating in a perceptible way the interwoven threads of these women's lives. As Alice explains in the "Pilot" to a skeptical colleague: "So the point is we're all connected. See? Through love, through loneliness, through one tiny lamentable lapse in judgment. All of us. In our isolation we reach out from the darkness, from the alienation of modern life, to form these connections." In this sense, community is a form of visibility that is arguably far more potent than many other, perhaps more radical, modes of lesbian political expression. In this model, everyone—straight women, men, and lesbians—can be rendered queer.

However, the case of Lara calls even this unifying notion of community into question. Before Dana and her friends, in Bette's words, "deploy a mission to ascertain the disposition and intent of one Miss Lara Perkins," Alice tries to use her online chart to find Lara amidst its homespun web of lesbian relationships. Her name is not to be found, and, compounded with the failure of the club espionage expedition, Dana's surprise is understandable when Lara later approaches her in the locker room and kisses her without preamble. Lara is not presented as closeted or otherwise shy about her sexual orientation, so the reasoning for her absence from the chart and her lack of response to Shane's flirtations is never made clear. What Lara's unclassifiable presence does suggest, however, is that the lesbian community, like lesbian fashion, is not all-encompassing; despite the social and cultural cache, perhaps even the women of *The L Word* do not have the final say on what constitutes lesbian visibility or embodiment. Furthermore, when Dana is dissuaded by her friends from wearing a sundress on her first date with Lara in the next episode ("Longing"), Lara herself shows up in a dress, noting with chagrin, "I overdressed . . . God, I feel like such a geek." Dana's response—"No, I'm a geek. For letting my friends tell me what to wear"—perfectly sums up the failure of a unified notion of (lesbian) fashion.

As the aforementioned scenes indicate, despite the show's explicit fore-grounding of connectivity, community, and diversity, the characters are often remarkably unaware of their own place in the construction of lesbian fashion and visibility. As Alice's slightly mocking reading of the hundred-footer and Dana's willingness to comply with her friends' fashion edicts both imply, the women of *The L Word* often fail to implement the tenets of feminist egalitarianism and individual freedom that provide the groundwork for their positions as visible and politically viable lesbians despite their heteronormative appearances. In fact, when gender is in question—rather than just sexual orientation—the women are often even more perplexed by the potential visual confusions.

For example, at the end of the first season, Kit finds herself increasingly attracted to Ivan, a possibly transgender sometime drag-king. Kit's attraction to Ivan initially leaves her feeling confused and guilty because she knows it is not founded on a changing sexual orientation, but rather because, in her eyes, Ivan appears and acts masculine enough to garner her attention. However, their flirtation ends abruptly at the beginning of the second season not because, as we may expect, Kit decides she cannot handle Ivan's gender complexity, but because Ivan cannot come to terms with Kit accidentally seeing his naked and very feminine body. Although Kit, an ostensibly heterosexual woman, is willing to accept Ivan for his named gender rather than his biological sex, Ivan cannot overcome the failed representation of himself as a woman in Kit's eyes.

In another example of confused gender and its visible ramifications, Alice briefly dates a self-identified male-lesbian named Lisa. Physically male, but identifying across genders, Lisa is simultaneously not very feminine-looking and yet very stereotypically feminine in his demeanor; he is overly sensitive and nurturing, constantly wants to talk and refuses to have genital intercourse with Alice because he does not identify with his penile anatomy. Despite her bisexuality, Alice cannot come to terms with Lisa's gendered contradictions and ends the relationship. Both Lisa and Ivan, and their respective partners, complicate sexuality and gender in a way that unsettles notions of lesbian visibility (how much more invisible can a lesbian get than actually being a man?). However, even though the women of The L Word do not seem to understand the problematic and compelling nature of these visual conundrums, it does not mean that the attentive viewer must fall completely in line with the characters' perspectives. In other words, the characters are often foiled by the same visual stereotypes of femininity, masculinity, and gender's deceptive juxtaposition with sexuality that the show itself arguably is trying to disbar. However, rather than allow these contradictions to disavow the show's subversive potential, I believe the tension between the presumed diversity of the women and their problematic enactment of that collectivity is one of the most fruitful and compelling sites for political viability.

In conclusion, I wish to offer an example of confused appearances, failed diversity, and uncertain readings of fashion, class, and sexuality from the just-concluded third season. In what may be one of the most compelling and/or problematic plotlines to date, in the episode "Lobsters" Jenny returns from an extended trip to the Midwest with shy, working-class butch Moira in tow. Her presence is a startling contrast to the glamorous, fashion-conscious, upper-middle-class world of *The L Word*'s core cast. While Moira is initially unapologetic about her style of dress and self-gendering—upon first meeting, addressing Shane through the collective "us butches" while Shane looks at her incredulously—she is treated in a surprisingly patronizing way by the other characters (except Jenny and Shane). At a dinner in honor of Jenny's return, Bette even goes so far as to unselfconsciously speculate that Moira is "the way she is" (butch in a decidedly un-chic way, in torn jeans and old t-shirts) because she is from rural America and is yet to be liberated from what Bette sees as the confinement of lesbian gender binaries. And Tina's startling suggestion that Jenny must have been lonely in the Midwest clearly implies that Jenny would have never found anything attractive about Moira if she had been in L.A. What is amazing is that almost all the women make the same essentializing assumptions about Moira's butchness without any mention of their own investment in the unquestionable femininity of their L.A.-lesbian fashion.

However, the structure of the show itself does not let the ladies off the hook. Just as their earlier attempt to classify Lara is portrayed as an absurd espionage adventure, Moira's subsequent homesickness and breakdown is rendered much more sympathetically than the core cast's refusal to accept her. And it is telling that she is not self-conscious about her appearance or gender position until her lack of any intentional style is juxtaposed with the readily apparent yet subconscious fashion concerns of the other women. Their eventual acceptance of Moira is made all the more disturbing as it comes on the heels of Moira's co-option of an expensive men's suit jacket to complement her t-shirt and jeans at a party and her not entirely surefooted decision that she is transgender. The clarity of the ladies' prejudice—moored in notions of class, fashion, and gender—and their obvious inability to recognize their own place in the style hierarchy of lesbian visibility and gender politics has heretofore not been as starkly rendered as in this third season story arc. This narrative highlights the characters' collective failure to enact the tenets of their own supposed stylistic liberalism. However, it also foregrounds the show's continued commitment to confronting the relationship between femininity, fem(me)ine dress, style, class, and the politics of lesbian visibility, thus simultaneously instilling and critiquing the mythology of lesbian chic.

NOTE

I would like to thank Professor Beth Buggenhagen, April Miller, and Fred Viebahn for their encouragement and insight during the writing of this chapter.

WORKS CITED

Charlies Angels. ABC. 22 Sept. 1976–24 June 1981.

Cottingham, Laura. *Lesbians Are So Chic . . . That We're Not Really Lesbians At All*. London: Cassell, 1996.

Dittmar, Linda. "The Straight Goods: Lesbian Chic and Identity Capital on a Not-so-Queer Planet." *The Passionate Camera: Photography and Bodies of Desire*. Ed. Deborah Bright. New York: Routledge, 1998. 319–39.

Everett, Karen, dir. *Framing Lesbian Fashion*. Videocassette. Frameline, 1992.

Eves, Alison. "Queer Theory, Butch/Femme Identities and Lesbian Space." *Sexualities* 7.4 (2004): 480–96.

Faderman, Lillian. *Odd Girls and Twilight Lovers: A History of Lesbian Life in Twentieth-Century America*. New York: Penguin, 1991.

Halberstam, Judith. *Female Masculinity*. Durham: Duke UP, 1998.

The L Word. Perf. Jennifer Beals, Erin Daniels, Leisha Hailey, Laurel Holloman, Mia Kirshner, Katherine Moennig, Pam Grier, Daniela Sea, Rachel Shelly, and Sarah Shahi. Showtime. 18 Jan. 2004–Present.

"Let's Do It." *The L Word* 25 Jan. 2004.

"Lobsters." *The L Word* 22 Jan. 2006.

"Longing." *The L Word* 1 Feb. 2004.

"Looking Back." *The L Word* 28 Mar. 2004.

Nielsen, Kate. "Lesbian Chic, Part Deux." *Advocate* 17 Feb. 2004: 9.

"Pilot." *The L Word* 18 Jan. 2004.

Pottie, Lisa. "Hierarchies of Otherness: The Politics of Lesbian Styles in the 1990s, or, What to Wear?" *Canadian Women's Studies/Les Cahiers de la Femme* 16.2 (1996): 49–52.

Sedgwick, Eve Kosofsky. "*The L Word*: Novelty in Normalcy." *The Chronicle of Higher Education* 50.19 (2004): B10–11.

Solomon, Alice. "Not Just a Passing Fancy: Notes on Butch." *The Passionate Camera: Photography and Bodies of Desire*. Ed. Deborah Bright. New York: Routledge, 1998. 263–75.

Walker, Lisa M. "How to Recognize a Lesbian: The Cultural Politics of Looking Like What You Are." *Signs* 18.4 (1993): 866–90.

CHAPTER 6

"READING FOR IT": LESBIAN READERS CONSTRUCTING CULTURE AND IDENTITY THROUGH TEXTUAL EXPERIENCE

SHEILA LIMING

Abstract: *My research here concerns lesbian readership and stems from a study I conducted among twelve lesbian interview participants (18–24 years old) who comprised a generational view of this particular issue. I interviewed these women in order to gain insight into texts that they found particularly instrumental, or applicable, to their individual coming out processes and to the ways in which they have managed to construct both their personal lesbian identities and conceptions of modern lesbian culture. On average, I found that lesbian women continue to rely upon somewhat outdated lesbian texts and are otherwise made to "read for it" in heterosexual culture with an awareness of otherness.*

ADRIENNE RICH, WHO HAS STATED that "Re-vision—the act of looking back, of seeing with fresh eyes . . . is an act of survival," understands the threat that inactivity poses to culture ("When" 35). If we are to understand her words to the extent that culture (and its applications) is made to survive through revision, we can interpret popular gay culture (and gay culture more generally) as well on its way to total deceasure.

Though these grave consequences threaten all facets of queer culture, lesbian culture in particular, I believe, remains especially vulnerable to such systematic

86   SHEILA LIMING

annihilation. For lesbians, progress and movement have always been difficult to acknowledge or grasp because lesbianism itself has been largely unsure of its own beginnings. Literature has long served as a vessel by which lesbian women might come to terms with their identity and has helped to contextualize lesbianism more broadly, however it has done so through a rather meager ration of lesbian texts and authors. Bonnie Zimmerman, speaking in 1992, stated that "We are certainly not as badly off as we were in the early seventies, when the only lesbian novels in print were *The Well of Loneliness*, Isabel Miller's *Patience and Sarah*, and Rita Mae Brown's *Rubyfruit Jungle*" ("Lesbians" 51). Now that another decade has passed, though, and provided us with more wisdom and assumptions of progress, where is the proof of our evolution? Where is the evidence of advancement that Zimmerman alluded to in describing her relief over not having to rely on texts such as Brown's?

At the age of sixteen, I was reading *Rubyfruit Jungle*. I was also reading Radclyffe Hall's *The Well of Loneliness* and, only a few years later, Miller's *Patience and Sarah*. What is more, the young lesbian women with whom I had interaction—the women who, in fact, constituted the only feasible, recognizable sampling of lesbian culture available to me at that time—were also reading these books. Like me, they were also made to cling to texts that offered up yellowing pages, outdated scenarios, and the only obtainable representations of real lesbians. These texts, however, were integral to the formation of our lesbian identities because they constituted for us some semblance of history; with and within them, we were able to glimpse where lesbianism had been and, perhaps, indications of where it might be going. The repute and ubiquity of these texts to lesbian culture also cemented their value in our lives and experiences; they were important to us as lesbians because they were important to other lesbians.

In considering the connections between lesbian readers and these seemingly obsolete, old-fashioned texts, I set out to conduct a study that would get at the heart of lesbians' requirements and the texts, both old and new, that serve to fulfill them. I outlined a general population from which to locate research subjects, choosing to place them between the ages of eighteen and twenty-four as a means of comprising a generation of readers in which I would also be able to participate. Thirteen subjects, including myself, were secured and interviewed for the purposes of this study, and their separate locations and identities spanned issues of geography, race, and ethnicity to provide, in my view, a reasonably balanced population within which to study issues of lesbian readership and subjectivity in relation to standard lesbian texts. The subjects' upbringing varied as well, providing an intriguing validation of this body of literature when a young woman living in Salem, West Virginia, for example, was discovered to have been reading the same lesbian material as girls in Portland, Oregon, and Seattle, Washington.

The discussion at hand seeks to investigate the use and usefulness of lesbian literature in constructing aspects of identity for lesbian women among this generational population. It is approached from a fundamental understanding that, while gay pop culture purports to offer an ample supply of images appropriate to young, modern, homosexual women, the media still lacks authentic and viable representations of lesbians and, as such, lesbian women, in confronting the truth of their sexual identities, are forced to refer to literature for verification of themselves and their culture. While celebrated series such as Showtime's *The L-Word* pretend to confront and furnish issues of lesbian visibility in the media, the show features few lesbians among its regular cast members; in an interview with *The Advocate*, series actor Jennifer Beals identified only two such cast members while citing her own hesitations about acting lesbian (Stockwell). As a result, *The L-Word* may present an aesthetically pleasing rendition of lesbian culture, but it ultimately fails to provide us, its lesbian audiences, with a reliable model against which we may affirm our identities. Given this general lack of media representation, literature continues to be central to popular lesbian culture and must be revisited and revised in order to promote the survival not just of lesbianism, but of lesbians as a visible, existent body within society. It is my intention to investigate and discuss popular lesbian culture in terms of the texts that constitute the bulk of its applications, including such standards as Hall's *The Well of Loneliness* and Brown's *Rubyfruit Jungle* alongside another vital, more pressing contingent: lesbian Young Adult literature. Finally, I pay attention to considerations of lesbian readership in an effort to discuss the modes and motives of lesbian reading that fall in conjunction with lesbian texts or, on occasion, heterosexual texts that entertain lesbian interpretations.

At the age of sixteen, I did not have friends to consult about being gay. Though my perceptions of my moderately progressive suburban high school in my moderately progressive neighborhood had suggested to me that my friends would be supportive, I had no way of beginning to speak to them about what I was going through, and no reason to believe they might understand if I did. Now, as I reflect on past conversations with other gay and lesbian individuals, the disaffected quality of the coming out process itself becomes apparent to me; the process through which an individual is able to come out and acknowledge certain essential truths about their sexuality is always a process of alienation, marked by feelings of loneliness and singularity. Though environmental factors and upbringing may support or further complicate this process, it is ultimately one that we endure alone. The sources of these feelings of alienation are all around us—on television, in the newspaper, in our own families—and given that these institutions do not generally reflect images of gay and lesbian people, it is easy, if not inevitable, to feel as though you are the only one.

"NOTHING TO REMEMBER": HISTORY, PRESENT, AND THE ROOTS OF LESBIAN LITERATURE

Perhaps even more disturbing for a young lesbian woman than the lack of a media-inspired contemporary context is the apparent lack of a historical one. Lesbians have, as the authors Laura Doan and Sarah Waters remind us, a genealogy that is disrupted by "the suppression or absence of lesbian activity from the historical record" (13). Our history, even from its earliest representatives, is constructed as a literary one with its beginnings mysteriously rooted in the obscure personae of Sappho of Lesbos, the sort of default model for ancient lesbianism. Not much is actually known about Sappho, except that she loved women and wrote poetry about them. The combination of these two identities, lesbian and poet, has established Sappho, much like Radclyffe Hall and Rita Mae Brown, respectively, as an integral piece of lesbian history. She has become our alpha and our omega, and where do we go from there? To the library, it seems.

"There is only the present and nothing to remember" (24). Doan and Waters' statement here is a painfully true one for many lesbians today and yet is somewhat speculative in asserting that lesbians have a present. If we do, it is a nebulous one, and one that is hardly visible to the greater majority of society. For many lesbian women, it seems literature, in all its forms but especially in novels, memoirs, and autobiographical stories, holds both a past and a present, or at the very least access to both. As Julie Abraham puts it, "before Stonewall, novels were the primary (textual) source of popular understandings of lesbianism" (qtd. in Bachmann 378). Though terms such as "popular understandings" are contentious in themselves (are popular understandings the only ones legitimized for unpopular lesbian populations?), and though I would argue that our post-Stonewall era has not seen a digression from this method of understanding, Abraham's argument begins to speak to the importance of texts in the construction of lesbian identity.

Keeping in mind that lesbian history—indeed, lesbian existence as we know it—survives in essence as a literary one, I became intrigued with the concept of the lesbian reader. In particular, I wanted to know what lesbians read for when they approach texts such as The Well of Loneliness, or Sappho, or Rita Mae Brown; how does one read when they are charged with the task of seeking out and formulating a historical and contemporary context in the pages of fiction or even classical poetry? What do these women glean from these texts, and how does that information shape their lives as lesbian women, as individuals, and as modern people in modern society? Most importantly, though, how does this literature help, if at all, to fill the void left by popular media that generally excludes images of lesbians or lesbianism?

Approaching a wide range of lesbian literature for the purpose of this study, I was confronted all too inevitably with the issue of my own subjectivity.

While asking what it meant to read as a lesbian and to interpret texts in this manner, I was suddenly challenged by an onslaught of memories and textual experiences contained in my own brief lesbian past. In discussions with other women, I began to recall tenderly the exact emotions and feelings connected with the afternoons I spent reading *The Well of Loneliness*, locked away as I was in my bedroom and voraciously consuming the notes left for me by previous readers. I realized that I could not ethically begin to discuss the lesbian reader without applying and analyzing the power of that concept upon my own experiences as a reader, and so began formally my interview process with a self-interview. This material, quoted as subjective source information alongside responses from other participants in the study, would provide a basis and touchstone to which I would return time and again throughout the project to reflect, remember, and just breathe.

There came the natural but also important struggle with the term "lesbian literature" itself, a vague one warranting elucidation for the purposes of this study. At long last, I chose to allow each participant the opportunity to outline, as specifically or tenuously as each may desire, her own definition of lesbian literature. In general, these separate definitions came to include either works written by lesbian women, works written specifically for lesbian women (though usually difficult to identify), or works written with a main lesbian character or issue as their primary focus. Though many seemed to argue that lesbian texts could only be written accurately and effectively by actual lesbians (and most of the works discussed here, consequently, are), some of the texts that entered into the conversation were also those whose authors are heterosexual, homosexual male, or whose sexualities were not clearly designated or revealed. In addition, conversations and interviews also paid special attention to the experience of reading straight literature as a lesbian, and the consequences of imposing a consciousness of lesbianism upon these texts. As Zimmerman points out, this is an issue with which lesbians are particularly but also inevitably faced; lesbians "have had to begin with a special question: 'When is a text a "lesbian text" or its writer a "lesbian writer"?' Lesbians are faced with this special problem of definition: presumably, we know when a writer is a 'Victorian writer' or a 'Canadian writer' " ("What" 204).

What Zimmerman labels as lesbian women's special problem is an integral one; after all, it is not merely with detached entertainment that a lesbian woman may read through such a text, but with concentrated and passionate attention. Identifying a text for what it is or what it may be permitted to be is an important task for a lesbian reader, and one that, like lesbian reading, follows no set definition or set of standards. On the whole, it seems that human representation was ultimately at the core of lesbian experience and information to be relayed to these women in a given text, and that representation might stem from fictional sources (from the characters themselves) or from a more factual, authoritative presence (the author herself). Despite this relative criteria, however, many of the women I spoke with were hesitant about applying the lesbian label to some of their first reading experiences of this nature. Participant Twelve, while discussing the novel *Foxfire* by Joyce Carol Oates, demonstrated such hesitation when saying that it "wasn't really, like, the first lesbian book I ever read or anything, I mean it's probably not even a real lesbian book, whatever that's supposed to mean . . . but it was definitely the most important for me. It's probably the most important book of my life to date."[1] She was obviously reluctant about identifying a written text for what it might not be in the eyes of anyone other than herself, but she was simultaneously emphatic about its personal significance as a lesbian text.

Finally, I borrowed and adapted a rather handy and deceptively linear spectrum of coming out stages from Dr. Richard Niolon of the Chicago School of Professional Psychology.[2] These stages I arranged along a so-labeled "coming out continuum" and asked interview participants to place their important lesbian texts, coming out experiences, and shaping lesbian moments along the continuum in order to gain and assess a sort of progression of lesbian consciousness in each of them. This growth of lesbian consciousness was then matched to the lesbian texts cited by each respondent as having occurred or been experienced simultaneously. The continuum thereby became a reference point for understanding the coming out process and, while it was not always accepted by the interview subjects, helped them to track the evolution of their own lesbianism.

One of the interview respondents, during the course of our conversation together, hesitated before placing her own lesbian literary highlights along the familiar "Coming Out Continuum," asking me, "What if I read this book before even really thinking about being gay?" I realized that the continuum itself left only a small amount of space for the respondents to list their reading experiences in any chronology that might have preceded their awareness of their sexuality, however slight that awareness may have been. The reason, for I had intended it to be that way when devising the continuum, was the focus and direction of my research; my primary concerns were with lesbian readers. Anything that came before self-awareness and lesbian identity therefore seemed, at least cursorily, to be slightly beyond the scope of my project. If we are, however, to interpret lesbian women as always having been lesbians regardless of their own recognition (for this seems to be the favored opinion among my respondents), then we must acknowledge and allow space for earlier experiences influenced by assumptions of heterosexuality.

Most of the women I spoke with could identify as having read from a lesbian perspective before even knowing that they were, indeed, lesbian. As Participant Two put it, "Even if I'd wanted to be gay then, I couldn't have because of my family, so I was . . . reading for it, but I didn't know it."

Her choice of words in this statement communicates many things, among them the fact that her lesbian identity was not the one she had seriously considered at this point so that, even if she had been aware of it and had wanted to assume it, familial and environmental pressure would have prevented her from doing so. Participant Two was thereby experiencing reading as a lesbian ("reading for it") without yet identifying as one. Similarly, Participant Five recalled the experience of reading heterosexual texts without inclinations that would have allowed her to read and accept them as anything but truth for her personally. In response to the books she read while in high school, she said, "I wasn't even thinking about being gay then. I didn't come out until I was in a very safe place—that includes to myself." For her, concerns for her own safety and security prevented her from thinking about her sexuality or its relevance to the literature she was reading.

Participant Four, who began to identify and acknowledge her lesbianism at the relatively early age of twelve, remembers reading books from the *Nancy Drew Girl Detective* series including titles such as *The Mystery at Lilac Inn* and *The Clue of the Whistling Bagpipes* (Keene) and described, along with an obsession with the character of Nancy, being sympathetically drawn to the boyish, short-haired character of George; in looking back, she described this character as "totally gay." In her interview, Participant Four regarded this as an early lesbian reading experience, important, if not completely legitimate. Sherrie Inness has likewise approached the subject of Nancy Drew as a lesbian icon and states that "Reading the Nancy Drew books from lesbian perspective entails being a resistant reader who refuses to accept the books' apparent messages about society, cultural values, and gender" (84). It seems that Participant Four was, in many ways, ahead of her time in developing the skills of a resistant reader—by all means necessary and indispensable to lesbian readers—at such a young age.

I once heard someone say that to be a lesbian means to live on the scraps and morsels occasionally offered to you by heterosexual society. In this way, the occasional mention of lesbianism in a television show or the slightly ambiguous gay female character in a movie would persist to haunt me, providing only a taste of what I came to believe must exist in a greater, more explicit totality elsewhere. For years, I experienced heterosexual texts as a lesbian, desperately reading for those scraps and morsels, dog-earing their pages and remembering them with startling lucidity. Stacey Donovan asserts her stance regarding this practice: Lesbians "look for meanings that lurk behind the text's apparently heterosexual surface, knowing that lesbian experiences, whether in fiction or reality, are rarely overt. When lesbians read, they actively disassemble the dominant heterosexual plot, demonstrating that heterosexuality does not hold its culturally prescribed central role for all readers" (qtd. in Inness 123). Lesbian women, having inferred from their surrounding culture the covertness of their own lives and experiences, appear to read more intensely in search of them. Remember also that, for a lesbian reader, one would be more often engaged in reading against a given text than reading toward it, seldom encountering works where lesbianism would be overt enough to place us on our home turf.

Many of the women I interviewed intentionally chose to avoid more mature, adult novels and subject matters in their reading in order to obviate situations where they would be faced with explicit illustrations of heterosexual sexuality. Participant Nine admitted to sticking to young adult novels "perhaps too long" in her reading so that she might not have to confront such direct representations of sexuality that would have been contrary to her own. As she seemed to feel, avoiding sex—even in literary representation—was a means by which she might avoid the truth about herself and her own sexuality. Participant One employed similar methods, recognizing only that she felt uncomfortable with sexual situations in literature (all of which were hetero-sexually based), and not that her discomfort might be in any way significant of an underlying issue. Both women, however, enjoyed literary representations of real relationships in any context, gay or straight, and Participant Nine even cited having read Nancy Garden's classic young adult lesbian text *Annie on my Mind* as a young, assumedly heterosexual female, and not having been significantly affected by the lesbian relationship described there. She remem-bered only that the relationship was sweet and innocent to the point of being relatively sex-free. In another conversation, Participant One related her feelings of reluctance when approaching the subject of sex and sexuality at a younger age. She said, "I didn't feel like most people seemed to be . . . feeling at seventeen and I really didn't want to read romance stuff with lots of sex on every page." The latent assumption in this statement is, of course, that most seventeen-year-olds growing up normally, and without the intrusion of societal pressure upon their true desires, would be feeling an interest in sex and would be, by this age, exploring their own personal sexuality. Though the subject did not directly express this reluctance as deriving from her undiscovered homosexual inclinations, I think it is safe to argue that, in this case as in many others, those inclinations are nevertheless at work in wielding influence. Participant One added, "I was seventeen but I wasn't like most people at seventeen," further evidence of the separation she was already sensing even before identifying as gay.

Jean E. Kennard's theories of lesbian reading address the issue of preles-bianism as well as the subsequent appropriation of heterosexual texts that so often results from these implicitly felt inclinations. She has termed this process one of "lesbian re-reading" and describes it as involving the relentless pursuit of details or, as she says, "finding something else to do than substitute woman where the word man appears" (66). This substitution is simply not enough for lesbian readers to engage with a text and so the process of their

reading becomes a somewhat painstaking procedure in which texts must be
revised, mentally rewritten and, as such, reread.

APPROACHING "THE CLASSICS": INNOCENCE, SEX,
AND SEXUALITY IN LESBIAN LITERATURE

Of all texts discussed by interview respondents, three surfaced as the most
popular and, thus, most widely identified, discussed, and read among young
lesbian readers today. Listed in order of popularity, they are *Annie on my
Mind*, by Nancy Garden, *Rubyfruit Jungle*, by Rita Mae Brown, and *Tipping
the Velvet*, by Sarah Waters. Particularly, *Annie on my Mind* arose as an
influential text for all but one woman I spoke with. Nancy Garden's highly
controversial young adult novel has received its fair share of attention since its
initial publication a few decades ago. In that time, it was consistently celebrated and simultaneously denigrated, to varying degrees and for different
reasons, but now it has a place on the American Library Association's "The
100 Most Frequently Challenged Books of 1990–2000"—having itself been
banned for various periods of time in locations across the United States.
Inness describes its history, stating that, "Even critically acclaimed books,
such as Nancy Garden's *Annie on my Mind* are not free from censorship. Her
novel was burned on Kansas City School District grounds in 1993 and was
the subject of a lawsuit instigated by a group of parents and children" (105).
In spite of—or perhaps due to—*Annie on my Mind*'s infamous rapport, many
of the subjects interviewed in my research encountered the novel as their very
first lesbian reading experience.

Participant Four, in our conversation, had the following statement to offer
regarding Garden's novel:

> I had a problem with the fact that none of the books—really none of the
> books—spoke to me or spoke to my personality . . . I found that there were
> books written for people like me, people who were so young and who wanted to
> read about other people a little bit older than them who may have been strug-
> gling with ideas about their sexuality, and *Annie on my Mind* was . . . something
> that was . . . amazing. Inspirational.

A key portion of this response is the phrase "people like me." For a young
woman on the verge of constructing an identity for herself, recognizing at
least to some degree that this identity is, in essence, a contradiction of what is
considered normal in society, the discovery of people like herself could be
nothing short of phenomenal. What is more, the realization that there exist
books and written material designed specifically for *these* people is further
verification: proof of not only their existence but also of their recognition in
the world. Says Inness, "Gay and lesbian youth continue to have a difficult

time gaining access to reading materials that relate to their own lives" (102). For Participant Four, this relation, as well as the books that made it possible, was an essential part of constructing a lesbian identity: "it made me feel like my own sexuality was validated, like it was okay and still, like, an innocent impulse or whatever." Note the word "innocent"; since popular conceptions of homosexuality have historically portrayed it as something perverse, dirty, and immoral, the idea of innocence is one that seems to often become absent in lesbian and gay consciousness. Additionally, it must be remembered that Participant Four was only thirteen at the time of reading *Annie on my Mind*. Innocence may not hold much significance for a lesbian of twenty-five, but one has to consider its potential importance for a lesbian of thirteen. This concept of innocence is, I believe, one of the more redeeming aspects of Garden's novel, aside from its very existence as one of the few texts of its kind available and published for young readers.

Participant Six, however, related to me how Garden's novel had initially "freaked her out," citing that its closeness to her own life had made her feel "doomed" in heterosexual society. It seems that the book paralleled her own feelings and experiences so assiduously that she interpreted this as confirmation, though of a negative sort. Instead of feeling empowered by the text, she felt found-out by it: "Reading a story that was almost my life made me feel doomed to be gay and whatever happened in that book might as well just be the story of my life or my future. I felt, like, good, and comforted, but I cried and cried and cried."

One of Garden's most impressive achievements made through *Annie on my Mind*, however, may be its ability to turn lesbian readers on to other lesbian textual sources. Garden, now the author of many young adult novels with the majority of them concerning (if not blatantly focusing on) issues of sexuality in young readers, is no stranger herself to the importance of literature and its wide-ranging influences. She intentionally injects this knowledge into her texts and, in *Annie on my Mind*, includes a scene where Annie gives the bewildered Liza a copy of Isabel Miller's *Patience and Sarah*.[3] Liza narrates, "I did read the book, and Annie reread it, and it helped us discuss the one part of ourselves we'd only talked around so far . . . I felt as if I were meeting parts of myself in the gay people I read about. Gradually, I began to feel calmer inside, more complete and sure of myself, and I knew from the way Annie looked as we talked . . . that she did also" (144). Liza's mature tone in this passage, coupled with Garden's implicit suggestions for further reading, serve, or at the very least have the potential to serve, as a guide for the young, questioning, lesbian. The theme is repeated in another scene where Liza and Annie do some investigating while house-sitting for two of their female teachers. Liza again narrates the discovery in the teachers' bedroom of a bookcase containing additional lesbian texts, and the reading list grows to include Hall's

The Well of Loneliness, Female Homosexuality by Frank S. Caprio, and *Sappho Was a Right-On Woman* by Sydney Abbott and Barbara Love.

The subject of young adult fiction in particular is an interesting one where a lesbian population is concerned. At first, having conducted only a few interviews, I was shocked by the constant reference to the title *Annie on my Mind* in these responses. This novel was written for and remains aimed at a young adult audience, yet the majority of my respondents—not only these early ones, but many others to follow—encountered this book at a later stage, one at which we would assume such literature to be below the level of concern, intrigue, or value for such women. The image of an eighteen-year-old lesbian female forging her identity through the pages of a young adult novel featuring main characters who are younger than herself seems, at least initially, to be somewhat consternating. It must be remembered, however, that an emotional and sexual awakening tends to come hand in hand with one's own self-revelation of homosexuality and, thus, a developmental delay of sorts can be observed in individuals who are not able to experience this awakening until a later age.

For the heterosexuals of this world, literature has always been able to move along in tandem with basic human growth and development—one need only to take a stroll through their local bookstore's young adult section in order to realize this. The shelves of this section are often filled with novels that attempt to tenderly, gently approach subjects such as sexuality and early romantic relationships for audiences of adolescent and preteen kids. Junior high and high school health curricula spend considerable amounts of time on these subjects, and television and media portrayals supplement the imaginations of young adult viewers. When it is remembered that not all young adults are inclined to accept and respond to this sort of sexual prepping, a problem suddenly becomes visible, the results of which can be seen in lesbian and gay individuals who suddenly, at the ages of seventeen, eighteen, or much later down the road, must come to terms with what heterosexuals have already learned long ago. Given this lack of integration into popular consciousness, the interest that young lesbian women often have in young adult fiction and literature is not only elucidated, it is also afforded social and developmental logic. Participant Eight echoed this view in her responses to Garden's novel:

> When you begin that process of coming out, you are developmentally at a different, like, emotional age. You are at the sexual and emotional equivalent of a thirteen or fourteen year-old because you are experiencing then what you should have already experienced emotionally and sexually. And, you know, if we lived in a healthy society, children at that age would be able to have that sexual and emotional awakening regardless of its direction or its gender specification, and then I don't think you would have that delay.

I believe her assertions in this matter to be direct articulations of an issue that is central to my motivations in this research. Young lesbian women are denied access to their own development, systematically and consistently, through a society that negates their existence and self-awareness via this denial. Young women, by age and inexperience alone, are forced into belonging to the heterosexual majority and are not presented with options that would enable them to arrive at the truth about their own sexual identity. No one will talk to us about it, in schools or on television, and hence we are driven, many years later, back to the starting point to begin the process of self-discovery all over again. Participant Eight said additionally, "If you come out later, you're going back to *that* stage." The implications of the stage in question are apparent; *that* stage denotes ground zero, and lesbian women are henceforth required to make up for lost time.

There is always, it seems, a delay for us. Writing this, I am suddenly reminded of Adrienne Rich and, in particular, a few lines from her epic poetic sequence, "Twenty-One Love Poems." Rich says, "Since we're not young, weeks have to do time/for years of missing each other" (237). Of course, Rich's subject in this poem does not concern lesbian women of eighteen, but rather of forty-five. Nevertheless, a sense of self-awakening and rebirth—of starting over from ground zero—is communicated in her poem. She also feels pressed to make up for lost time, to recover for years of misconstrued identity and falsification. At eighteen, I felt so behind. I am hardly able now to consider the sensation of having been twenty-some years behind.

Lesbian literature, as a body and collected genre of texts, continues to exist perpetually behind the times. Why else would my interviews with lesbian women produce, among the top three most popular titles, two texts written almost three decades ago? It seems that standards such as *Annie on my Mind* (1982) and, even more importantly, *Rubyfruit Jungle* (1973) have become instilled as relics of lesbian history that must be read by all good lesbians. Lillian Faderman, in her monumental work *Surpassing the Love of Men*, describes the value that modern lesbians may continue to find in Rita Mae Brown's thirty-year-old novel: "The novel is so popular among [lesbians] because it gives them what they have long awaited: a character with whom they can identify, who is bold, brave, always in the right, an avenger of all the wrongs done to lesbians in twentieth-century life and literature" (407). Indeed, Brown's character, Molly Bolt, is a great many things. Participant Four, reflecting her own opinion and mine as well (and no doubt that of many other women), stated simply: "She was my hero." And why shouldn't she be? Faderman's identifying of Molly as a lesbian avenger of sorts is incredibly apt given the body of work and lesbian characters that had, for years, preceded this character and any representation of a strong, self-assured and (dare I say it?) *happy* lesbian woman.

In contrast to the self-deprecating, bemoaning Stephen Gordon as depicted by Hall, or even the polite, desexualized characters of Patience and Sarah as written by Miller, Molly Bolt has all the makings of a lesbian hero and has, I believe, earned her status as such. Additionally, Molly Bolt retains a degree of iconicity in current lesbian culture. It has been said, on many occasions and by many individuals in my presence, that one simply cannot be a lesbian without having read *Rubyfruit Jungle*. It is considered by groups of lesbian women to be a prerequisite of sorts, required reading that serves to place lesbian women in the context of the culture they are either explicitly or implicitly a part of. This view, in preserving the popularity and atemporality of the novel, continues to draw a consistent and obligatorily charged readership. Several of the women I spoke with described their motivations for reading *Rubyfruit Jungle* as having stemmed from a sense of duty, one which was not necessarily supported by a genuine interest in the book itself. While issues of race and class are both likely inhibitors preventing some lesbian readers from finding connection in Brown's novel, I believe the expectation of that connection itself surfaces as a preliminary and rather central obstacle.

Respondents such as Participant Eight, however, remained adamant in their feelings for Brown's book: "that book went from being, like, totally shocking to being . . . a resource. After a while it became this really cool thing, this liberating thing . . . It was liberating, especially after I started to come to terms with some things personally. I identified with the characters and I identified with their situations." While Participant Eight's upbringing may not in any way seem to parallel that of Brown's fictional character, she was able to make explicit and vivid connections between herself and Molly, a fact that may be attributed to many factors but, I would argue, is verified most significantly in having been the subject's first exposure to lesbian literature. The pure authority of it and the forthrightness of its subject matter had served, in this case, to overshadow all other details. Participant Eight, identifying with the characters' situations, was doing so primarily from the situation of sexual otherness.

The tremendous amount of emotion and intensity conveyed by this subject continues to impress me and, reading back over the interview's transcript, I am stirred to emotions of my own. I can no more make sense of her connections to a 1960s, poor, Southern lesbian woman than I can of my own with an early-twentieth-century, wealthy, English, aristocratic lesbian portrayed by Radclyffe Hall. With complete disregard for specifics of any kind, both of us had somehow given ourselves completely to these texts, blind to differences that might have marred our otherwise unwavering devotion to their characters.

We read, it seems, to insert ourselves within the greater design of things. We read for a sense of connection, for belonging. To cite Stanley Fish's opinions on the subject, reading "is self-sharpening and what it sharpens is *you*" (99).

That is, the act of reading is often an act of self-definition that is a necessary and requisite aspect of world-definition; you cannot place yourself within a context of others without first understanding yourself. Participant Eight and I, we both read and found inclusion. Years later, I sat in her living room and we discussed what we had read. Suddenly, it seemed, we were doing it all over again, seeking out and finding the inclusive community we needed—this time with each other.

PROOF OF LIFE: LITERATURE
AS CULTURAL VALIDATION

My concerns for the subject of popular gay culture begin, quite naturally, with considerations of lesbian literature; it is a connection that is afforded to me not only on the basis of my sexuality and experience but also as a tangible, accessible body of work that, I believe, succeeds in affirming lesbian existence where other aspects of culture fall short. In general, lesbians and homosexual people as a contingent are denied culture so as to deny them their existence. The meager collection of morsels, to recall an earlier discussion presented here, are primarily offered to us by the hands of the heteronormative majority and, as such, fail spectacularly when put to the test. Just as Showtime's *The L-Word* pretends to provide lesbian women with images of themselves, the popular comedy *Will and Grace* has similarly managed to lull us into false satisfaction at seeing a gay character as part of the accepted media mainstream. What audiences are generally unable to grasp while viewing *Will and Grace*, however, is a larger spectrum of detriment and damage caused by such a trite, atypical rendition of a homosexual character; instead of being furnished with an image of gay sexuality on our prime-time viewing schedule, we are being force-fed a contrived, shallow depiction that reassigns gay men—and women, vicariously—to all the old stereotypes that have historically kept them from participating in the mainstream. In short, gay images, when crafted by heterosexual majority, cannot be trusted or accurately understood as gay images. They are merely lifeless effigies, ventriloquist's dummies.

Literature exists now as one of the few authentic sources by which information about and indications of true gay identity may be conveyed in popular culture today. For lesbian women, this means delving into the work of past decades in order to locate verification of lesbian culture. The majority of the interview participants I spoke with who identified works by Brown, Hall, or Garden cited difficulties in connecting with the main characters in these works. They, however, read them—as lesbian readers will continue to so long as popular gay culture remains kowtowed to gay popular culture—in order to be able to participate in their lesbianism and in the culture, however slight, that defines it.

Lesbian literature has been hard at work to provide a context of lesbianism for some time now and to varying degrees, though, as I have argued, it has been primarily maintained through an embarrassingly small collection of texts. Circumstances—in which scandal, celebrity, criticism, and accessibility, all play their various parts—have served to keep these few works at the forefront of this canon, a fact that is at once both intriguing and profoundly unsettling. Although it has been demonstrated that literary reflection and verification is necessary to lesbian women during their coming out process and, additionally, into the later stages of their lesbian identity, works such as *Annie on my Mind* and *Rubyfruit Jungle*, while fundamental to that body of literature, are simply not enough. What is more, lesbian women consistently encounter obstacles when trying to access this literature, evidence of the fact that this genre—as well as the population it predominantly serves—is, far from what it needs to be, not a part of popular literary consciousness.

Adrienne Rich, in a line from "Twenty-One Love Poems," states that "The story of our lives becomes our lives" (245), speaking to the power that narrative invention often has over the way we live as people and, more specifically, to the way we envision and construct ourselves as lesbian women. As a sixteen-year-old, I forged a connection with the literary personae of Stephen Gordon whose story, though by all means different from my own, opened up and created a space for the story that would be mine. Participants One, Four, and Eight, in our conversations together, were able to identify this same sort of collection established between them and Brown's character of Molly Bolt while Participants Four, Five, Six, and Nine were doing the same with *Annie on my Mind*. In each case, the literature we read was informing us even as we were transforming it; these stories were creating a basis for our own and, in doing so, were becoming part of our experiences as lesbian women and active elements of our history together.

Today, popular gay culture stands irrefutably at a turning point in its progress and movement. As the gay marriage debate rages and small, incredibly vocal facets of the American homosexual population mobilize for gay rights, the culture itself remains encased in the same old torpor that has defined it for so many years. If change and progress is to be made, popular gay culture must be revitalized with both a respect for its past and a realistic understanding of its future. Within lesbian literature, texts such as those by Brown, Hall, and Garden must continue to spark inspiration and lay the groundwork for lesbian writers. In addition, though, lesbian writers themselves, and queer writers of all definitions and identities, must follow suit; we must actively engage ourselves in the production of popular gay culture that exists by and for ourselves. We must not make ourselves content with the picture-perfect, insultingly subcutaneous representations of homosexuality that are mass-marketed and deemed "gay pop culture." We must increase the knowledge, awareness, and accessibility of our history; texts such as *Rubyfruit Jungle* must be made easily available to lesbian women so that dialogue can begin and, additionally, our interactions with true lesbian and gay culture must not end there if we are to stimulate and enforce survival as a means of becoming a viable, legitimate force in society.

I feel for Hall's character Stephen Gordon when she tells Puddle, "I mean that my work could be much more vital; I feel it, I'm holding it back in some way, there's something I'm always missing" (217). The irony is, of course, that my reverence for Hall's works stems from the decision she made to *not* hold back, to deliver with compassion, honesty, and integrity the truth of her existence and the truth of lesbianism in the world. It is a charge that lesbian writers—myself among them—must not lose sight of, now that there exist a few works that do not hold back. To write as a queer voice means to resist our society's attempts to hold us back, to fight against forces that prevent the illumination of that experience and, consequently, to kindle a system of connections between readers and writers as part of the vital, requisite task of constructing culture. At the same time, reading with a queer conscious requires a similar amount of resistance; gay readers are required (to borrow from Peter J. Rabinowitz) to participate in a particular process of transformation when approaching a text (43). It is only through transformation that queer readers may extract true meaning from texts and may ascribe the significance of that meaning to their own lives. Such is the basis of culture, a necessary force that transforms us while we transform and challenge the elements that comprise it.

NOTES

1. Interview subjects are referred to as numbered participants. Interviews were conducted with the expectation of confidentiality. While the original study included brief biographies about the participants, I chose not to assign pseudonyms in order to stay true to the focus of this project that, I believe, primarily concerns identity and the claiming of personal ownership in one's experiences, thoughts, and reactions.

2. The stages are outlined and adapted as follows: "Stage One: Self-recognition as gay: confusion, curiosity, denial, anger. (What is homosexuality?) Stage Two: Disclosure to others: 'coming out' to close friends, family, studying stereotypes. (How does one be gay?) Stage Three: Socialization with other gays: feelings of camaraderie, seeking gay 'role models'. (Who is gay?) Stage Four: Positive self-identification: seeking and making positive gay relationships. Stage Five: Integration and acceptance: fulfillment in gay relationships" (Niolon).

3. This is especially significant considering that the majority of participants I interviewed stated that they received their books from other lesbians. Book-lending was the most common means by which lesbians gained access to these somewhat elusive texts, and is exemplified here in Garden's novel as well as in another of hers, *The Year They Burned the Books* (1999).

WORKS CITED

Abbott, Sydney, and Barbara Love. *Sappho Was a Right on Woman.* New York: Stein, 1972.

American Library Association. "The One-Hundred Most Frequently Challenged Books of 1990–2000." *ALA.org.* 2005. American Library Association. 10 Nov. 2005 <http://www.ala.org/ala/oif/bannedbooksweek/bbwlinks/100mostfrequently.htm>.

Bachmann, Monica. "Someone like Debby: (De)Constructing a Lesbian Community of Readers." *GLQ* 6.3 (2000): 377–88.

Brown, Rita Mae. *Rubyfruit Jungle.* New York: Bantam, 1973.

Caprio, Frank S. *Female Homosexuality; A Psychodynamic Study of Lesbianism.* New York: Citadel, 1954.

Doan, Laura, and Sarah Waters. "Making up for Lost Time: Contemporary Lesbian Writing and the Invention of History." *Territories of Desire in Queer Culture: Refiguring Contemporary Boundaries.* Ed. David Alderson and Linda Anderson. Manchester, Eng.: Manchester UP, 2000. 12–24.

Faderman, Lillian. *Surpassing the Love of Men.* New York: Morrow, 1981.

Fish, Stanley. "Literature in the Reader: Affective Stylistics." *Reader-Response Criticism: From Formalism to Post-Structuralism.* Ed. Jane P. Tompkins. Baltimore: Johns Hopkins UP, 1980. 70–71.

Garden, Nancy. *Annie on my Mind.* New York: Farrar, 1982.

———. *The Year They Burned the Books.* New York: Farrar, 1999.

Hall, Radclyffe. *The Well of Loneliness.* New York: Anchor, 1928.

Inness, Sherrie A. *The Lesbian Menace: Ideology, Identity, and the Representation of Lesbian Life.* Amherst: U of Massachusetts P, 1997.

Keene, Carolyn *The Mystery at Lilac Inn.* New York: Grosset, 1961.

———. *The Clue of the Whistling Bagpipes.* New York: Grosset, 1964.

Kennard, Jean E. "Ourself Behind Ourself: A Theory for Lesbian Readers." *Gender and Reading: Essays on Readers, Texts, and Contexts.* Ed. Elizabeth Flynn and Patrocinio Schweickart. Baltimore: Johns Hopkins UP, 1986. 63–80.

The L Word. Showtime. 18 Jan. 2004–Present.

Miller, Isabel. *Patience and Sarah.* New York: Fawcett, 1973.

Niolon, Richard. "Stages of Coming Out." *Psychopage.com.* June 2004. Chicago School for Professional Psychology. 10 Nov. 2004 <http://www.psychpage.com/gay/index.html>.

Oates, Joyce Carol. *Foxfire: Confessions of a Girl Gang.* New York: Dutton, 1993.

Participant Eight. Personal Interview. 21 Nov. 2004.

Participant Five. Personal Interview. 4 Nov. 2004.

Participant Four. Personal Interview. 27 Oct. 2004.

Participant Nine. Personal Interview. 29 Nov. 2004.

Participant One. Personal Interview. 10 Oct. 2004.

Participant Six. Personal Interview. 8 Nov. 2004.

Participant Twelve. Personal Interview. 31 Dec. 2004.

Participant Two. Personal Interview. 11 Oct. 2004.

Rabinowitz, Peter J. *Before Reading: Narrative Conventions and the Politics of Interpretation.* Ithaca: Cornell UP, 1987.

Rich, Adrienne. "Twenty-One Love Poems." *The Fact of a Doorframe*. New York: Norton, 1984. 236–46.

———. "When We Dead Awaken: Writing as Re-Vision." *On Lies, Secrets, and Silence*. New York: Norton, 1984. 33–49.

Stockwell, Anne. "Soul of *The L Word*." *The Advocate* Jan. 2006: 43.

Waters, Sarah. *Tipping the Velvet*. New York: Riverhead, 1999.

Will and Grace. NBC. 21 Sept. 1998–18 May 2006.

Zimmerman, Bonnie. "What Has Never Been: An Overview of Lesbian Feminist Literary Criticism." *The New Feminist Criticism: Essays on Women, Literature, and Theory*. Ed. Elaine Showalter. New York: Pantheon, 1985. 200–20.

———. "Lesbians Like This and That: Some Notes on Lesbian Criticism for the Nineties." *New Lesbian Criticism: Literary and Cultural Readings*. Ed. Sally Munt. New York: Columbia UP, 1992. 1–17.

CHAPTER 7

READING AND QUEERING PLATO IN HEDWIG AND THE ANGRY INCH

WENDY HSU

Abstract: Hedwig and the Angry Inch, *a musical film about a queer punk rocker, alludes to a part of Plato's* Symposium *in which Aristophanes narrates a mystical origin of love: that bifurcation of gender types yields sexuality types. After Judith Butler's idea of gender binary as a by-product of the oppressive practice of hetero sexuality, I want to consider the use of Plato in the movie not as a simple reproduction of the Greek mythology, but as a disruption or a subversion of the mythology's seamless unidirectional connection between sex, gender, and sexuality. Here Hedwig serves as a symbolic queering agent in the oppressive, constructed binary gender and sexuality categories. I show this through a close reading of Hedwig's songs and their diegetic performances in which aspects of Hedwig's gender and sexuality are highlighted within the context of her personal history. I interpret the deployment of the punk rock aesthetics in performance, a style that definitively celebrates the abject, to be indicative of Hedwig's positive outlook on life as a stigmatized queer individual. The ending of the film gives a politically progressive message that gender division is neither essential nor universal and, echoing Butler, is conditioned by the oppressive norms of the heterosexual society. The film's conventional narrative structure encourages the viewer to empathize with Hedwig despite and for her queer gender and sexuality. The identification with Hedwig thus makes the film politically queer and activist.*

HEDWIG AND THE ANGRY INCH, A FILM OFFSHOOT from the original off-Broadway theater production, rocks the world of identities into a sensual and rational disarray. Identity categories are thrown together and taken apart.

I cannot help but be perplexed and at the same time mesmerized by the disorienting gender and sexuality signifiers of the characters. In an interview, John Cameron Mitchell, who wrote, directed, and starred in the movie, reveals his intention of portraying a world "where identification and categories are fluid, changing and confusing, as they are, really, in real life." Gender-and-sexuality vertigo resonates with some of the familiar rhetoric about queerness in the twenty-first century Anglo-American world.

As a rock musical, *Hedwig and the Angry Inch* states its queer politics via a few expressive vehicles: the characterization of Hedwig, the musical performances, and the ongoing narrative reference to Plato. The film's narrative focuses on the gender and sexual transformations of our queer punk rocker hero/heroine Hedwig Schmidt, played by Mitchell. Hedwig's story begins with Hansel, a boy growing up in East Germany. At the age of twenty-six, Hansel falls in love with American G.I. Luther Robinson. In order to marry Luther and go to the United States with him, Hansel has to get a sex-change operation, becoming a woman named Hedwig (Hansel's mother's name). Unfortunately the operation gets botched. Not a typical male-to-female transsexual, Hedwig is now a biological he/she with neither-female-nor-male genitals which s/he refers to as "an angry inch."[1]

The film's musical numbers, individually set in a franchised seafood restaurant in a suburban strip mall, remain in the format of the original theater production: a drag show backed up by a punk band.[2] Punk musician Stephen Trask, who scores the production, makes several punk and glam rock references. Being dumped by her husband while living in the stark trailer-trash Midwestern United States, Hedwig suddenly realizes her penchant for punk rock. With a band named The Angry Inch, Hedwig sings about her past and enacts her present sentiment toward different points of her personal history. By using punk rock conventions, marked by masculine aggression, Hedwig expresses anger while celebrating her abject position in her world. Also, Hedwig adopts the style of glam rock to highlight her gender ambiguity. Glam rock, most famously represented by David Bowie's gender-bending Ziggy Stardust incarnation, is a flamboyant celebration of sexual freedom especially signified by Bowie's ostensible bisexuality.[3]

The makers of the movie borrow from Plato's *Symposium* to characterize Hedwig and to develop the movie's overall message about queer genders and sexualities. In Plato's *Symposium*, Aristophanes tells a mythical story about the origin of love and desire. In it, the original three human types—female, male, and androgynous (having both female and male qualities)—are split into two halves by the gods because of their discontent with decadent human behavior. As a result of the division, the individual halves desire to find their other half. The birth of love is thus the emergence of the human desire to recover the wholeness of the original form (Plato).

The mythology presents a neatly sketched picture of the different sex/gender types and sexuality types. The splitting of the original sex types results in three different sexualities—female homosexuality, male homosexuality, and heterosexuality. The mythology conveniently explains away any identities that fail to match the man/woman and the homosexuality/heterosexuality binaries. And there are other queer gender and sexuality identities, for instance, transgender, transsexuality, and bisexuality, that do not fit into these categories. Invariably tied to binarism, Aristophanes's story echoes with the heteronormative ideology and perceptions of gender and sexuality in the twenty-first century United States.

Queer theorist Judith Butler offers an alternative theory about the connection between sex, gender, and sexuality in *Gender Trouble*. Butler argues that sex and gender differences do not exist naturally, but as culturally constructed differences in our world. Both sex and gender differences have been enforced as a norm necessary for human reproduction; and the heterosexual norm oppresses the minority sexuality groups through the reinforcement of the binary gender system. So, compulsory heterosexuality is not an effect, but a cause of gender and sex binaries. Plato's Aristophanes and Butler seem to propose opposing ideas about the connection between sex, gender, and sexuality. While Aristophanes narrates that sexualities emerge from the binary pairing of two sexes, whether it is based on sameness or difference, Butler argues that it is heterosexuality, the dominant sexuality, that creates the binary gender and sex categories.[4] In a hermeneutic style representative of queer studies culture in academia and inspired by Butler, I consider the use of Plato's *Symposium* in *Hedwig and the Angry Inch* not as a simple reproduction of the Greek mythology, but as an attempt to disorient or *queer* the mythology's seamless linear connection between sex, gender, and sexuality.

Most narratives about transsexuality or sexual inversions center around a character who has felt as if she or he has been trapped in the wrong gendered or sexed body. So the sex change operation is usually a means to liberate the individual, allowing the individual's gender to be coherent with her or his sex. Unlike conventional narratives about transsexuality, *Hedwig and the Angry Inch* tells a story of an individual who does not have complete agency in her gender and sexual transformations. Hedwig's queerness not only is narrated and affirmed in her musical performances, but it also comes out of her defiance, both as a symbol for and a victim of the oppressive heteronormative forces in her world.

To engage with the movie's details, I interpret Hedwig's songs' lyrical contents and their diegetic performances in relation to the narrative progression of how Hedwig becomes a rock star.[5] There I explain Hedwig's sex and gender transformation and its connection to the notion of division, borrowed from Plato's *Symposium*. Then I delve into the idea of wholeness, also from Plato, as Hedwig contemplates and deals with issues of sexuality, by examining Hedwig's sexual and gender identities in the context of each of her relationships with the men in her life. Finally, I will offer a reading of the movie's ambiguous ending, illuminating the movie's potentially progressive message.

DIVISION: HEDWIG'S SEXUAL AND
GENDER TRANSFORMATION

Before launching into close examinations of the film, I want to complicate the description of Hedwig's gender performances by asserting that they are *gender-y*, a term I borrow from queer scholar Eve Sedgwick that refers to the quantity rather than quality of gender signifiers. The usage of this term also permits the coexistence of multiple gender axes—such as butch-femme, masculine-feminine, effeminate-butch. Hedwig's gender-y performance makes her sometimes both effeminate and femme, for example, in "Wig in the Box"; femme and feminine, for example, in "Wicked Little Town"; and masculine and butch, for example, in "The Angry Inch" and "Tear Me Down." Hedwig's gender is beyond the simple description of just being androgynous, or masculine, or feminine. Read through Sedgwick's multidimensional gender paradigm, Hedwig's complicated gender-y gender performances depart from and break down the conventional one-dimensional gender dichotomy between masculinity and femininity.

In the beginning of the film during the performance of "Tear Me Down," with a high-pitched dykey voice, the biker-jacket-clad backup singer Yitzhak announces Hedwig's metonymic identity with the Berlin Wall: "Hedwig is like that wall/Standing before you in the divide/Between East and West/ Slavery and freedom/Man and woman/Top and bottom." Using the trope of the Berlin Wall, which divided Berlin into two halves with opposing political ideologies, Hedwig implies that she stands in the crack between the two different sexual and gender spheres—she is neither a woman nor a man, neither a he nor a she. Hedwig is not of the predivision androgynous type, accounted by Aristophanes. Hedwig's self-proclaimed in-between identity is not a point of orientation for people's identification, but of disorientation. Recognizing her symbolic existence as an object of abomination in the world, Hedwig pleads for her listener to "tear her down" and challenges the world to reconsider the ideological binaries.

With the lyrics of "The Angry Inch" that directly tell about Hedwig's botched sex-change, the juxtaposition of conflicting gender signifiers borrowed from different performance styles pushes the gender confusion of the scene into an overdose of gender vertigo. There are several punk references in this scene. Hedwig's girly halter-top says "punk rock." Singing "Six inches forward and five inches back/I got a/I got an angry inch," Hedwig boyishly gropes her genitals and hops around on the stage while passively flinging around her stiff appendages like a ventriloquist femme dummy. Musically, "The Angry Inch" uses a punk-like straight-ahead rhythm and simple harmonic progressions consisting of power chords on the guitar.[6] The musical and kinesthetic minimalism is expressed with a punk masculine aggression; at the same time, it is juxtaposed by feminine signifiers such as Hedwig's glitter makeup, an elaborate blonde wig, and lacy, black gloves like Stevie Nicks'. Moreover, Hedwig sings with vibrato, which is not characteristic of punk, but of glam or Broadway vocal style (or hair metal). When juxtaposed against punk aesthetics, vibrato seems relatively effeminate and feminine because of its decorative quality.

The depicted audience response to the performance deserves mentioning. After Hedwig's explicit narration about her botched operation while groping her neither-penis-nor-vagina crotch and looking straight into the audience aggressively and provokingly, one large macho-looking man from the audience calls out "faggot." Then Yitzhak jumps on the man to start a fight that then grows into a large group fight in which the members from the band and the audience throw food and punches at each other. I read the man's defensive remark as reflecting his discomfort with Hedwig's spectacular crossing of gender and sexual boundaries. The derogatory term he uses to refer to Hedwig should not be read literally. Faggot, a readily available derogatory term referring to queer and stigmatized identities, is used by the man to repudiate Hedwig and distance himself from Hedwig's queer gender and sexual performance. Hedwig's castration narrative threatens to emasculate the man's symbolic control of his own reaction to Hedwig's performance.

Hedwig sings, "The train is coming and I'm tied to the track/I try to get up but I can't get no slack." Here the train can refer to either Luther or the stipulations imposed by the heterosexual marriage institution. I prefer the latter reading because it allows one to see Luther and Hansel—both stigmatized because of their gay sexuality—as human agents, as opposed to subjects of free agency, within the context of the politically oppressive world. In the spirit of punk, Hedwig performs to lament and celebrate her abjection. Her neither-female-nor-male sexed body ruptures the sexual and gender binary boundaries by its accidental and brutal containment of opposing binaries in one.

In the performance of "Wig in a Box," Hedwig shows her epiphany about gender transformations. Hedwig reclines on a beat up couch like a confined Victorian woman. With only minimal accompaniment in the background, she begins singing a slow lyrical passage depicting imageries of darkness symbolic of her mundane and miserable life in Midwestern United States as a result of being left by Luther. As the tempo of the music and the volume of her band pick up, she sings about her transformation from a boy into a woman (now with makeup and a wig). Yitzhak brings Farrah Fawcett's wig on a serving tray. Hedwig turns to it and smiles into the camera singing, "This is the best way that I've found/To be the best you've ever seen."

With a transition marked by a drum fill and glissando on the keyboard, the music progresses into a fast-tempo section. At this point, Hedwig's trailer home turns into a performance stage. Now standing in the middle of the stage, she is wearing a long straight blonde wig (resembling Cher's long straight rarified blonde hair) and a white two-piece outfit with long frills and tall white pleather boots. With a vocal exclamation, she sings: "Suddenly I'm this punk rock star/Of stage and screen/And I ain't never/I'm never turning back!" Shagging and groping the microphone stand (like Tina Turner), Hedwig is now a rock star. Her body gesture and her outfit make her look like an oversized wig. I read this moment to be Hedwig's full gender transformation as it coincides with her new identity of a rock musician. The performer's identity legitimizes the fluidity of her gender identity and performance. As her name and title of this song imply, Hedwig is now an embodiment of a wig, a quintessential cross-dressing accessory.

For Hedwig, this round of gender transformation can be characterized as do-it-yourself, similar to the DIY premise of punk aesthetics (Hebdige). Feeling disenchanted by Luther's leaving her, at the same time, oppressed by the heterosexual institution that rejects her ambiguous body, Hedwig takes the existing resources—her musical talent and her ambiguous gender "Angry Inch"—to remake herself into a glamorous punk rock star. While the sonic constitution of "Wig in the Box" is devoid of the aggressive punk sonic and gestural signifiers, it is in the lyrical and performance context of this song that Hedwig openly identifies and announces her new identity as a punk rock star. The punk style is not literally employed, but the punk spirit is evoked through Hedwig's DIY, defiant, and self-empowering attitude against the world that has victimized her. With her neither-nor anatomical sex, now enhanced and legitimized by her power to perform as a punk rocker, Hedwig wields her queer body symbolically to defy the clean-cut sex and gender division in Plato's *Symposium*.

WHOLENESS: HEDWIG'S RELATIONSHIPS AND SEXUALITY

Hedwig never explicitly identifies herself using any of the three sexuality labels from Plato. I explore the dimension of Hedwig's sexuality in the context of her relationships with the three men in her life—Luther, Tommy Gnosis, and Yitzhak. As a way to position Hedwig's attitude toward love, I begin by discussing the movie's most conspicuous allusion from Plato's *Symposium* in the musical number "The Origin of Love."

Hedwig's voiceover narrates how she was "touched by many people" in her life—first as a seven-year-old boy in East Berlin by his American G.I. father. The picture then transitions into Hansel's drawing of two male bodies lying in bed. At this point, the music begins and the camera shows a very femme Hedwig onstage solemnly singing "The Origin of Love" with stick-figure animation projected on the screen behind her. The song's lyrics and the animation narrate the Aristophanic mythology starting from the original human forms to the gods' dividing them into halves. The song ends with Hedwig's voiceover stating her desire to find her other half. She then poses a series of questions about the gender attributes of that person, whether that person is a he or a she, whether that person is identical or complementary to Hedwig in appearance. She then questions whether sex is the way to put the halves back together and the possibility of that recovery.

I read the introduction of the song, about Hansel's being touched by his father, as crucial for establishing the onset for Hedwig's curiosity, if not inclination toward, male-to-male eroticism. The song's literal reference of Aristophanes' mythology should be read in the context of the narrative progression, especially since the song comes back in a different rendition in the end (which I will discuss in the next section). Occurring early in the film, the "Origin of Love" sequence can be interpreted as Hedwig's contemplation about sexuality in general—reading her ruminations as being literally enacted by the animation onscreen. And the questions she poses about her sexuality set the movie off as a quest for the answers to these questions. Before tackling these questions, I should turn toward the other people who have touched Hedwig on her quest for her love.

With Luther, a very macho black American G.I., Hansel is a bottom gay boy. The story of meeting Luther begins when Hansel remembers his leftist mother's lesson that "it's better to be powerless." Upon first meeting him, Luther first assumes that Hansel is a girl. Luther gives Hansel a bag of candy establishing his identity as a Sugar Daddy to Hansel. After having sex with Hansel, Luther says that he cannot believe Hansel is not a girl, revealing his satisfaction with being Hansel's top. Hansel then analogizes his satiating experience of being penetrated to the sweet taste of "power" in his mouth. The lyrics of "Sugar Daddy" are explicit about Hansel's position of orally receiving Luther's penis. Hedwig sings, "I've got a sweet tooth/For licorice drops and jelly roll,/Hey Sugar Daddy/Hansel needs some sugar in his bowl." The jelly roll reference echoes with its euphemistic signification for either female or male sexual organs within the traditional blues repertoire. Though the sexual ambiguity could connote a queer sexuality, what seems more primary is the reference that further accentuates Luther's Americanness and blackness, considering the history of blues as an African American aesthetic form. Read with the stereotypical cultural image of threatening hypersexualized working-class black men in the United States, Luther's blackness along with his Midwestern trailer-trashiness can feed into the characterization of Luther as Hedwig's sexual top (Collins). Later in the song, Hedwig sings about disco, a gay-male signifier based on its historical existence as a dance subculture dominated by white and black gay men in urban centers in the United States (Dyer; Hughes). The song ends with a spoken part by Luther who pleads for Hansel to cross-dress for his satisfaction. The extent to which Luther tops Hansel is shown by Luther's eventual success in convincing Hansel to literally become a woman by getting a sex-change operation.

With Tommy Gnosis (formerly Tommy Speck), Hedwig is a bottom femme. At work as a babysitter for Tommy's baby sibling, Hedwig sees Tommy Speck, the androgynous seventeen-year-old pretty-faced white boy, frustrated with his adolescent attempt to get off in a bathtub. Hedwig, being older and more sexually experienced, gives Tommy a hand job. Hedwig subsequently falls in love with Tommy. Their sexual relationship marks Hedwig as the bottom whose role is to give Tommy sexual pleasure through blowjobs and hand jobs. Beyond sex, Hedwig is a source of knowledge for Tommy. Hedwig's drawing of the symbol of gnosis on Tommy's forehead is symbolic of her giving Tommy a new life as Tommy Gnosis the rock star.[7] The name Gnosis, which is the Greek word for knowledge, is important because it is the object passed down from a teacher to his young disciple in ancient Greece.[8] As we find out later in the plot, Tommy co-opts Hedwig's original songs and publicly claims authorship over them. Their relationship in terms of creativity and knowledge resonates with their sexual relation: Hedwig gives while Tommy receives.

Hedwig never gets what she wants from Tommy—love. The relationship is not reciprocal in a way that satisfies them emotionally. Being maternal and nurturing to the young Tommy, Hedwig has unconditional love for him. In a coffee shop, Hedwig sings and dedicates "Wicked Little Town" to Tommy. Looking femme and fragile with subdued makeup and a shoulder-length blonde flip, Hedwig sits on a stool with her legs crossed tightly. Gazing straight into the camera, which then connects her gaze with Tommy's, she expresses her desire to love and protect Tommy: "And if you've got no other choice/You know you can follow my voice/Through the dark turns and noise/Of this wicked little town." In a couple of scenes later, Tommy refuses to engage in sexual activities that involve the front of Hedwig. We find out that it is Hedwig's not-so-womanly genitals that repel Tommy. This dynamic allows Tommy to continue to top Hedwig emotionally and sexually. This is reinforced by Hedwig's femme gender, of her onstage and offstage appearance, in the context of her relationship with Tommy.

Hedwig and Yitzhak have a regular sexual relationship as well as a legal marriage, though their relationship is never at any point marked by love. Hedwig's total dominance over Yitzhak is consistent throughout the movie. Onstage, Hedwig is ambivalent and sometimes aggressive toward Yitzhak. When Yitzhak wants to perform in drag, Hedwig bars him from doing so.[9] When Yitzhak wants to divorce, Hedwig refuses to sign the paper. Yitzhak's Bosnian nationality and his legal status as an immigrant in the United States impinge upon his marital affiliation with Hedwig. Yitzhak's ambiguous sexual and gender identity is ostensibly brought out by the incoherence of his high-pitched, feminine singing voice and his overtly masculine physical features, that is his uneven facial hair, a bandanna, and biker's leather jacket. In an interview, John Cameron Mitchell discussed the deliberate intention to cast confusing signifiers about Yitzhak's gender—as a way to express his endorsement of gender fluidity—by having a woman play Yitzhak (Mitchell). Though Yitzhak is located in a subordinate position in terms of his legal existence and his role in Hedwig's emotional and musical life, his unstable gender identity complicates his sexual relationship with Hedwig. This in turn obscures Hedwig's position on the sexuality typology.

Hedwig's sexual object choices vastly differ from one another in terms of gender and sex—Luther, a macho black gay man; Tommy, an androgynous young white man with a more or less straight sexuality; and Yitzhak, ambiguous with his masculine appearance and feminine voice. Moreover, Hedwig changes his anatomical sex and gender for Luther and his gender again to be more femme for Tommy. Certainly more complex than the three sexuality types in Aristophanes's speech, Hedwig's sexuality is hard to pin down. My reading of the first performance of "The Origin of Love" points to the idea that Hedwig contemplates and searches for her other half as the movie's narrative progresses forward. The ending of the movie is then crucial in solving the mystery about Hedwig's gender and sexuality and the connection, or disconnection, between the two.

A DIFFERENT KIND OF WHOLENESS: HEDWIG'S
FINAL TRANSFORMATION

The open-endedness of *Hedwig and the Angry Inch* is a point to puzzle over. The dense musical material in this part, with five musical numbers back-to-back, picks up the narrative pace and puts the viewer on a roller-coaster ride. Here Hedwig and Tommy Gnosis, now a famous rock star (whose looks resemble Lou Reed, an American glam rocker), reunite and their reunion causes a series of media scandals. After (or because of) the high media exposure, Hedwig appears onstage at Times Square, New York, where she is welcomed by a round of applause by the audience.

With hair like Dolly Parton or Tina Turner and a short fur coat over a transparently layered "dress" covering a two-piece outfit, Hedwig sings a lyrical ballad called "Hedwig's Lament" with a piano-only accompaniment. Looking femme and fragile, Hedwig's compelling lyrics are about the tragic events in her life—her botched operation and broken heart from her relationship with Tommy—all connected to the theme of division as figured by East Berlin, "a town ripped into two."[10] Just when the melancholy saturates the atmosphere, the guitar picks up the rhythm by striking a few dry and aggressive chords that lead into another song "Exquisite Corpse."[11] At this point, Hedwig takes off her fur coat and kicks her left leg to sing about her "sewn up," "collage[d]" body. Contrasting the previous style, the music is now played with a fast masculine aggression. Kinesthetically, Hedwig enacts the brokenness of her body by flinging her body parts jaggedly. Even more butch and aggressive than her punk gestures in "The Angry Inch," Hedwig starts banging the guitar on the sound system. With a musical chaos created by heavy guitar distortion and rhythmic irregularity, Hedwig takes off her wig, tears open her dress, and reveals her flat-chested he-she body. The song goes, "And all the rest's illusion/That there's will and soul/That we can wrest control/From chaos and confusion." Crosscutting with Hedwig's shedding of her drag accessories is a series of flashing images of her relationships with her father, Tommy, and Yitzhak.

Without the wig, which is symbolic of her last gender transformation, Hedwig's gender is once again transformed. I interpret this moment of yet another drastic femme-to-masculine gender transformation to be closely tied to Hedwig's frustrated sexuality. Hedwig's abjection is induced first by his gay sexuality (as Hansel) leading him onto the path of sexual and gender ambiguity. Her gender ambiguity eventually leads to her failed attempts to find love, that is to consummate her relationship with Tommy. Hedwig is fed up with the way she has to conform to one of the binary gender types. The peeling off of his/her drag appearance can be read as a deliberate act to regain his/her gender autonomy in spite of his/her attraction to Tommy.[12] Hedwig realizes that s/he does not have to be femme in order to complement Tommy's boyish effeminacy anymore.

Now with a bare chest of a man, Hedwig walks into Tommy's performance space next door. Hedwig's newly emerged gender makes him/her more like his/her previous pre-operation self—the young Hansel—or like Tommy who is standing at the opposite end of the screen. Let me consider the first reading that leads to the conclusion that Hedwig's gender is reversed back to that of the young Hansel before meeting Luther. Read with Aristophanes's mythology, is this a gesture that reverses the mythical splitting? This interpretation will take Eros out of the picture, implying that love simply does not matter. I should point out that loving Tommy Gnosis and finding the other half constitute the driving force of the plot, which is structured around Hedwig's performances. Hedwig schedules the same tour dates and locations as Tommy Gnosis's concert tour, hoping to recover her relationship with him. In other words, without love or Tommy, the story would not exist.

So, does the new Hedwig look like Tommy? I should mention an important narrative detail that this Tommy—now with the name Gnosis—is not the same as the old Tommy Speck, the Jesus-loving youth from a small town. The transformation from Tommy Speck into the rock star Tommy Gnosis is actually Hedwig's creation (or cocreation with Tommy himself). It is Tommy Gnosis (now with the body of Iggy Pop and the face of Lou Reed) who is an imitation of Hedwig, not vice versa. Furthermore, Tommy Gnosis is Hedwig's musical copycat because he claims all the songs that Hedwig wrote as his, without giving Hedwig any credit. On stage, to Hedwig, Tommy sings Hedwig's tune "Wicked Little Town" with altered lyrics expressing his apology for not reciprocating Hedwig's feelings. Tommy rejects Hedwig by singing that he does not believe in preassigned "cosmic lovers."

Hedwig's response to Tommy's rejection is crucial. I want to read the subsequent musical number "Midnight Radio" as Hedwig's emotional response to Tommy and his/her new self. Now back on his/her own stage, wearing dark makeup, Hedwig is singing triumphantly with a positive reassurance while wearing on his/her forehead the same cross symbol as Tommy's. I argue that the meaning of this symbol remains the same on either of the two. For Hedwig, the cross symbol is a sign of a new life marked by knowledge, in this case, self-knowledge: "Breathe feel love/Give free/Know your soul/Like your blood knows the way/From your heart to your brain/Knows that you're whole." Hedwig wants (his/her audience) to love and be in love, to feel and be affected by Eros, while at the same time be in touch with oneself, not get overinvested in a relationship. Wholeness resides in oneself. Wholeness is not a self-contained sex or gender type, like the predivision human forms in Aristophanes's story. It is a process of becoming aware of one's gender identification and allowing it to transform through the experience of love. Departing from the Platonic idea of finding the predestined other half, wholeness is a vision of love that sees it as a journey in itself.

In "Midnight Radio," Hedwig is not only singing to him/herself, s/he is also singing to "all the misfits and the losers." To those living on the fringe of the society, especially to Yitzhak; Hedwig encourages them to be confident in their queer identities, to wield their power and to perform their identity. Hedwig's attitude toward Yitzhak changes here. Hedwig dances with Yitzhak for the first time. The closeup shot on their hands shows a sense of reconciliation. Singing "You're shining like the brightest star," Hedwig lets go of Yitzhak's hand as Yitzhak puts on a wig. This gesture signifies that Hedwig finally allows Yitzhak to cross-dress, an act that the latter has longed to do.

Similar to Hedwig's liberation, Yitzhak is now free to be himself without succumbing to Hedwig's control.

Before the ending credits begin, an alternative version of "The Origin of Love" animation appears on the screen. Here, the two opposing halves attempt to fuse into one and nevertheless bounce off of one another until they eventually merge into a larger, horizontally stretched oblong entity that differs from the circular figure of the original pre-split human forms in the first animation. I interpret the new oblong figure to mean a relationship that allows the two halves to coexist without having to conform to the original or prescribed shape. Echoing with Tommy's rejection of the notion of predestined lovers in his reprise of "Wicked Little Town," this idea disrupts the teleological order of Aristophanes' story. With that, the film's final message can be one that queers the idea that there is one predefined, essential sexuality type, be it homosexual or heterosexual. Instead, one's sexuality is defined and redefined moment-to-moment by the particular gender of the other person involved and the dynamic between the two people. This takes us back to the queer perspective that I discussed in this chapter's first section regarding the ideological and political stance that sexuality is fluid and unconstrained by binary gender and sexuality categories as well as by the norms that they implicate in our society.

The audience in the "Midnight Radio" scene departs from previous performance scenes in the way it is completely attentive to Hedwig's performance. These are the fans who not only accept Hedwig but also appreciate and celebrate her/him for who s/he is. The celebratory ending makes the movie a success story about a queer individual in terms of his/her sex, gender, and sexuality. John Cameron Mitchell and Stephen Trask cleverly incorporate conventional narrative themes—namely, self-discovery and finding true love—in order for the viewer to identify with Hedwig *despite* and *for* both her gender and sexuality.[13] *Hedwig* is different from *The Rocky Horror Picture Show*, a classic musical film starring Tim Curry—infamous for his transsexual performances as mere spectacles with no points of empathy. *Hedwig and the Angry Inch* is a drama that represents queer identities in positive light.[14]

As a theater performance, *Hedwig and the Angry Inch* continues to be produced by theater companies around the nation and is received with positive attention—a testimony to its popularity; the film has made its way across the country on both large screens and home video screens. At a live performance of *Hedwig* that I recently attended, I was impressed by the positive vibe in the audience and was touched by how the show brought together many individuals from the local queer community. During the ending chorus of "Midnight Radio," I too "lift[ed] up [my] hands" in celebrating queer liberation. On the Internet, there are a number of active fan sites, populated by Hed-heads that are devoted to the interpretations of the songs and the movie. While most of the reviews and interpretations I have found on the Internet (on discussion forums on fan sites and imdb.com) revolve around the movie's message of self-acceptance, I think the fans' collective effort in discussing their interpretations makes the film's message of self-acceptance a collective acceptance of queer identities. Many Hed-heads are queer individuals themselves and their forum discussion about *Hedwig* becomes a safe space for queer expressions and affirmation. I see this active Hed-head community as a subcultural movement of queer resistance. I consider myself a participant of that same resistance movement hereby having offered a perspective on the movie's political implications in our oppressive heteronormative society today. Ultimately I want to say that self-acceptance is not enough. Moreover, through my intellectual and sensual identification with the queer *Hedwig*, I hope to solicit my readers to consider and practice the societal acceptance of queer identities.

NOTES

1. The movie does not indicate whether Hedwig is on hormones. Hedwig's exposure of her flat chest in the end of the movie may indicate that Hedwig has not been on hormones.
2. This is discussed by the makers of the film in the documentary on the movie's DVD.
3. This is most evident in David Bowie's album *The Rise and Fall of Ziggy Stardust and the Spiders from Mars* released in 1972 and the concert performances associated with the album. Furthermore, during the first musical number "Tear Me Down," Hedwig gets down on her knees and bites the wammie bar of her sideman's guitar. This is a conspicuous reference of David Bowie's Ziggy Stardust performance in which Bowie kneeled down to bite Mick Ronson's guitar, which was held in front of his crotch. This interaction suggests male-to-male oral sex.
4. Butler's paradigm also stands out in its account of power, and therefore of the oppression of women and minority sexuality groups, which are absent in Plato.
5. In a similar vein, Judith Peraino's uses *Hedwig and the Angry Inch* as an example in her lengthy chapter on popular music as a means of resistance against "technologies of power" that govern and regulate gender and sexuality (195). My interpretation, however, is more attentive on tracing the specific instances in which the film references Aristophanes's mythology to substantiate ideas about queer theory and politics.
6. I should note that the soundtrack of this scene is studio-recorded, just as all the other songs in the film. The production quality of the recording is polished, thus unlike the rough or do-it-yourself criterion evident in some of the recordings definitive of the punk genre. This tension between professionalism and amateurism is an ongoing internal debate among the people in punk scenes.

CHAPTER 8

DIVA INTERVENTIONS: DANA INTERNATIONAL AND ISRAELI GENDER CULTURE[1]

AMALIA ZIV

Abstract: *Dana International, the Israeli transsexual pop Diva who won the Eurovision Song Contest in 1998, has made a profound impact on Israeli gender culture through her performative, textual, and political interventions. This chapter examines this impact from a number of perspectives: Dana's substitution of a glamorous image of transsexuality for the older abject representations; the contestation of the medical paradigm of transsexuality implicit in her affirmation of a transsexual identity and continuing affiliation with the gay community; her subversion of the Zionist gender project of reforming Jewish masculinity; and her rejection of the clear-cut distinction between gay men and transsexuals (hence, between gender identity and sexual identity) that underpins contemporary gay identity.*

DANA INTERNATIONAL, THE ISRAELI TRANSSEXUAL SINGER, attained worldwide celebrity, when, in 1998, she won the Eurovision Song Contest. At that time she was already a successful recording and stage artist in Israel, diva of the gay dance scene, but also acquiring increasing mainstream popularity, especially with the teenage public. Her music was also a hit in the neighboring Arab countries, in particular Egypt and Jordan, where her first album, though officially banned, sold huge numbers of illegal bootleg copies.[2] In addition, she became, for a while, a focal figure in the culture wars between orthodox and secular Jewish Israelis, with the former pronouncing her an "abomination"[3] and expressing outrage at her election to represent the Jewish state, and the latter embracing her as the symbol of a liberal ethos of personal freedom and individual quest for happiness, and as a representative of the struggle against religious fundamentalism.[4]

Located at the intersection of some of the structuring tensions of Israeli society—between religious and secular, Ashkenazi and Mizrahi,[5] high culture and low culture, nationalism and individualism—Dana International epitomizes many of the contradictions that characterize contemporary Israeli reality: she represents queer political struggle and yet rejects identity politics in favor of a universalizing human-rights model; she stands for the fight against religious coercion yet declares herself faithful to Judaism; she defines herself as international yet expresses patriotic sentiments. To the critic observing her various cultural performances (her music, public statements, press interviews, performative style), she presents a slippery object of interpretation that eludes easy classification and confounds stable categories. However, despite these contradictory aspects of her persona—or perhaps all the more so because of them—it seems clear that Dana's overall effect on Israeli culture is a significantly subversive one.[6] This effect is due not merely to a certain conjunction of historical conditions through which she has come to represent secular Israel, or gay pride, or post-Zionism, or the New Middle East; rather, through her statements, performances, and musical repertoire, Dana International emerges as a radical cultural agent that troubles and contests categorical boundaries, and that has contributed tangibly to concrete processes of social change.

As a cultural phenomenon, Dana International can be read from a number of interrelated perspectives. While some critics have focused on issues of ethnicity and (trans)nationality, this chapter will discuss Dana mostly in the context of Israel's gender culture and contemporary queer politics.

DANA AND ISRAELI TRANSSEXUALITY

> There was a stigma about transsexuals that it's a terrible thing, vulgar, aggressive, but I knew from the start that I was going to fight it and shatter the conventions. (International, "Interview" 7)

> If they shout at you "faggot" you're offended only if you feel inferior. So they call me "coccinelle," isn't that the truth? (International, "Where" 2)[7]

Dana International has radically altered the public image of transsexuality in Israel.[8] Before the 1990s transsexuals were a highly stigmatized and persecuted group. Until the early 1980s, transsexuals used to suffer from severe police harassment including arbitrary arrests, and their situation improved only by slight degrees during the 1980s.[9] The harshness of transsexual existence was complemented by a public image that identified transsexuals with prostitution and social deviance. Before Dana International, the representation of transsexuality in Israel was dominated by the figure of one notorious transsexual, Zalman-Shoshi. Zalman-Shoshi—who for many years, in a time when the largely closeted lesbian and gay community lacked official representatives, acted in the Israeli media also as spokesperson for the gay community—was associated with prostitution, violence, and mental illness. The heteronormative representational regime assigned hir the role of the tragicomic, quasi-wretched-quasi-dangerous representative of a dark and sordid world. The fact that s/he was consistently referred to by masculine pronouns indicates that hir femininity was never taken seriously and was construed more as a ludicrous, failed aspiration. The very fact that s/he was known by a compounded male-female name (Zalman is a male name and Shoshi a female one) attests that hir chosen gender identity was never respected and that s/he was perceived as a kind of hybrid.[10] Similarly, when other local transsexuals were mentioned in the media, it was almost always in the context of prostitution and criminality.

Dana International has completely overturned this representation. In fact, one can hardly imagine a starker contrast to the figure of Zalman-Shoshi: a successful and glamorous pop star who boasts of not only gold and platinum albums, "singer of the year" titles, and the 1998 Eurovision victory that brought her international celebrity, but also of wall-to-wall affirmations of her femininity and heterosexual allure. In the early stage of her career, before her Eurovision success, nearly all newspaper stories about her engaged in a ritual affirmation of her femininity, whether performed by the journalist him/herself or attributed to others, for example, "she has a captivating femininity . . . everything is natural and feminine in the purest sense" (a popular songwriter) (International, "What" 62); "I simply can't imagine that this girl was once a guy" (fashion photographer) (Kerem 50); "she's a real woman," "it's incredible how feminine she is" (members of the audience in one of her concerts) (International, "I Sell" 11); "a perfectly amiable young woman that looks no different from any other woman her age" (reporter for a popular women's magazine) (International, "Dying" 36). The ritual repetition of this credo attests to its function as an act of exorcism—the ghost exorcized being that of the transition as process, the ghost of the intermediary stages, the middle ground between man and woman. The ritual affirmation of Dana's absolute and natural femininity is a kind of incantation aimed to counter the threat of gender fluidity that the transsexual presents for a system of gender dimorphism. Sandy Stone, in a landmark essay, pointed out how the discourse on transsexuality, including accounts provided by transsexuals themselves, constructs a myth of instantaneous and complete transition from unambiguous masculinity to unambiguous femininity in the service of bolstering the dominant conception of gender as binary and oppositional (280–304). The warm embrace that the Israeli mainstream offered Dana International (talk shows, teen magazines, and, above all, her election to represent Israel at the Eurovision song contest) is conditional on the reiterated practice of exorcism (through avowals of her unquestionable femininity) that seeks to occlude the existence of any middle territory or potential mixture between genders.

However, Dana herself conveys a far less unambiguous message. Alongside declarations that she had always felt like a woman, she continues to identify as a transsexual and even refers to herself by the derogatory slang term "coccinelle." Derived from the stage name of a famous French transsexual entertainer who performed in Israel in the 1960s, "coccinelle" was for many years the prevailing colloquial term for transsexuals and drag queens and served as a slur directed against sissy men in general. Far from being a merely descriptive term, the word "coccinelle" epitomizes the stigma attached to transsexuality in Israeli society and carries connotations of abjection and demimonde existence that are perhaps best typified by the figure of Zalman-Shoshi. Male to female (MTF) transsexuals have always employed the term in their inside community parlance (attaching, however, a feminine suffix to the French word that in Hebrew has the form of a masculine noun, thereby asserting their femininity), but Dana International has not been afraid to embrace it in interviews not only in the gay press but in the straight media as well (for example, "as a child, I don't think I would have dared to rank a coccinelle at the top of the chart," or "many people think I can occupy an important slot in Europe . . . the slot of an international coccinelle"), thereby contesting its stigma and resignifying it through its very deployment by a glamorous and desirable pop star. By holding on to the term "coccinelle," Dana evokes the very ghost of the transition or the middle territory, that the straight press—and public discourse on transsexuality in general—attempts to disavow.

Her continuing embrace of a transsexual identity also stands in opposition to the prevailing medical model of gender reassignment. According to this model, postoperative transsexuals are expected to settle quickly into their new gender, cut off their ties to the past, and become normal heterosexual women or men, and the success of the gender reassignment procedure is judged by the transsexual's ability to pass as a genetic member of his/her gender of choice. As Stone poignantly puts it, "the highest purpose of the transsexual is to erase him/herself" (295). This conception of therapeutic success both reflects and serves to bolster an essentialist, binary, and heterocentric view of gender: the notion that gender is a stable inner essence; that there exist only two genders (man and woman), which are polar and mutually exclusive opposites; and that heterosexual object-choice is part of a healthy gender identity. It also exacts a heavy personal price from transsexuals, since, as Stone points out, to pass successfully means to efface one's personal history and individual experience.

By continuing to identify as a transsexual, Dana International defies the injunction to pass and contests its underlying assumption that "transsexual" is only a temporary and abject identity that one would hasten to cast off once one has completed the reassignment process. Both the medical discourse on transsexuality and popular opinion assume that only those transsexuals who are unable to pass convincingly, and hence cannot assimilate into straight society, cling to their transsexual identity and maintain their ties to the transsexual and gay community. Yet Dana subverts the dichotomy between successful straight transsexuality and failed abject transsexuality: not only does she make a convincing woman, she even possesses the paradigmatic femininity of the female star, yet—despite this fact and despite being embraced by the musical establishment and the media—she has not ceased to identify as a transsexual and to manifest her affinity to the gay community. Further, the double gesture she performs of asserting that she has always been a woman and of continuing to identify as a transsexual undermines the alleged contradiction between the category "real woman" and that of "transsexual."[11] For Dana, to claim the label of real woman does not necessitate relinquishing that of transsexual; asserting an ontologically full femininity does not entail disowning her past.[12]

THE FIRST LADY OF THE GAY COMMUNITY

As noted above, Dana International has always presented herself as part of the gay community and even as its representative. She used to be a regular participant in the annual Gay Pride celebrations, occasions in which she addressed the crowd as "brothers and sisters" and made political statements, such as calling other artists to come out, and encouraging lesbians and gay men to stand up for their rights.[13] She also performed in the local Wigstock drag festival, a fundraiser for AIDS activism, and in December 1996, when Ezer Weizman, the president in office at the time, made a public homophobic remark, Dana gave voice to the rage of the entire LGBT community, when she was quoted on the front page of the gay journal *Hazman Havarod* (*The Pink Time*), saying that Weizman was not her president and was unfit for that role.[14] Dana expresses her identification with and commitment to the gay community not only in acts and performances addressed to a queer public, but also when addressing a general public. Thus, for example, when the British television program *Eurotrash* came to do a story about her, Dana chose specifically queer locations for the production, such as the gay strip of the Tel Aviv beach located right below the city's largest gay cruising park, and a gay club.[15]

Following her Eurovision victory, Dana became a gay icon worldwide. She was asked to perform in the opening ceremony of the 1998 Gay Games in

Amsterdam and has since performed in Gay Pride events in both England and the United States. On the occasion of the 1998 Gay Games, her status as gay icon was recognized by Amnesty International, when it selected her to star in its gay rights campaign. The poster Amnesty International issued shows Dana in an unspecified ethnic costume that evokes representations of third world women with the caption "Gay Rights Are Human Rights."[16] That gay men and lesbians indeed perceived Dana as representing them was evidenced by the predominance of rainbow flags in the spontaneous celebration that erupted in Tel Aviv's main square on the night of her Eurovision victory. Moreover, around the time of the contest, rumors circulated that in a number of European countries gays organized to vote collectively for Dana, and many people attributed her victory to such mass voting. This, if true, confirms that not only gay Israelis but gay Europeans at large regarded Dana as representing them, and that this sense of representation was not merely a consequence but possibly a cause of her victory.[17]

Dana's unequivocal outness and her outspokenness as a champion of gay rights single her out in Israeli popular music. For several years, Dana was the only out singer in Israeli pop with the exception of one lesbian musician in the alternative music niche.[18] In the 1990s, when Dana was fighting her way into mainstream acceptance, some of Israel's most popular and established pop and rock musicians chose to remain entrenched deep in the closet (a closet that was in many respects a glass closet, an open secret often maintained as such through the collaboration of knowing journalists), fearing damage to their career as a result of disclosure of their sexuality.[19] Many of those artists have since come out, and their coming out can be attributed not only to the change in the public climate around homosexuality but also, more specifically, to the successful precedent set by Dana herself, whose popularity—despite the strong stigma on transsexuality and her clear ties to the gay community—demonstrated that their fear of ruined careers was unfounded. Nevertheless, against the backdrop of other musicians' slow and tortuous way out of the closet, and the continuing closetedness of still others, Dana, from the outset, remains unique in founding her public persona on an ethos of openness. Also, while other singers who came out of the closet position their sexuality as an individual lifestyle or identity, she has been the only one to understand herself as representing the LGBT community and to display queer political awareness.

Dana's conjunction of broad mainstream acceptance and a queer political stance is all the more interesting in light of the internal hierarchies of the LGBT community. Since 1993, Israel's LGBT community has taken a giant leap forward: significant legal and political achievements were won (among them the abolishment of discrimination in the military, the equation of some of the economic rights of gay couples to those of heterosexual couples, a supreme court ruling in favor of adoption of children in lesbian families by the nonbiological mother, etc.); the visibility and public legitimacy of the lesbian and gay community increased exponentially; and the community itself grew, developed institutions, and became politicized. During this time period, the image that the community has projected to the straight world is one of educated, professional gay men and women who have served in the military, live in long-term relationships, and raise children—that is, who correspond in all points to the prevailing heterosexual model.[20] Further, the public face of the community did not include feminine men or masculine women.

As Esther Newton has noted, the effeminate man (and especially the drag queen) symbolizes the stigma of homosexuality in general (283). As such, he occupies the bottom of the gay social hierarchy, since many gay men (and lesbians too) wish to distance themselves from this stigma-bearing figure.[21] One of the things that make gay men uncomfortable about drag queens is their visibility. While most lesbians and gay men can pass as heterosexual, most drag queens cannot, thus they in effect wear their stigma for all to see. This visibility has made them symbolize the potential vulnerability of all gays, but on the other hand it also made them adopt and represent a stance of proud defiance: it is no coincidence that drag queens played a major role in the Stonewall riots that sparked off the gay liberation movement—their active confrontation of the police reflected the fact that they had less to lose than gay men and lesbians who had lesser visibility and hence greater immunity from violence and discrimination. Similarly, it is no surprise that it is a transsexual singer who came to represent the gay community in Israel, rather than straighter looking artists whom one would think had a greater chance of acceptance by mainstream culture.[22] Dana's queer political stance combined with her great success brought about a paradoxical situation, whereby the LGBT community, whose major political strategy has been one of underlining its resemblance to straight society as a ground for its demands for equal citizenship, found itself represented by a transsexual who, in terms of the community's own internal hierarchy, belongs to its most marginalized and excluded minority.

And indeed, it seems safe to state that the notable change in the status of transsexuals within the LGBT community owes much to Dana International's impact. In 1997 Israel's major gay organization, The Society for the Protection of Personal Rights, changed its name to The Association of Gay Men, Lesbians and Bisexuals (the old closeted name dated back to the late 1970s when sodomy was still a criminal offence), and some time later transgendered people were added to the title as well. This symbolic redrawing of the boundaries of the community was not only a reflection of similar developments in U.S. gay politics but was also made inevitable by Dana's role as an icon of gay pride. The reversal in the attitude toward transsexuals was so complete that only a few years later, in 2003, an MTF transsexual, Nora Greenberg, was elected as chair of the association. Greenberg, a middle-aged Ashkenazi professional, is a far cry from the old abject image of the "coccinelle," but the community proved itself capable of embracing less straitlaced figures as well—in that same year, Gila Goldstein, the most prominent older generation transsexual, who has been involved in prostitution, received an honorary title in recognition of her contribution to the community.[23]

Dana International has not merely changed the status of transsexuals as a minority within the LGBT community; more controversially, she disputes the very existence of an essential difference or clear categorical distinction between MTF transsexuals and gay men, thus contesting what is an article of faith in both transsexual discourse and modern gay politics. Gay identity after Stonewall is founded on the rejection of the inversion model of homosexuality and posits a disjunction between gender identity and sexual object choice. Dana, however, proposes the notion of a continuum between sissy gay men and MTFs. In an interview for the queer magazine Tat-Tarbut she said:

> What is a coccinelle? Merely a variation on a homosexual. I'm sure that every homosexual has entertained the wish to be woman at least once. . . . Seventy percent of the patrons of the Playroom [a gay club] address each other in the feminine. . . . The roots are the same. The difference is in the lifestyle and the outlook. So a coccinelle looks like a woman, she had an operation and grew breasts, but both she and a homosexual like to have sex with men. (International, "Where" 6)

Several years later, in an interview for Israel's largest newspaper, she offered the observation that 99.9 percent of gay men have a sissy soul and suggested appending a feminine postfix to the word "homosexual" (Asheri).

Ofer Nissim, her former personal manager and musical producer, describes the continuum in similar terms: "A coccinelle is a homosexual who went further. The first step is sleeping with a man, then dying your hair and becoming a feminine man. The hormone phase is for someone who has the mental strength to do it and come out as well" (6). Nissim himself incontestably fits the description of a feminine gay man, and Yair Qedar who interviewed him described him as having the mannerisms of the opposite sex (5). The notion of a continuum of male femininity that spans both transsexuals and effeminate gay men is borne out by the close relationship between Dana International and Nissim, a relationship that dates back to the gay club scene where he discovered her when she was still male.[24] This idea of a continuum represents not the community's official politics but its popular wisdom that retains sediments of older identity paradigms. In one respect it is a reactionary notion since it abolishes homosexual difference, explaining it as a gendered difference (gay men love men because they are really women); yet in another respect, which I believe is the pertinent one today, it is a radical notion since it affirms the potential for gender fluidity that both the medical model of transsexuality and mainstream gay culture deny.

THE TRANSSEXUAL BODY AND
THE ZIONIST DREAM

In recent years, Daniel Boyarin, Michael Gluzman, and other scholars have underlined the gendered dimension of the Zionist project, highlighting Zionism's preoccupation with Jewish masculinity and especially with the male body (Boyarin; Gluzman). Boyarin describes the centuries-old European tradition that defined the Jewish male as feminine, a tradition whose most concrete manifestation was the belief that Jewish men menstruate (210). He also calls attention to the fact that the representation of the Jewish male as feminine was not merely an anti-Semitic stereotype projected from the outside, but also an internal Jewish representation that expressed a positive self-image and fulfilled an identitarian function of distinguishing Jewish culture from the surrounding gentile culture (211–12). This representation, as Boyarin and Gluzman show, became problematic in the nineteenth century with the emergence of the invert as a pathological figure that combined cross-gendered characteristics with same-sex object choice (Boyarin 211–16; Gluzman 146–47). The feminized Jewish male resembled the invert too much, and Zionism, as Theodor Herzl and Max Nordau envisioned it, set out not only to provide a homeland for the Jewish people but also to rehabilitate Jewish masculinity, that is, to replace the scholarly and antiheroic Jewish model of masculinity with the gentile one (Boyarin 271–312; Gluzman 148–49). In Herzl's novel *Altneuland*, the very move from Europe to Palestine is depicted as transforming the Jewish body—and especially the male Jewish body—from a slender, weak, and deformed one into a healthy, tall, and robust one (Gluzman 154–55).

Today it seems clear that Zionism's gender project—the project of fashioning a new Jewish man in accordance with the gentile paradigm of normative masculinity—has succeeded far more unambiguously than any of the other parts of the Zionist program. True, the most recent embodiment of this "new Jew" is not Herzl's sunburned farmer, nor any longer the Israel Defense Forces (IDF) soldier in combat fatigues, but rather the bearded, Yarmulked settler with a gun slung across his shoulder—a figure Herzl and Nordau could not have foreseen in their wildest dreams—but even this figure finds its origin in their civilized fantasies of duels and sports clubs. In light of this legacy, which has left its mark on Israel's national identity in the form of

far-reaching gender imitation possible. In transsexuals, gendered imitation is so complete that it extends its scope to the flesh itself. If drag "reveals the imitative structure of gender itself" by disrupting the expected coherence between the performer's anatomy and the gender being performed, then transsexuality first disrupts this coherence and then restores it—but it restores it by reversing the normative direction of causality: anatomy does not determine gender, rather anatomy is modified to correspond to gender (Butler 137).[32]

Dana International began her stage career as a drag artist doing parodic imitations of female pop stars.[33] Her first hit, "Saida Sultana," was conceived as a takeoff on Whitney Houston's "My Name Is Not Susan" and was first performed in the context of a mock "Pre-Eurovision" contest in a gay club.[34] This imitation of femininity gave rise to a woman who is a paragon of femininity ("everything is natural and feminine in the purest sense"); the imitation of stardom bred a star; the loving Eurovision parody produced a Eurovision winner. Dana, therefore, provides a perfect illustration to the understanding of gender as performative and as an imitation that constructs its own origin. As the epitome of femininity—and femininity as an artifact— she *is* the ontological equivalent of the one hundred percent man, but as such, and as opposed to the speaker in the poem, she can never behave like a nonwoman and can never fail to be an object of male heterosexual desire. But while the position of one hundred percent woman is presumed to lack any critical dimension, Dana in her very choice of this poem by Wallach, and in many other of her textual and performative practices, adopts a self-reflexive and critical stance vis-à-vis the feminine ideal she embodies. She does not allow us to forget the continuum that links femininity to drag, but as one who has chosen performance—both as a stage artist and as a woman by will, she celebrates the joy of performance and its potential for nearly infinite diversity that runs counter to any attempt to reify a "natural" femininity.

NOTES

1. An earlier, shorter version of this chapters was published in Hebrew in *Theory and Criticism (Special Issue: Fifty to Forty-Eight)* 12–13 (1999): 401–11.
2. Estimates range between 50,000 and five million copies. For the former see Sweedenburg, 88–119; the latter is cited in Moriel, 225–37.
3. This particular pronouncement was made by Rabbi Shlomo Benizri of the religious Shas party, who served as minister of health at the time.
4. For an analysis that situates Dana International in the context of Israel's culture wars, see Solomon, 149–65.
5. Ashkenazi are Jews of European origin; Mizrahi (formerly known as "Sephardi") are Jews of Middle-Eastern or North-African descent.
6. The dense web of contradictions spanned by Dana International is explored by Aeyal Gross. See Gross, 227–36.

7. "Coccinelle," "ladybird" in French, is a derogatory term in Hebrew for transsexuals and drag queens. Its etymology is explained later on in this section. See International, "Where" 2–6.

8. Throughout this chapter when I speak of transsexuality, I am referring to male to female (MTF) transsexuals. Female to male (FTM) transsexuality was entirely unknown in Israel before the late 1990s.

9. This information is derived from a newspaper article about transsexuals in Israel published shortly after Dana's Eurovision victory. See Levertov. As the timing of the article proves, Dana's high media exposure promoted public interest in transsexuality.

10. The hybridity of the name is exacerbated by the fact that Zalman is an old-fashioned diasporic name, whereas Shoshi (short for Shoshanna = Rose) carries connotations of younger and often low-class women.

11. Significantly, in an interview to a local gay magazine, she counters such assertions and explains: "In front of a journalist you need to prettify things. I never felt a woman. I felt different. If a woman who had been pregnant and miscarried would sit here I couldn't feel what she feels, never. I didn't feel a woman, I felt different" (International, "Where" 2). This statement indicates her awareness that the assertion "I have always felt like a woman" forms a necessary article of faith not only for the medical establishment that controls the access to sex change technology, but also for the heterosexual public that can accept the fact of transsexuality only if it does not disrupt the notion of gender as natural and innate and even contributes to its naturalization.

12. This refusal to disown her past is expressed even more explicitly in her answer to a journalist who asked what her associations to the name Yaron Cohen, her formal male name, are. Her response is: "How far. It was truly wonderful. With transsexuals there's this myth of 'how bad everything was before the transition, and how singularly good things have become since.' As far as I'm concerned, except for a few cosmetic changes, the brain is the same brain and the heart too." See Segev.

13. Gay Pride has been celebrated publicly in Israel since 1993, and Dana first performed in the Pride event of 1994.

14. See *Hazman Havarod* 1. Interestingly, Weizman's objection to gay men and lesbians, in that notorious comment, referred to their deviation from prescribed gender roles, so that, while he did not explicitly allude to transsexuals at all, his condemnation of homosexuality was on the ground of its supposed disruption of the gender system. Cf. Yael Ben-Zvi, who contrasts International's militant response to the conciliatory attitude of some of the mainstream leaders of the community who met with Weizman and accepted the weak apology he made. See Ben-Zvi, 26–28.

15. International also took care to point out the reputation of that strip of beach to a local reporter who covered the shootings. See Hakak, 24.

16. For an elaborate and astute reading of the image and the campaign, see Gross, 227–36.

17. The symbolic significance of Dana's victory is compounded by the fact that Eurovision, with its profoundly kitsch aesthetics, has a place of honor in local

gay male culture. Both in Israel and throughout Europe, Eurovision has a broad gay fandom, and the contest has acquired the status a gay cult event (e.g. some gay bars hold a weekly Eurovision music night), so that gay men sense a kind of ownership over it. For a discussion of the Eurovision's gay fandom and the significance of Dana's victory to gay fans, see Lemish, 41–63.

18. I am referring to Sharon Ben-Ezzer, who in the late eighties formed the band "Pollyanna Frank," and released two albums. Ben-Ezzer has always been out, and her lyrics included lesbian and feminist texts, but, both due the genre that she created in, and due to the fact that she made most of her career in England, she remained on the fringe of the local music scene, and never achieved such wide publicity and success as Dana International has.

19. Eve Kosofsky Sedgwick characterizes the structure and mechanism of this type of open secret in her *Epistemology of the Closet*, 79–80.

20. One such example is provided by Uzi Even and his partner Amit Kama. Even, a Chemistry Professor at Tel Aviv University, and formerly a high-ranking officer in the IDF, played a key role in changing the IDF's discriminatory policy by describing his discharge from the IDF on the grounds of his homosexuality in a celebrated speech in front of a Knesset committee. Later, Even sued Tel Aviv University, and won for his partner spouse benefits, and the two also adopted a gay teenage boy who had been thrown out of his home. The landmark achievements won by the two, and especially Even's pivotal role in bringing about a reevaluation of the IDF policy, were in large part owing to their respectable mainstream image: professional careers, long-term relationship, military background, and middle-class Ashkenazi origins.

21. I can even recall gay bars in Tel Aviv of the early nineties that in an attempt to foster a respectable image barred transsexuals and drag queens.

22. In this context it is also interesting to note that the exhilaration that followed International's Eurovision victory brought about a dramatic—if temporary—shift from a normalizing and assimilationist politics to a more confrontational attitude, when following early closure of the 1998 Wigstock festival by the police, for the first time 2000 gay men, lesbians, and transsexuals spontaneously took to the streets, blocked roads, and confronted the police. Once again, it seems like no coincidence that this demonstration erupted at the close of a drag festival, and that transsexuals were its moving spirit.

23. The announcement of the award winners stated that "all transgendered people are part of the community," and that the community "must not be ashamed of any chapter of its history." See Halperin.

24. I am coining this term with allusion to Judith Halberstam's notion of a continuum of female masculinities spanning both butches and FTMs, of which it is reminiscent. Halberstam's coinage of the term "transgender butch" contests the distinctness of transsexuality and lesbianism in a move that is parallel to the one preformed by Dana International. See Halberstam, 141–73.

25. My use of masculine pronouns here in referring to MTF transsexuals is merely strategic, for purposes of underscoring the contradiction to Zionism's project of masculinization.

26. Alisa Solomon makes a similar point: "[Dana International] challenges the dominant old story of Zionism as the making of a new Jewish man by proposing that Israel's *new* new Jewish man may be a woman" (151). While I share Solomon's reading, my analysis, first published in Hebrew in 1999, was developed independently.
27. Her mélange of musical styles, mostly Western dance music and elements of Arab music, has also been noted by critics. See especially Sweedenburg, 102–05.
28. On Dana's heterodox linguistic practices, see especially Sweedenburg, 100–02 and Moriel.
29. For a sample of Wallach's poetry and a short introduction to her work in English translation, see "Yona." On Wallach's poetry, see also Cohen.
30. The other poem, which I will only mention, is "Presomnolent Poem," whose first-person-masculine-plural speaker expresses a desperate wish for "a different kind of sex" (which could also be taken to mean "another sex"). The standard male wish for more thrilling sex is ironized when ventriloquized by someone who for the average male represents thrilling sex par excellence. At the same time, when at the end of the song Dana repeats the line "There is a different kind of sex," it acquires the valence of a liberating promise (Wallach, *Shira*).
31. In Hebrew, first and second person verb conjugations are gendered as well.
32. As Judith Shapiro explains, transsexuality, as a system of institutionalized gender crossing, works to maintain the gender system by detaching gender from the principle that provides its apparent foundation, i.e. the rule of anatomical recruitment to gender category membership. See Shapiro, 248–79. At the cost of sacrificing the foundational status of anatomical sex, as well as the assumption that gender membership is innate and fixed, transsexuality allows the maintenance of the gender system itself as binary, and reestablishes sex-gender coherence.
33. As late as the release of her first hit single, "Saida Sultana," Dana interviewed as Yaron Cohen, drag artist, using male pronouns and declaring that he performed as a woman only in order to make a living. See Porian, 68–69.
34. The story of the beginnings of International's career is told by Ofer Nissim, her former personal manager and the one who discovered her in an interview for a gay paper; see Nissim, 5–7.

WORKS CITED

Asheri, Ehud. "Mishak Milim" ["Word Game"]. *Haaretz* 28 Oct. 2005. 10 June 2005 <http://www.haaretz.co.il>.
Ben-Zvi, Yael. "Zionist Lesbianism and Transsexual Transgression: Two Representations of Queer Israel." *Middle East Report* (1998): 26–28.
Boyarin, Daniel. *Unheroic Conduct: The Rise of Heterosexuality and the Invention of the Jewish Man.* Berkeley: U of California P, 1997.
Butler, Judith. *Gender Trouble: Feminism and the Subversion of Identity.* New York: Routledge, 1990.

134   A M A L I A   Z I V

Cohen, Zafrira Lidowsky. *"Loosen the Fetters of Thy Tongue, Woman": The Poetry and Politics of Yona Wallach.* Cincinnati: Hebrew Union Coll. P, 2003.

Eurotrash. Channel 4. 1993–Present.

Gluzman, Michael. "Longing for Heterosexuality: Zionism and Sexuality in Herzl's *Altneuland.*" *Theory and Criticism* 11 (Winter 1997): 145–62.

Gross, Aeyal. "Queer Globalization and Human Rights: Dana International/Amnesty International." *Theory and Criticism* 23 (2003): 227–36.

Hakak, David. "Yoter Chatzufa, Harbeh Yoter International" ["Much Cheekier, Much More International"]. *Ma'ariv.* 11 Aug. 1996: 24.

Halberstam, Judith. *Female Masculinity.* Durham, NC: Duke UP, 1998.

Halperin, Yaniv. "Rami Hasman VeGila Goldstein Nivcharu leyakirey Hakehila" ["Rami Hasman and Gila Goldstein Won Community Award"]. 24 Mar. 2003. 24 Mar. 2006 <http://www.gogay.co.il/today/ItemDB.asp?CMID=2441>.

Hazman Havarod 4 (1997): 1.

Herzl, Theodor. *Altneuland.* Berlin: B. Harz, 1921.

International, Dana. "Re'ayon im Dana International" ["Interview with Dana International"]. By Yoav Birenberg. *Yediot Acharonot (Shiva Leilot) [Seven Nights].* 28 Mar. 1996. 6–7.

———. "Ani Meta Lehitahev Aval Holechet Lishon Levad" ["I'm Dying to Fall in Love but I Go to Sleep Alone: An Interview with Dana International"]. By Or Korel. *La'isha.* 23 Dec. 1996. 36–37.

———. "Ani Mocheret Ashlayot" ["I Sell Illusions: Interview with Dana International"]. By Eran Eisenhandler. *Ma'ariv.* 15 Sep. 1995. 10–11.

———. "Ma Shero'ot Ha'eynayim Ka'et Zot Lo Tamid Ha'emet" ["What the Eyes See Now Is Not Always the Truth: an Interview with Dana International"]. By Shai Kerem. *Yediot Acharonot (Shiva Yamim) [Seven Days].* 10 Dec. 1993. 61–62, 74.

———. "Bemakom Shehomo Mekabel Bakbuk Barosh, Coccinelit Mekabelet Hatza'a Meguna" ["Where a Homosexual Gets a Broken Bottle, a Coccinelle Gets an Indecent Proposal: An Interview with Dana International"]. By Tzipa Kampinsky. *Tat-Tarbut [Subculture]* 2 (1996): 2–6.

Kerem, Shai. "Mivtza Dana" ["Operation Dana"]. *Yediot Acharonot (Shiva Yamim) [Seven Days].* 19 July 1996. 44–46, 50.

Lemish, Dafna. " 'My Kind of Campfire': The Eurovision Song Contest and Israeli Gay Men." *Popular Communication* 2.1 (2004): 41–63.

Levertov, Michal. "Kama Aval Eifo Kol Hayeter?" ["Dana Has Risen, But Where Are All the Rest?"]. *Haaretz* 22 May 1998. 10 June 2006 <http://www.haaretz.co.il>.

Moriel, Liora. "Diva in the Promised Land: A Blueprint for Newspeak?" *World Englishes* 17 (1998): 225–37.

Newton, Esther. "The Mythic Mannish Lesbian." *Hidden from History: Reclaiming the Gay and Lesbian Past.* Ed. Martin Duberman, Martha Vicinus and George Chauncey Jr. New York: NAL, 1989. 281–93.

Nissim, Ofer. "Thank You for the Music." Interview with Yair Qedar. *Hazman Havarod* 4 (1997): 5–7.

Porian, Ronit. "Viduyo Shel Zameret" ["Confession of a Singer"]. *Tel Aviv.* 22 Jan. 1993. 68–69.

Sedgwick, Eve Kosofsky. *Epistemology of the Closet*. Berkeley: U of California P, 1990.

Segev, Amira. "Dana International." *Haaretz* 7 Sept. 2001. 10 June 2006 <http://www.haaretz.co.il>.

Shapiro, Judith. "Transsexualism: Reflections on the Persistence of Gender and the Mutability of Sex." *Body Guards: The Cultural Politics of Gender Ambiguity*. Ed. Julia Epstein and Kristina Straub. New York: Routledge, 1991. 248–79.

Solomon, Alisa. "Viva la Diva Citizenship: Post-Zionism and Gay Rights." *Queer Theory and the Jewish Question*. Ed. Daniel Boyarin, Daniel Itzkovitz, and Ann Pelegrini. New York: Columbia UP, 2003. 149–65.

Stone, Sandy. "The *Empire* Strikes Back: A Posttranssexual Manifesto." *Body Guards: The Cultural Politics of Gender Ambiguity*. Ed. Julia Epstein and Kristina Straub. New York: Routledge, 1991. 280–304.

Sweedenburg, Ted. "Sa'ida Sultan/Dana International: Transgender Pop and the Polysemiotics of Sex, Nation and Ethnicity on the Israeli-Egyptian Border." *Mass Mediations: New Approaches to Popular Culture in the Middle East and Beyond*. Ed. Walter Armburst. Berkeley: U of California P, 2000. 88–119.

Wallach, Yona. "Me'ah Achuz Gever" ["One Hundred Percent Man"]. *Or Peré [Wild Light]: Poems*. Jerusalem: Adam, 1983. 36.

———. *Shira [Collected Poems]*. Tel Aviv: Siman Qri'a, 1976. 79.

"Yona Wallach." *Poetry International Web*. 2006. Central Bureau of the Poetry International Web Foundation. 24 Mar. 2006 <http://israel.poetryinternational.org/cwolk/view/21730>.

Chapter 9

Arse Bandits: Exploring Nostalgic Representations of Queerness in Gangster Films

Sharif Mowlabocus

Abstract: *This chapter considers the British gangster film as a site of queer masculinity, contending that the counterhegemonic world of organized crime has proven a useful space in which queer identities can be formed and articulated. Countering postliberationist criticisms that such representations of homosexuality are wholly negative, this chapter considers how the specific sociohistoric context of post–World War II Britain has provided a cultural milieu in which homosexuality and crime can coexist, particularly within mainstream film. This chapter concludes that such an analysis demonstrates the need to revisit previously abandoned heteronormative texts in order to identify homosexualities that operate outside of the contemporary metropolitan gay male identity.*

SEARCHING FOR POLITICALLY USEFUL REPRESENTATIONS OF HOMOSEXUALITY in gangster films might at first glance appear a pointless task. A genre that celebrates archetypal heterosexual masculinity in its most crude and base forms, it is not the most obvious choice for developing queer readings, or for seeking to historicize queerness. This is a genre that uses racism, homophobia, and misogyny in an almost casual manner that rewards parasitic opportunism and glorifies violence to a degree verging on the pornographic. A brief look at the *International Movie Database* top 250 films illustrates the continuing popularity of the gangster genre, though I would argue that this has less to do with cinematic genius and more to do with upholding ideals of hegemonic masculinity in a world in which (at least according to British men's magazines such as *Loaded* and *Nuts*) masculinity is supposedly under attack. This celebration of "real men" (i.e., white heterosexual masculine supremacy) can be understood as a defense against the supposed encroachment of feminism, of lesbian and gay rights, of political correctness, and of equal opportunities legislation. Claire Monk has commented on the 1990s fashion within film culture for older British crime films, stating that a reverence for films such as *Get Carter* and *The Long Good Friday* demonstrates an "uncritical, backward-looking self-referentiality and unacknowledged nostalgia" (172). Given the fact that part of this nostalgic appeal must surely lie in the forceful reassertion of hegemonic masculinity, the gangster film would appear an odd place to start discussing *queer* representation and histories.

Despite this initial reading of the genre, however, I contend that such texts can operate as sites of sexual subversion, providing a counterpoint to the (over)represented metropolitan gay male lifestyle found in contemporary popular culture. I also believe that alternative queer narratives can be mined from such texts, providing a glimpse of historical configurations of homosexuality that, for reasons of class and politics, have been left unspoken. In writing off gangster films as emblems of smug heterosexual masculinity, I want to argue that we risk losing sight of the queer identities, nuances, and narratives evident in a number of these texts.

This loss may in part be because we are not looking at these films through the correct lens. Although they appear politically effective in the shaping of a positive gay male identity, postliberationist discussions of gay representation have not been free from their own ideological assumptions. As Matias Viegener comments, "in its history as a white, middle-class movement, gay liberation may be said to have fashioned gay identities suited to the bourgeoisie" (127). Searching for these identities in mainstream film may serve to obscure other representations that can be recuperated by some, if not all, gay/queer audiences. It is now time to pick over those films and genres that were previously discarded as homophobic, in order to begin exploring queer representations that do not fit in with these postliberationist models of representation.

My discussion centers on the analysis of gangster films either produced or culturally located (via set and/or characterization) in Britain, and the reasons for this are threefold. First, there is a comparative dearth of commentary on British crime cinema in comparison to its American counterpart. While there *are* several important critical commentaries on British crime cinema (Chibnall and Murphy; Monk; Chadder; Leigh), these are outweighed by the cannon of literature built up around American crime films. Arguably this reflects cultural differences between the two countries. While British organized crime has existed throughout the twentieth century, no one group has rivaled the size, power, or notoriety of the American syndicates. Eugene Rosow identifies the specific cultural milieu in which both the real and the cinematic gangster rose to prominence in the 1920s America. Twinned with an older, yet still powerful metanarrative of individualism, he cites prohibition, the drive toward consumerism, the poverty and hardship of immigrant life, and the hedonism of the age as providing the recipe for large-scale organized crime (41–42). Figures such as Al Capone, Meyer Lansky, and Lucky Luciano were the public faces of local, then regional, and finally national crime syndicates that stretched out across the nation, and these crime fraternities were "celebrated" in films of the time, such as *The Racketeer, Little Caesar*, and *The Public Enemy*.

The difference in migrant population; the social-class dynamic; and the specific legal, political, and social frameworks of British society meant that although criminal gangs were present in the poorer quarters of major towns and cities, they lacked the opportunities afforded their American brethren. As James Robertson asserts, "no large-scale British organised crime on the American model seems to have existed" (16). Steve Chibnall and Robert Murphy point out that compared to his American cousin, the British crim- inal has historically "kept a lower profile and provided less scope for mythology" (5). The British crime film has therefore had fewer cultural resources to draw on and this has sometimes led to criticism of it being "imitative of American originals and in poor taste" (1). The first reason for focusing on British films then is to build on and extend this limited cannon, providing an analysis of British gangster films that is acutely aware of the specific cultural contexts in which they are produced and received.

The second reason for this focus lies in the fact that one of the most notorious criminal personalities in recent British history was queer-identified. Together with his twin brother Reggie, Ronnie Kray remains the most infamous gangster in British history. Though the Kray Firm did not match the size, breadth, or might of the Mafia-controlled American outfits, the brothers (prior to their incarceration in 1969, for murder) ruled the criminal underworld in London and across the country for the best part of a decade. Even today, the family name continues to be mentioned in almost reverent tones in the autobiographies of retired gangsters, and knowing one of the Krays remains laden with subcultural capital in this sphere of British society. As icons, Ronnie and Reggie have remained integral to British culture, even in death and, as Chris Jenks writes, "[T]hey [have] retained, with a passive appreciation, the magnetism and public agitation that they actively sought and engendered in the heyday of their nefarious careers" (112).

Along with his schizophrenia, his temper, and his sadistic behavior, Ronnie's homosexuality is now commonly known. Publicly declaring his homosexuality was unthinkable at the time (homosexuality remained a criminal offence in England until 1967), yet Ronnie was not closeted in the

modern-day sense of the word. Although he identifies the fact that growing
up in the East End of London was not conducive to being out, John Pearson
writes that as an adult, Ronnie made "no bones about his homosexuality" and
in fact used it as a means of accessing close-knit communities of wealthy
homosexual men (qtd. in Higgins 196–97). In the 1950s and 1960s,
although Britain moved slowly toward law reform, Ronnie refused to identify
with such reform, nor did he describe himself as gay. Pearson later notes that
"there was no hint of effeminacy about [Ronnie]. 'I'm not a poof, I'm a homosexual' he would say, and was genuinely put out by the antics of effeminate
males. 'Pansies' he used to say, with the same cockney contempt with which
he pronounced the word 'women' " (Higgins 197).

Kray's queer masculinity has been central to the subsequent portrayals of
British gangsters, many of whom have been modeled on the infamous twin.
In *Villain*, the queer mob-boss, Vic Dakin, is widely understood as having
been modeled on Ronnie, while Peter Medak's *The Krays* offers a biography of
the notorious pair with an emphasis on Ronnie's homosexual relations. More
recently, Jake Arnott's book *The Long Firm* featuring the Kray-clone Harry
Starks has been adapted for television by the BBC. The iconic power of Ronnie
Kray continues to be felt in British culture today and, I believe, is the primary
reason behind British crime cinema's interest in the sexually dissident.[1] While
British gangster films are often considered staunchly heterosexual, the collision
of history and genre creates a space in which masculinity, dominance, and
control can occupy a queer identity. In the world of the British gangster, to
victimize the homosexual is to insult Ronnie Kray, and who in their right
mind would want to do that?

Finally, there is a certain logic in seeking queerity amongst films that
feature strong British characters, narratives, or contexts of production. For
the British, or more specifically, the Englishman, has historically been
regarded as somewhat queer, particularly in comparison to his American
counterpart. Vito Russo identifies the link between queerity and Englishness
within American cinema—and culture—when he discusses the response
from the Hays Office to the screenplay of Hitchcock's *Rope*. He quotes
Arthur Laurent, the screenplay writer who noted the censorship of apparent
homosexual phrases in the script: "And do you know what they were? It was
simply that they were saying things like 'My dear boy' to each other, and the
way the English talked was known as 'fruity' over here" (92–94).

The well-spoken Englishman carries with him connotations of queer
desire, particularly when placed within the context of American hegemonic
masculinity. As Russo notes, even the common American terms "fag" and
"faggot" are English in origin, "taken from its use in British boarding
schools as a term for underclass men 'fagging' for upperclassmen" (46). This
linguistic detail reflects how the Englishman has been used as an identifier of

homosexuality in many films including *It's Love I'm After, The Gay Divorcee, Gone With the Wind, Wuthering Heights,* and *Laura,* to name just a few. The relationship between Englishness and queerness continues even today and has recently been seen in *Gods and Monsters,* the biopic of homosexual film director James Whale. Sir Ian McKellen's portrayal of the *Frankenstein* director employs Englishness as a signifier of queer desire as he attempts to seduce the embodiment of working-class American masculinity (Brendan Fraser) under the guise of wanting to draw his portrait. Thus British masculinity in film is always contending with the specter of the queer via this link, providing any discussion of queerness in British film with an extra dimension, and it is this specter that my analysis shall draw out.

Chibnall and Murphy do not specifically discuss the issue of homosexuality in their analysis of British crime cinema, though they perhaps inadvertently imply a link when they label the British gangster film as the genre that "dare not speak its name" (1). Not a particularly common phrase within film criticism, it nevertheless apes Lord Alfred Douglas's concept of the "love that dare not speak its name," namely homosexuality, and this discursive echoing reflects similarities between the social histories of organized crime and homosexuality in Britain (57). Both have thrived during periods of social upheaval, most notably World War II, only to have faced increased policing and prosecution immediately afterward. Roy Ingleton has documented the changes in moral codes during wartime Britain and notes that "discipline appeared to have ceased to exist and even public officials accepted and adopted what, at best, might be called rule-bending, and at worst, unequivocal corruption" (327). This tolerance of crime is reflected in the "spiv" films of the immediate postwar period.[2] Andrew Clay has discussed this genre, in which "a contrast in fortune was often drawn . . . between the unrewarded demobilised servicemen and the 'spivs' who had unfairly prospered in their absence" (51). These films often portrayed the war as a period of criminal opportunism, be it in the form of black market goods that bypassed the ration system of the 1940s or more elaborate scams that took in and fleeced young and naive soldiers and sailors during their leave.

Likewise the war provided opportunities for the still unspeakable crime of homosexuality to flourish, albeit briefly. Quentin Crisp described London during the heaviest bombing campaigns as a golden age and celebrated night-time London during the war for its abundance of American servicemen, its devil-may-care attitude and its dimly lit party atmosphere, an atmosphere that allowed homosexual activity to thrive:

> Voices whispered suggestively to you as you walked along; hands reached out if you stood still . . . Once, when I emerged from Leicester Square Underground station, the outline of the buildings on the opposite side of the road looked so

unfamiliar that I thought I must have taken the wrong exit. When I asked an
invisible passer-by where I was, he kissed me on the lips, told me I was in
Newport Street and walked on. (154–55)

Echoing Crisp, more traditional oral history narratives note the comparatively
relaxed attitude that spread over the nation's capital as a result of the war
(Hall 44). Of course, during the aftermath of World War II, as Britain rebuilt
its towns and cities, social norms were also forcefully reaffirmed (David
153–54; Weeks 158–59). Ultimately, however, the ideological face of British
culture has shifted irrevocably, the war providing the seeds for second-wave
feminism and homosexual law reform, as well as for more organized criminal
enterprise (Morris 89–105).

In addition to these historical similarities, both subcultures have developed
similar relationships with hegemonic British society. First, both operate outside of, but continually collide with, normal society. The criminal, whether
he be fencing goods, blackmailing, or extorting money, relies on the regular
joe as a source of income. The preliberation homosexual, if we follow Crisp's
myth of "the great dark man," was not interested in other homosexuals but in
regular (i.e., heterosexually identified) men (62). Second, both the gangster
and the homosexual upset gender normativity, though in obviously different
ways. As the homosexual threatens normative masculinity through his disregard for the gender binary, the gangster, operating in homosocial spaces and
in homosocial groups, troubles stable gender relations and heteronormativity.
Esther Sonnet and Peter Stanfield identify this latter destabilizing process
when examining the hypermasculinized figure of the gangster in retro films
such as *Miller's Crossing* and *The Untouchables*. This masculinizing occurs
through two devices, "the resurrection of the dress code of hegemonic
masculinity and the literal and symbolic elimination of women" (177).

The final relational point to be observed is the relationship *between* queer
subculture and organized crime. The latter has historically provided spaces
for queer interaction, and even the legendary Stonewall bar was owned and
run by the "Mob" (Duberman 184). In Britain similar connections between
queer life and criminal enterprise have been identified and were an early target
of the Gay Liberation Front campaign (Weeks 193).

Yet despite these cultural and historical similarities, the relationship
between homosexuality and organized crime in film has rarely been discussed.
Carlos Clarens has commented on the use of "nonerotic homosexual
attachment" between characters in a variety of films, including *The Big
Combo*, and while he goes further than other film critics in acknowledging
the existence of homosexual relationships, he finds nothing useful in such
representation, writing them off as oddities (56). Gaylyn Studlar goes further,
developing a queer reading of three crime films in order to explore homoerotic

desire within this genre during the early 1940s. Studlar offers a convincing analysis highlighting incongruities and linguistic anomalies in her search for the invisible queer, but her discussion focuses on the unseen; the queer is hinted at but he never reveals his desire, though this is hardly surprising considering censorship laws at the time.

Where queer characters *do* appear the general consensus seems to be that such representations are at best flourishes added to make the film stand out, and at worst, signifiers of deviancy and moral decay. But their existence in this genre should neither be denied nor dismissed as singularly homophobic. Indeed, where American figures such as Fante and Mingo in *The Big Combo* live and die serving their boss, in British crime films, the queer can *be* the boss. I have previously mentioned Richard Burton's character, Vic Dakin, in *Villain* as an example of the queer mob-boss and, as I shall now demonstrate, Dakin is not alone in occupying the position of top dog.

While *The Italian Job* (1969) positions Michael Caine's character, Charlie Crocker, as the heterosexual hero of the film, he is ultimately subject to the rule of the quietly menacing—and quietly queer—Mr. Bridger, tellingly played by Noel Coward. Bridger never identifies himself as homosexual, though such identification is perhaps unnecessary—and unwanted. Bridger's queerness should be understood as operating outside the matrix of gay consciousness and as such the will to self-identify—to be out and proud as it were—is less apparent. Instead, the audience is given a string of clues that signify both Bridger's queerness and his status. His servant on the inside, Keats (played by Coward's offscreen partner, Graham Payn) embodies the best of British camp, while his business advisor Camp Freddy cuts a dash in garish cravats and pink two-piece suits, employing the piss-elegant speech of a bar queen to everyone except his boss.[3] To this must be added Bridger's obsession with *the* Queen—Queen Elizabeth II—and of course the queer credentials of Coward himself, cast for a specific purpose. Unlike Fante and Mingo, Bridger comes out on top. While Charlie Crocker grafts on the outside, Bridger treats his jailers like footmen and wanders about the prison with the grace and poise of an old Duchess; his Englishness serves as both a cover for and a signification of his queerness. Audiences can write Bridger off as an upper-class eccentric (he is not queer, he is just foreign or—for a British audience—posh) or they can identify his performance, along with the casting and extratextual details, as a specific breed of queer identity.

The 2003 homage to the *The Italian Job* lost nearly all traces of its British accent, the new (German-built) Mini Cooper perhaps being the only remaining signifier of the original text.[4] In this translation, Bridger (Donald Sutherland) undergoes a process of heterosexualizing (his daughter, Stella, becomes a member of Crocker's team) prior to being killed off before the big heist. Stella takes up her father's position as safecracker and provides a suitable object of desire for Charlie Crocker (Mark Wahlberg), as the excessive and queer desires that spill out of the original film are tempered into the satisfaction of classic Oedipal anxiety; Stella is Bridger's biological daughter; Charlie is positioned as the son Bridger never had, cast in the same mould—a chip off the old block.

There are two possibilities for Bridger's heterosexual conversion. Firstly, Bridger's closeted queerity flies in the face of political correctness and this may have proven too problematic for a film industry that has moved from representing homosexuality as evil or sinful to representing one version of homosexuality, namely the positive (and desexualized) metropolitan gay man (Sinfield 6). This maneuver has been at the expense of all other articulations of queerness, and Bridger may well have become a victim of the homogeneity of gay characterization. However, linking Bridger's sexuality and nationality may provide us with a more substantial reason for his disappearance. As discussed above, Britishness, or more precisely Englishness, has historically been used as a queer signifier in film and television. Bridger's sexuality is identified through his cut-glass accent, his fondness for the aristocracy, his ritualistic traditions of high tea, and his sartorial precision. Once more, the casting of Noel Coward plays an important role, as he embodied this effete, stylized, and comfortably upper-class stereotype. The transplanting of the narrative to American soil (the climactic heist is set in Los Angeles) left no space for such an oblique sexual reference (nor, arguably, for such a class-defined character) and in many ways Bridger became out of date, out of place, and out of fashion.

Bridger's disappearance serves to underline two important points. Firstly, it demonstrates that British-made and British-based crime films have a long-standing relationship with queer desire. This is not to say that American gangster films cannot contain queer figures, or that gay gangsters have not appeared in American films (most notably *The Mexican*, starring James Gandolfini of *The Sopranos*), but such figures are rare in comparison to their British cousins. Secondly, where contemporary American crime films occasionally utilize *gay* characters, contemporary British crime films feature *queer* figures. That is to say, in contrast to Gandolfini's brooding gay assassin, films such as *The Italian Job*, *Layercake*, *Gangster No. 1*, *The Krays*, *Endgame*, and *The Courier* include characters that operate outside of the metropolitan configuration of homosexuality indicated by the term gay.

For example, *Layercake* pays respect to Ronnie Kray and historicizes the queer through a flashback sequence. In a scene between Daniel Craig's anonymous character and Gene (Colm Meaney), the latter describes the death of Kilburn Jerry, a young hooligan and onetime boyfriend of Crazy Larry. Larry, the head of a crime fraternity, has a reputation for seducing young, straight men and it is suggested that Jerry's suicide is as a result of having been turned by Larry. While problematic from a liberationist perspective, it should be noted that queerness is here positioned as a site of masculine power. When asked if Larry was gay, Gene replies, "Larry was never gay." Larry's queerness is identified as masculine, as the flashback continues with Larry sneering to camera that "fucking females is for poofs."

Within the context of the upturned world of organized crime, this statement serves to invest a degree of power within the figure of the queer. At the same time it separates him out from other homosexualities, most notably the mincing queen or the metropolitan gay man. This separating out of queer from camp or gay identities is strengthened by the mis-en-scène, styling, and costume of the flashback, all of which suggest a period in the mid-1970s, a time when Gay Liberation was expanding across Britain and the metropolitan gay identity was beginning to emerge. Larry identifies himself as being outside of this emerging model yet continues to articulate sexual dissidence within ostensibly heterosexual space.

Of course, we must remember that Larry meets with a gruesome end, but even his death destabilizes the assumed heterosexuality of the gangster film. For it is implied that Gene was perhaps one of Larry's boys. When asked what happened to Larry, Gene suggests that one of his boyfriends shot him, adding that "he took liberties with too many straight lads"; it later transpires that it was Gene who murdered Larry. Again, this queering of the gangster figure appears somewhat problematic. The fact that Gene is driven to murdering Larry suggests a reestablishment of heterosexual privilege, not to mention the validation of the homosexual panic defense. Nevertheless, the small space created by Larry serves to undermine the assumed heterosexuality of Gene and reconstitutes queer desire outside of the now widely accepted norms of gay identity. The rupture that Larry causes within Gene's heterosexuality—and within the assumed heterosexual masculinity of the gangster film—echoes Studlar's assertion that such films "expose the continuum of 'male homosocial desire' " and the contradictions that can arise in such a continuum, namely the slippage between homosocial and homosexual, "these crime-centered films . . . explore the sexual complexity of the bond forged between men within a homosocial underworld associated with gangsterism" (122).

Similarly, *Gangster No.1* plays with the idea of nostalgized queerness, the film being framed around a single extended flashback. While Paul Bettany's eponymous character does not identify as queer, his rejection of women, obsessive behavior toward his boss, and naked approach to torturing his subjects serve to undermine normative assumptions of heterosexuality. Indeed Gangster and his boss, Freddie Mays, rub shoulders with the sexually dissident as they dine at a nightclub. In one of the most important scenes in the film (that sees Gangster's erotic devotion to his boss betrayed as Freddie meets his future wife), Gangster swaps looks with a pair of passing drag queens before looking back to his table, only to find that the object of his desire is desiring someone else.

Gangster's obsession is not missed by his boss who instructs the club owner to send over a couple of dancers remarking to Gangster that "two blokes on our own drinking wine? Bit suspect innit?" This of course raises questions as to why Freddie is so concerned that people see him as heterosexual. But Freddy *is* heterosexual. He is narcissistic and he enjoys Gangster's hero worship but his relationship with his right-hand man ends there. Gangster on the other hand is far more "problematic." Earlier in the scene, Gangster also identifies their suspicious coupling, commenting that their choice of drink is "a bit suspect." However, unlike Freddy, Gangster seems less willing to erase this queer suspicion. Immediately after he makes eye contact with the two drag queens, he leans forward and pours Freddy more wine as if asserting their queer coupling.

Paul McGuigan uses Bettany's character to explore the nervous and uncomfortable boundary between the homosocial and the homosexual as identified by Studlar. In turn, queer audiences are offered a barely disguised narrative of excessive desire and passionate longing. The techniques employed by McGuigan may be heavy-handed—the mirroring of Freddie's mannerisms by Gangster, Karen's spit made to look like semen streaked across the protagonist's face, the intense scrutiny of clothing and style—but are these not the tools with which queer audiences have historically excavated sexually dissident readings from otherwise hegemonic texts?

Films such as those discussed here are predominantly deviant in nature, though they may include elements of rehabilitation. Their narratives and characters draw on subversive elements of British culture, elements that society prefers to ignore where possible. As Chibnall and Murphy state, "the English underworld is no less mean or nasty than it ever was but it continues to provide inspiration for tales of treachery, courage and troubled sexuality which enriches British cinema" (14). While the representation of queer sexuality may not be unproblematic in the films discussed here, it should be remembered that this genre of film depends on such problematics; the world of the gangster is not normative and heterosexuality is just as troubled as homosexuality. Through a discussion of the queer elements such as those identified here, we can uncover a history—perhaps I should say one history—of queerness within British society. While the Gay Liberation Front attempted to marry left-wing politics to the emerging gay consciousness, by and large the remnants of this radicalism have been superseded by an economically defined lifestyle-based identity.

But the dominant model of gay masculinity identified by the likes of Alan Sinfield and Michaelangelo Signorile runs the risk of obscuring the history of other homosexualities, particularly those that operate within spheres that are less than politically correct. Gangster films, such as those discussed here, serve to provide a critical route back to identities and activities that prefigure the formation of a gay identity, while allowing us to identify articulations of queer desire other than the idealized vision on offer today. This is not to suggest that there are countless queer men in the audience longing to become criminals or that there are countless gangsters dreaming of being queer, but rather that there are queer men out there today who no longer identify as— or indeed have never identified as—gay, finding the implications of this label either too binding or too exclusionary.

The glimpses of queer desire and identities that erupt within British crime films serve as examples of homosexualities that have not been politicized or commodified. They also historicize queer desire and serve as a reminder that male-male desire did not begin in the 1970s. Organized crime is not something to be celebrated. It is exploitative, violent, racist, homophobic, and misogynist. It ruins lives, communities, and nations, leaving its victims emotionally, physically, financially, and sexually scarred. I am not celebrating organized crime. But while crime films *do* seek to celebrate such activities, the defiance of the queer within such texts and his ability to permeate—and sometimes even control—these closed networks of homosociality and masculine primacy suggest that elements of the crime film can be recuperated by queer audiences. Such a project may offer divergent and potentially empowering notions of masculinity to otherwise emasculated homosexual men. Although queer gangsters are problematic when read through a postliberationist framework that demands positive role-models, it should be remembered that notions of heterosexual masculinity are often flawed and renegade— Bruce Willis (as John McClane in *Die Hard*), Humphrey Bogart (as Phillip Marlowe in *The Big Sleep*), and Sylvester Stallone (as Rambo in *First Blood*) to name just three examples. The strength of such characters is intimately tied up with their deviance, their waywardness, and their refusal to toe the line. But because only the good are seen as worthy, the existing framework of gay representation struggles to accept queer renegades. What I have demonstrated here is how the queer gangster can be identified, not as some kind of postgay savior (as perhaps Genet would suggest), but as an acknowledgment that homosexuality is not homogenous but comes in different flavors, some of which are not so sweet.

NOTES

1. Ronnie and Reggie Kray were featured in Britain's *Gay Times* magazines as recently as November 2004; see Watson.
2. "Spiv" is the British term for the low-level, smartly dressed criminals who flourished during World War II. They commonly peddled black-market luxury goods and ran small confidence tricks.

3. I am indebted to Andy Medhurst for this insightful piece of information.
4. Paramount Pictures stressed that the film was not a remake but a homage to
    the original 1969 film that has since become something of a cult classic.

WORKS CITED

Arnott, Jake. *The Long Firm*. New York: Soho P, 1999.

The Big Combo. Dir. Joseph H. Lewis. DVD. Allied Artists Pictures, 1955.

The Big Sleep. Dir. Howard Hawks. Perf. Humphrey Bogart. Warner Bros., 1946.

Chadder, Viv. "The Higher Heel: Women and the Post-War British Crime Film."
    British Crime Cinema. Chibnall and Murphy, 66–80.

Chibnall, Steve, and Robert Murphy. "Parole Overdue: Releasing the British Crime
    Film into the Critical Community." Chibnall and Murphy, 1–15.

———, eds. *British Crime Cinema*. London: Routledge, 1999.

Clarens, Carlos. *Crime Movies*. London: Secker, 1980.

Clay, Andrew. "Men, Women and Money: Masculinity in Crisis in the British
    Professional Crime Film 1946–1965." Chibnall and Murphy, 51–60.

The Courier. Dir. Frank Deasey. Videocassette. Vestron Pictures Ltd., 1988.

Crisp, Quentin. *The Naked Civil Servant*. London: Fontana, 1985.

David, Hugh. *On Queer Street: A Social History of British Homosexuality 1895–1995*.
    London: Harper Collins, 1997.

Die Hard. Dir. John McTiernan. Perf. Bruce Willis. 20th Century Fox, 1988.

Douglas, Lord Alfred (1999) "Two Loves." *Nineteenth Century Writings on
    Homosexuality: A Sourcebook*. Ed. Chris White. London: Routledge, 1999. 57.

Duberman, Martin. *Stonewall*. London: Plume, 1994.

Endgame. Dir. Gary Wicks. DVD. TLA Releasing, 2001.

First Blood. Dir. Ted Kotcheff. Perf. Sylvester Stallone. Orion, 1982.

Frankenstein. Dir. James Whale. Universal, 1931.

Gangster No. 1. Dir. Paul McGuigan. DVD. FilmFour, 2000.

The Gay Divorcee. Dir. Mark Sandrich. Videocassette. RKO, 1934.

Get Carter. Dir. Mike Hodges. MGM, 1971.

Gods And Monsters. Dir. Bill Condon. DVD. Lions Gate Films, 1998.

Gone with the Wind. Dir. Victor Fleming. MGM, 1939.

Grieveson, Lee, Peter Sonnet, and Esther Stanfield, eds. *Mob Culture: Hidden
    Histories of the American Gangster Film*. Oxford: Berg, 2005.

Hall Carpenter Archives Gay Men's Oral History Group. *Walking After Midnight: Gay
    Men's Life Stories*. London: Routledge, 1989.

Higgins, Patrick. *A Queer Reader*. London: Fourth, 1993.

"IMDb Top 250 Films." IMDB.com. Jan. 2005. 13 Mar. 2006 <http://www.
    imdb.com/chart/top>.

Ingleton, Roy. *The Gentlemen at War: Policing Britain 1939–45*. Maidstone:
    Cranborne, 1994.

The Italian Job. Dir. Peter Collinson. DVD. Paramount, 1969.

The Italian Job. Dir. F. Gary Gray. DVD. Paramount, 2003.

It's Love I'm After. Dir. Archie Mayo. Videocassette. Warner Bros., 1937.

Jenks, Chris. *Transgression*. London: Routledge, 2003.

The Krays. Dir. Peter Medak. Videocassette. Rank Film, 1990.

Laura. Dir. Otto Priminger. 20th Century Fox, 1944.

Layer Cake. Dir. Matthew Vaughn. DVD. Columbia TriStar, 2004.

Leigh, Danny. "Get Smarter." *Sight and Sound* 10 (2000): 22–25.

Little Caesar. Dir. Mervyn LeRoy. Warner Bros., 1931.

The Long Firm. Dir. Billie Eltringham. DVD. BBC, 2004.

The Long Good Friday. Dir. John Mackenzie. Paramount, 1980.

The Mexican. Dir. Gore Verbinksi. DVD. DreamWorks, 2001.

Miller's Crossing. Dir. Joel Coen. 20th Century Fox, 1990.

Monk, Claire. "From Underworld to Underclass: Crime and British Cinema in the 1990s." Chibnall and Murphy, 172–88.

Morris, Terrence. *Crime and Criminal Justice Since 1945*. Oxford: Blackwell, 1989.

The Public Enemy. Dir. William A. Wellman. Warner Bros., 1931.

The Racketeer. Dir. Howard Higgin. Pathe Exchange, 1929.

Robertson, James C. "The Censors in British Gangland, 1913–1990." Chibnall and Murphy, 16–26.

Rope. Dir. Alfred Hitchcock. Warner Bros., 1948.

Rosow, Eugene. *Born To Lose: The Gangster Film in America*. New York: Oxford UP, 1978.

Russo, Vito. *The Celluloid Closet: Homosexuality in the Movies*. New York: Harper, 1987.

Signorile, Michelangelo. *Life Outside; The Signorile Report on Gay Men: Sex, Drugs, Muscles, and the Passages of Life*. New York: Harper, 1997.

Sinfield, Alan. *Gay and After*. London: Serpent's, 1998.

Sonnet, Esther, and Peter Stanfield. " 'Good Evening Gentlemen: Can I Check Your Hats Please?': Masculinity, Dress and the Retro Gangster Cycles of the 1990s." Griveson, Sonnet, and Stanfield, 163–84.

The Sopranos. HBO. 1999–Present.

Studlar, Gaylyn. "A Gunsel Is Being Beaten: Homoeroticism and the American Movie Gangster 1941–1942." Grieveson, Sonnet, and Stanfield, 120–45.

The Untouchables. Dir. Brian De Palma. Paramount, 1987.

Viegener, Matias. "The Only Haircut that Makes Sense Anymore." *Queer Looks: Perspectives on Lesbian and Gay Film and Video*. Ed. Martha Gever, John Greyson, and Parmar Pratibha. London: Routledge, 1993. 116–33.

Villain. Dir. Michael Tuchner. DVD. MGM, 1971.

Watson, Howard. "A Bit of Rough." *Gay Times* Nov. 2004: 24–29.

Weeks, Jeffrey. *Coming Out: Homosexual Politics in Britain from the Nineteenth Century to the Present*. London: Quartet, 1990.

Wuthering Heights. Dir. William Wyler. United Artists, 1939.

CHAPTER 10

STRAIGHT SHOOTERS, STAINLESS-STEEL STORIES, AND COWBOY CODES: THE QUEER FRONTIER AND AMERICAN IDENTITY IN A POST-WESTERN WORLD

CHRISTOPHER LE CONEY AND
ZOE TRODD

Abstract: Brokeback Mountain *(2005) is the latest in a series of challenges to the cowboy code of an exclusively heterosexual frontier. From* Midnight Cowboy *(1969) onward, pop culture has confronted the West, and with it the whole mythic weight of American identity. Brokeback and the "Rawhide Kid" series challenge the frontier language of George Bush, just as protestors and artists had challenged the cowboy code of the Vietnam era. But if attentive to the limitations of straight-shooting masculinity,* Brokeback *and "Rawhide" offer no vision of an alternate frontier. Instead, the true revision of America's cowboy code comes from real-life gay rodeos. A cultural site that allows the revision of conceptual stereotypes, the gay rodeo recasts the West as a queer frontier.*

It is . . . a perversion of Westerns. All Western heroes have been portrayed as straight shooters—and that just doesn't mean hitting a target with a gun
—Robert Knight, Director of Concerned Women for
America's Culture and Family Institute, on Marvel Comics'
gay cowboy series, "The Rawhide Kid" (2003)

[In the West] storytelling was regarded as revealing secrets or the underside of things . . . They told an official, stainless-steel story . . . what the family was about, what the community was about . . . The West, of course, has good stories, but . . . because of the official mythology, they mostly never got told.

—Novelist William Kittredge (2001)

The Cowboy must never shoot first, hit a smaller man or take unfair advantage . . . He must not advocate or possess racially or religiously intolerant ideas . . . The Cowboy is a patriot.

—Gene Autrey, "Cowboy Code" (1939)

JOHN BECK PAUSED HIS STORY and looked at the scene around him: gay cowboys chatting over beers in a hotel lobby in Mesquite, Texas, at the November 2005 Final Round Competition of the International Gay Rodeo Association (IGRA). "I filed for divorce in 1981, but didn't get it until 1985; she wouldn't sign the papers," he continued,

During that time my barn caught on fire—mysteriously, ya know. I bought a brand new car, set it in the garage, went to jump in it on a Saturday night . . . on the windshield was written in blood: "Move or die." I got out of that car so fast that I sprung the door . . . it was raccoon blood. The KKK. That was their message to get out of there. So I slept with a 30–30 and a 4–10 for almost a year and half. Gun on each side of my bed. I was often run off the road. Back then it was serious.

Beck turned again to look at the gay cowboys, their beers provided by one of the IGRA's now numerous corporate sponsors, and mused: "kinda amazing, isn't it? We've come a long way since that time."

The growth of IGRA has been phenomenal; founded in 1981, it now has member associations across most states and two Canadian provinces. Another gay cowboy at the rodeo, Oscar, explained: "The thing I've seen change most is the professional growth of the organization . . . I remember in the late '90s, ya know, we had, one of the lubes. Then we started getting the beer competition . . . Now we have airlines and rental cars that give us discounts." Or another, T.J., observed: "All I've seen is it grow, grow, grow . . . get more acceptable with men and the communities when you travel around." Yet another, Ken, commented that the gay rodeo "has come a looong way . . . our competitors now are world class, the horses that are running are as good as anything on any circuit." And Beck described the organization's early days, when "it was rough—we weren't welcome." He recalled an incident when a sheriff blocked the roads, handcuffed him, drew a gun, and said, "gay people couldn't feed horses." But "everything has changed in the last 20 years," Beck added. While even ten years ago, many contestants used aliases and wore armbands indicating they should not be photographed, today the number is less than 10 percent by one cowboy's estimate.

The gay rodeo is a physical space where gay cowboys can operate free of fear, but it is also a cultural site that allows the revision of conceptual stereotypes. As Harley, a devoted gay rodeo attendee, put it: "I grew up in a community of 200 people, and there I developed the stereotypes that led me to think that I wasn't gay, because the stereotype was composed of all these effeminate things, which weren't anything that I could relate to." When he discovered the gay rodeo, it seemed a "very natural" place; "a lot of my past came into fulfillment . . . and I felt very at home." Similarly, Ken remarked that he treasures "this place where you can enjoy your love of rodeo and your love of horses and not constantly feel judged because you happen to be gay." He "lost a lot of good years," believing there was "nowhere to go." T.J. called the rodeo "one big family," and Oscar described a "camaraderie" and a "selflessness that you really don't see everyday." The rodeo, Oscar added, is where "we can be ourselves."

John, Harley, Ken, T.J., and Oscar, several of whom are taciturn cowboys who do not swish, find in the gay rodeo a space that reconciles homosexuality with the traditional image of the American cowboy—an image that, as Harley noted, often represents something "anti-gay, red-neck, hyper-masculine . . . that bars gays from its genre." The gay rodeo is an even more extraordinary subculture of America's gay community because it transcends the butch/femme divide: a royalty competition accompanies each rodeo, and after bucking broncos and roping cows all day long, the cowboys join together at night to watch shows put on by the royalty; men performing as men (dubbed Mr.), men performing as women (Miss.), women performing as women (Ms.), and women performing as men (MsTer). "They're part of the community," explained Beck.

At one point during the rodeo, a drag queen named Pussy LeHoot, "Miss IGRA 2005" (see figure 10.1), commented that it was a significant achievement for the gay rodeo to compete at the Resitol Arena in Mesquite, for it is a legendary site on the mainstream rodeo circuit. The bronze statue at the arena's entrance, a famous bronc-rider of yore, suggests a temple to the old cowboy myth. But the gay rodeo's presence is a rewriting of that myth and a recasting of both an imaginative and a physical space. Some would rather ignore this rewrite: "There ain't no queer in cowboy and I don't care for anyone suggesting there is," snapped straight Wyoming cowboy Jim-Bob Zimmerschied in December 2005, responding to questions from a journalist about Ang Lee's film *Brokeback Mountain* (qtd. in Sherwell par. 10). The gay rodeo, going from strength to strength, suggests otherwise, but Zimmerschied continued: "I've been doing this job all my life and I ain't never met no gay cowboy . . . John Wayne and Will Rogers, they made real cowboy movies.

Figure 10.1   Christopher Le Coney, "Pussy Lahoot, Miss IGRA 2005," Texas, November 2005.

They portrayed us like we are" (qtd. in Sherwell pars. 1, 10). Nearly thirty years after his death, John Wayne continues as a poster-boy for heterosexual, cowboy masculinity and has been invoked repeatedly in interviews and articles sparked by the release of *Brokeback Mountain*. "They've gone and killed John Wayne with this movie," concluded Zimmerschied (qtd. in Sherwell par. 1).

Yet Lee's film—and the IGRA rodeos—are not the first challenge to the cowboy code of an exclusively white, all-male, heterosexual American frontier. Beginning in the late 1960s, this cultural myth has been under attack. In *Gunfighter Nation*, Richard Slotkin documents how the Western genre was beset by "counterculture Westerns" in the late 1960s and early 1970s, and he links this to antiwar and race-based protest: "The rehabilitation of the Native American and the recognition of African-Americans as pioneers . . . substantially altered the visual style and ideological burden of the genre," he explains (633). The 1960s marked the beginning of the end for the hegemonic legacy of Theodore Roosevelt's conception of the American West; though nineteenth-century cowhands were a group of diverse races and ethnicities, Roosevelt had whitewashed those demographic realities in his popular representations of the West. But while Slotkin explores how race defined Roosevelt's frontier, he largely ignores the gender dynamics at work. Gail Bederman's *Manliness and Civilization* goes some way toward correcting this oversight, explaining that Roosevelt's racial philosophy was inextricably related to his schematic understanding of gender roles. Bederman offers only a cursory comment on sexuality, however, noting that Roosevelt "may well have been ambivalent about unleashing . . . new public affirmation of male sexuality" (205). Equally, Martin Pumphrey singles out feminism to argue that 1960s protest movements asked modern audiences to view the Western as anachronistic and ironic. But gay rights activists had also challenged the cultural myths and stereotypes enshrined in the form of Wayne's Westerns (93). Questioning the acceptance of an exclusively heterosexual American frontier, some activists even proposed an exclusively *homosexual* space instead. Amid these calls for a new frontier space, gay cowboys began to peek further out of the proverbial closet. Clones appeared within the queer community—gay men whose overtly butch fashions looked to traditional images of masculinity (the biker, the lumberjack, the construction worker, the cowboy).[1]

John Schlesinger's *Midnight Cowboy* and Andy Warhol's *Lonesome Cowboys*, both released in 1969, then reclaimed the silver-screen as a space for gay cowboys—much to Wayne's consternation: "It's a [perverse] . . . story about two fags," he said of *Midnight Cowboy* in a 1971 *Playboy* interview (76). Both films began to topple the macho cowboy myth and rewrite its code. As Joe Buck leaves Texas in the opening of *Midnight Cowboy*, he passes an abandoned movie theater still advertising the last film shown, *The Alamo*. This film has a special place in Wayne's filmography, for he not only starred in it but also directed and produced it as his pet project. The abandoned movie theater suggests an icon in peril and anticipates the situation in New York, where gay cowboy clones further undermine masculine signifiers. In fact, another toppling strategy employed by Schlesinger is to focus on the largely performative foundations of the cowboy code. Joe wears a tight-fitting cowboy outfit complete with western boots and a hat, and the camera frequently dwells upon booted feet walking or cowboy hats bouncing. Yet women wear faux Western outfits, and gay male hustlers dress as cowboy clones. Schlesinger's clones emphasize the fragility of the macho cowboy myth, as Rizzo explains: "That great big dumb cowboy crap of yours don't appeal to nobody, except every Jackie on 42nd street! That's faggot stuff! You want to call it by its name, that's strictly for fags!" In reply, Joe stammers: "John Wayne?! You're gonna tell me that John Wayne's a fag?!"[2]

Warhol's cowboys would not even need to ask this question. The camp aesthetic of *Lonesome Cowboys* took surefire aim at the self-important mythology that had infused Westerns since the 1930s. Warhol shot his film at the Old Tucson set in Arizona, where Wayne had filmed on numerous occasions; undermining Wayne's hyperstraight cowboys with its fake fellatio and naked all-male romps, the film simultaneously soils the myth's physical space. Warhol mocks the abandoned mausoleum and—like Schlesinger—topples an artificial myth. The film then ends with the pairing of Louis and Tom, gay cowboys who ride into the sunset toward a frontier space with "lots of beautiful men," as Louis promises, adding: "It's great, you can get anything you want out there." Not abandoning but rather adapting America's cowboy dreams, Warhol seemed to offer a renewed vision of the West. John Wayne would be skeptical, but Ang Lee's Jack Twist would surely approve.[3]

One possible result of these challenges to America's cowboy code was that the Western fell out of favor. During the 1980s and 1990s, Hollywood and the broadcast networks rarely offered new productions of the classic genre. The Native American, civil rights, feminist, and gay rights movements had perhaps rendered ridiculous the John Wayne myth of a white, all-male, heterosexual frontier, and the antiwar movement had certainly rejected that frontier's warrior-identity. Some Vietnam films of the 1980s tried to rehabilitate the lost myth of warrior-masculinity: *Uncommon Valor, Missing in Action,* and *Rambo: First Blood Part II* ask the question, phrased by Rambo in this last movie—"Do we get to win this time?" The films' plots all answer— yes. President Reagan's self-conscious cultivation of his image as a western president marked another attempt to rehabilitate the cowboy myth; Reagan, who had starred in the 1953 Western *Law and Order,* and eulogized Wayne in a 1979 article called "Unforgettable John Wayne," was frequently photographed in cowboy attire riding around Sky Ranch, and two famous photographs taken in 1982 and 1984 show him raising a white cowboy hat and triumphantly waving cowboy boots. "We lit a prairie fire a few years back," concluded Reagan in 1988. "But we can never let the fire go out or quit the fight, because the battle is never over. . . . There's still a lot of brush to clear out at the ranch, fences that need repair and horses to ride" (Reagan, "Remarks" par. 52–53).

Just over a decade later, George W. Bush's self-styled cowboy identity and smoke 'em out rhetoric relit this prairie fire. Six days after the terrorist attacks of September 11, 2001, Bush, when asked at a press conference whether he wanted Osama Bin Laden dead, responded: "I remember that they used to put out there in the old west, a wanted poster. It said: 'Wanted, Dead or Alive.' All I want and [what] America wants [is for] him [to be] brought to justice" (Bush, "Guard"). On other occasions he expressed a determination to "ride herd" over resistant Middle Eastern governments, and he branded Iraq as "an outlaw regime" (qtd. in Baard 27). Reverence for this frontier rhetoric was so great that in May 2005, Wyoming senator Craig Thomas introduced a resolution establishing July 23 as the National Day of the Cowboy. Thomas wrote to Bush seeking his support, from "one cowboy to another" (qtd. in Hardy, "SRES"). In July, Bush signed the resolution into law and it was featured on the cover of *American Cowboy Magazine,* next to the headline "The Cowboy Gets His Day." The resolution, which affirmed the cowboy's "sound family values," left sexuality markedly absent from its otherwise inclusive reach: "membership in rodeo and other organizations surrounding the livelihood of a cowboy transcends race and gender and spans every generation" (Hardy, "SRES"). The gay cowboy, it would seem, remained "a man for whom there is . . . no room" in the West, as Isabella L. Bird put it of one outcast in her 1880 travel narrative (93).

But just as protestors and artists had challenged the frontier language of the Vietnam era, so did the protest literature of the early twenty-first century challenge America's cowboy code. Some even connected the two historical moments. The Vietnam veteran Ron Kovic, whose war-wounds left him impotent, had challenged the potency of the warrior myth in his 1976 memoir *Born on the Fourth of July*, observing: "I gave my dead dick for John Wayne" (98). In his 2005 introduction to *Born on the Fourth of July*, he then explained: "I have watched in horror the mirror image of another Vietnam unfolding" (Kovic, "Introduction" 10). Yet again, Kovic wrote, he had "the task of . . . pleading for an alternative" (14). Numerous poems submitted to the group Poets Against the War linked the Iraq and Vietnam wars (forty-one explicitly and dozens more through allusion) and, like much Vietnam literature, these new poems allude to movie-Westerns. One, Jim Harrison's "Poem of War," reads: "The theocratic cowboy forgetting Viet Nam rides/into town . . . Clint Eastwood/whispers from an alley, 'George, they/were only movies' " (98). If the 2003 Iraq invasion was yet another attempt to kick "the Vietnam syndrome once and for all!" as Bush Sr. infamously claimed of the Gulf War, then the protest voices of Saigon would rise up from the sands of Baghdad (qtd. in Dionne A21).

Another rising protest voice came via Stonewall. In 2002, Marvel Comics announced that it was pulling from retirement a gun-slinging cowboy character that had lain dormant in its archives since 1979. First introduced in 1955, and one of the most popular comic-book cowboy heroes ever published, the Rawhide Kid was now gay (see figure 10.2). The five-issue series follows Toby, the preadolescent son of the town's ineffectual sheriff, Matt, as he finds a new male role-model in the Kid. When a gang of thugs rides into town to loot and pillage, the Kid's presence is the only thing protecting the luckless sheriff from death. The town, while perplexed by this "daisyboy" (Zimmerman *Issue 2*), respects him as a fighter and when villains mock his "sissy talk" (Zimmerman *Issue 3*), he shuts them up with bullets. He is also the object of intense admiration for the town's boys, whose appreciation of his unclothed body is one important difference marking the new series: the first issue ends with the Kid, stripped down to skimpy briefs and doing crunches atop his sleeping bag, unaware that a group of boys is watching his rippling back, defined pectorals, and bulging biceps (Zimmerman *Issue 1*). The original 1950s series had no such scenes. The literary critic Carla Freccero argues that the series deals "with the crisis of masculinity" and critiques "mainstream

Figure 10.2   Marvel Comics, "Rawhide Kid #1," February 2003.

masculinity" (qtd. in Shiels), and the *Marvel* editor-in-chief Joe Quesada later confirmed that the series took "what has been for decades a symbol of American hetero masculinity (think John Wayne, Clint Eastwood)," and showed "a whole different point of view on the heroic ideal" (Quesada, "Week 37"). It was a new cowboy code.

Like Warhol, Schlesinger, and the 1960s protest groups that came before, *Marvel* offered a subversive challenge to frontier mythology infusing contemporaneous political discourse. But it also *explicitly* critiqued Bush's cowboy identity. In the second issue, "Mayor Bush" (or "Walker") explains to Matt: "We're comin' up on election time and I need a second term. People are still a little shaky cuz I only won by a few votes last time." Matt responds: "And we know yore daddy and brother bought those." Then, in issue four, Bush tells the Kid: "I will bring these evil-doers to JUSTICE. Terrorism will not be tolerated and the evil ones will be punished. Cisco Pike may think he can hide, but I promise you, we will be holding him accountable. BET ON IT!" The Kid insists upon a united effort to punish the terrorists, asking Bush to "gather the townsfolk." He explains: "I'm gonna need some help taking care of these hideous outlaws. . . . We've got to work TOGETHER." Announced in December 2002, with the first issue published in February 2003, the Kid series critiqued the bypass of the United Nations' weapon inspection process: on August 28, 2002, the Bush administration stated they would seek to oust Saddam Hussein regardless of whether UN inspectors were allowed back into Iraq; on September 18, the administration formally rejected Iraq's offer to allow the UN unfettered access and called for "regime change"; and on September 20, Bush presented his new doctrine of pre-emptive invasion. Now, as the Kid asks "Mayor Bush" to "work together" with the "townsfolk," "Mayor Bush's" sidekick calls this strategy a "tired cliché." "Mayor Bush" agrees, with a bonus sideswipe at Bill Clinton (Will Kane): " 'member when Will Kane pulled this kinda stunt, tryin' to rally up townsfolk to stand up against outlaws? He damn near got everybody killed. . . . I'll be damned if I'm gonna let that fancy-pants gunfighter rope us into a thing like THAT" (Zimmerman *Issue 4*). Echoing Wayne's famous 1971 assertion to *Playboy* that he was no "panty-waist" (92), Mayor Bush's misguided resistance to the hero's request for a united effort is the *real* "tired cliché." By implication, the foreign policy of *President* Bush, whose initial "W" stands for Wayne (according to jubilant right-wing Web sites) and whose self-fashioning creates another "symbol of American mythology: cowboy . . . agent of empire" (as *The New York Times* described Wayne in 1974), enters the realm of bygone fictions (Kifner 41).

The following year, journalist Erik Baard pointed out that the "doctrine of preemptive war" meant that the president had in fact *broken* the "cowboy code" (27). In an article for the *Village Voice* on September 28, 2004, Baard explained that the code, written by screen cowboy Gene Autry, demanded that "The Cowboy must never shoot first, hit a smaller man, or take unfair advantage" (27). And in interviews at the 2005 gay rodeo, real gay cowboys described *their* cowboy code—again a far cry from both Senator Thomas' narrow resolution and the lone-ranger attitude of President Bush and "Mayor Bush": "cowboys have been known for years to be rough, tough, and mascu-line," said Randy; "it's just an image, you know. But it's in your heart, it's what you believe in. . . . A true cowboy is open, honest, trustworthy, loyal, treats people like he would want them to treat him." Harley added that the cowboy was "what I would like to project to the rest of the world, of what America is." He went on to explain that Bush was giving cowboys a bad name: "I've been overseas, and when I hear someone say 'cowboy,' you know they're talking about us as Americans—it's a synonym. But 'cowboy' represents the good side of America . . . something that I think we tend to tarnish with the current politics." The phrase "gay cowboy" was no "oxymoron," Harley concluded, and in fact might rescue America's image: "The gay cowboy has always been a good guy, and the icon of what American society at its best, when you helped out your neighbor." While Quintard Taylor questions whether the West might have been "a racial frontier beyond which lay the potential for an egalitarian society" (17), Harley and other rodeo participants seek an egalitarian society beyond the *sexual* frontier.

Gay cowboys are rewriting the cowboy code. Yet, unlike Harley's rewrite, *Marvel*'s was hardly serious. Quesada explained to CNN on December 12, 2002: "the Western genre seems to be really kind of dead in today's modern media, so we were looking at ways of reviving a Western, and we started with the idea of a comedy" (Quesada, "Interview"). In their search for a comedic twist on classic Westerns, the *Marvel* editors settled upon the gimmick of making the Kid gay. For, though gay pop culture characters were everywhere by 2002, their standard bearers were the characters from the hit prime-time NBC comedy *Will and Grace*; defending his company's decision, Quesada invoked the show's popularity as evidence of America's readiness for a gay cowboy. "I watch it too. Jack's hysterical; 'Just Jack!' " responded the CNN anchor, referencing the flamboyant moments when the show's character Jack epitomizes a cultural stereotype of effete, campy gay men (Quesada, "Interview"). While one cowboy at the gay rodeo, Aubrey, explained that the rodeo busted "a lot of stereotypes," because it exposed "a huge collection of gay and lesbian people who are . . . a long way from Jack on *Will and Grace*" (adding, "we each have very different stories"), the Kid's campy persona reinforces the Jack stereotype. *Marvel* had not answered the hope (expressed by another gay cowboy at the rodeo, Don) that "people will realize there is a difference between gays" because "most people think of all gays as queens and that's just not the way that life is."

In addition, the townspeople of the series remain unaware that the Kid is gay, the "Just Jack" style double entendres flying over their heads. The Kid is the apotheosis of Warhol's campy characters in *Lonesome Cowboys* but remains half in and half out of the closet, as though caught in a bad time-warp. The series then ends with a metareference to previous Westerns: as the Kid leaves town Toby calls, "come back!" and the Kid comments, "Doesn't he know that's not how this works?" (Zimmerman, *Issue 5*). The self-consciousness of this moment, and of the double-audience construction, confirms that *Marvel*'s series, rather than an attempt to fashion a new cowboy code (one neither excluding homosexuality nor rendering it a campy joke), was instead a signal that America had truly entered a post-Western moment. Perhaps closing the chapter that Warhol had begun, the comic-book series seemingly marked the Western's final frontier, and the fast-approaching twilight of America's cowboy dreams.

That twilight seemingly descended even faster when Ang Lee proclaimed *Brokeback Mountain* as "post-western" in December 2005 (Huston par. 4). For Lee, "post-Western" did not mean his film had "killed John Wayne," as Jim-Bob Zimmerschied had protested (qtd. in Sherwell par. 1). Rather, Lee explained, it marked a break with the "codes of westerns" (Huston par. 4). This break, and the post-Western tone of *Brokeback*, is conveyed by the film's portrayal of the rodeo as a tired site of physical trauma and insipid showmanship: in an early scene, Jack's parody of bull-broncing mocks the contrived bravado of rodeo cowboys, emphasizing their mediocre imitation of reality. Even this imitation is not what it used to be: the "rodeo ain't what it was in my daddy's day," Jack explains later. Equally indicative of the film's post-Western sensibility is the observation by one character that to expect "big handsome Marlboro Men" is to be "behind the times," or the fact that Ennis's ranch no longer signifies frontier independence but rather loneliness: "Can we move to town?" complains his wife. "I'm tired of these lonesome old ranches." Another post-Western moment comes when Jack's father-in-law insists upon his grandson watching television, commenting, "Want your boy to grow up to be a man, don't ya? Boys should watch football." This scene is one of the few not included in Annie Proulx's original short story: a self-conscious moment of cinematic reflection, it connects performative masculinity to the visual spectacle of a two-dimensional screen.[4]

Quesada could only note, in February 2006, that "*Brokeback Mountain* is considered revolutionary and will win all sorts of honors without a word that we did it first . . . ours was more of a comedy, but it still dealt with the issues" (Quesada, "Week 36"). Hinting that the decision to employ comedy emerged out of an awareness that America was not ready for a serious examination of the queer frontier, Quesada also observed:

> perhaps someday when we decide to do another Rawhide series . . . a movie like *Brokeback Mountain* will have cleared a wide enough path where . . . a gay cowboy will no longer be an issue . . . once again Hollywood will have trumped us at our own game and managed to break ground where we couldn't, even though we dug out the first few shovelfuls. (Quesada, "Week 37")

Yet in 2005 and 2006, America still seemed unwilling to recognize that new ground. Reviewers have repeatedly proclaimed the film as a universal love story, and print and TV advertisements have offered shots of the male leads with their wives but not each other—relegating Lee's gay cowboys back between the lines of Senator Thomas's exclusive senate resolution, or the lines of what Gore Vidal once called a "sonnet": "As for overt homosexuality in pre-1960 films, it was not attempted and not possible," Vidal explained. "Sonnets have fourteen lines. You wrote sonnets then and there was never an extra or an odd line . . . but subtexts did occasionally insert themselves" (qtd. in Russo 62). Lee did claim in an interview that the homoerotic subtexts of earlier Westerns were now moved from "subtext" to "text" (Huston par. 8), but reviewers have held tight to the old cowboy code of Roosevelt, Wayne, "Mayor Bush," President Bush, and Senator Thomas.

Brokeback itself perhaps assisted this vanquishing of the queer frontier. If attentive to the limitations of straight-shooting masculinity, Brokeback offers no vision of an alternate frontier, and no revised cowboy code. Marvel's series was one form of post-Western (high comedy, campy innuendo, and effete cowboys in the Warhol vein) and Brokeback is the other extreme: high tragedy that completes the chapter opened by Schlesinger in Midnight Cowboy. For while Warhol had offered a potentially radical vision of a utopian space on a queer frontier—a revised cowboy dream—Schlesinger's utopia was a no-place. New York is no promised land for Joe, and Florida is always out of reach for Rizzo. Rizzo dies on the bus to Miami leaving Joe alone, and Joe discards his cowboy costume. Now, though Jack and Ennis continue the search for that elusive utopia, both come up short. The film even ends with a scene, not part of Proulx's story, where Ennis agrees to attend his daughter's wedding, observing: "I reckon they can find themselves a new cowboy." His new son-in-law is an oil refinery man, channeling the resources of the frontier like nineteenth-century cowboys driving cattle up through the plains. Far from offering a queer frontier space, Brokeback restores the straight-shooting frontier of old: this new cowboy is unambiguously straight. Ennis's daughter confirms that her husband-to-be is in love with her and Ennis is left alone in his trailer.

The film ends with a shot of an open window and a field of flowers beyond but any suggested future of hope is for Ennis's daughter and her husband. Juxtaposed with the window is a postcard of Brokeback, which remains on the inside of Ennis's closet door. There is no space beyond the closet where Jack and Ennis might stake out a life: "This thing grabs hold of us—wrong place, wrong time—and we're dead," Ennis had warned Jack and at the end of the film there remains no *right* place. Even their supposedly safe space atop Brokeback had been violated by Joe Aguirre, who with hyperpowered binoculars observed them having sex , and Brokeback then became a lost paradise—as legendary as El Dorado: the bright red MOTEL sign, adorning the motel where Jack and Ennis go for their first reunion, recalls the bright red MOTEL EL DORADO sign in *Midnight Cowboy*. Just as that mythic land kept the Spaniards searching in vain, so the effort to find a new American frontier is thwarted for Joe and Rizzo, and Jack and Ennis.

While the gay rodeo's presence at the Restinol Arena is a rewriting of the cowboy myth, in both an imaginative and a physical space, Hollywood imaginative space remains a celluloid closet. *Lonesome Cowboys* and even *Midnight Cowboy* had spoken the unspeakable ("you're telling me John Wayne's a fag?"), acknowledged the possibility of a queer frontier, and cracked open that closet door. And Warhol had rejected this tragic queer-frontier narrative: *Lonesome Cowboys*, originally titled *Ramona and Julian*, inverted Shakespeare's *Romeo and Juliet*, its camp the opposite of tragedy. The tragic narrative that dominates *Brokeback Mountain* felt to some like moving backward: responding after a special screening at the IGRA rodeo, one gay cowboy, Don, observed that it was "still the same old, stereotypical, old gay type movie." He explained: "You got to kill off one or two gays somewhere in the movie to make it palatable, seems like. In the end, they did the same thing. It's a very depressing movie." Some gay cowboys at the rodeo, before seeing the film, *were* hopeful that it would finally tell an untold story: "I think its time has come— it's here," said one, Kevin; "It's probably about time that something like this was made . . . my god, its been going on for hundreds of years." Another believed the film would give "the whole scene that was missing in all the previous movies of what was going on out on the prairie." This gay cowboy, Oscar, also anticipated the film would be subversive: "I'm excited because GW's heart is going to explode, and the Right Wing is going to have a panic attack—which is good," he explained. Yet Ennis's new son-in-law, whose marriage looms large at the end of *Brokeback*, perhaps stands in for the new cowboy of Ang Lee's—and Oscar's—twenty-first century world: "GW" himself, a cowboy president and former Texas oilman.[5]

Bush embodies the old cowboy code, explained by *American Cowboy Magazine* in 2004 as the creed of "five Westerners who changed America" and "helped define the American kind"—"Cody, Roosevelt, Rogers, Regan, and Wayne" ("Five Westerners" 34). The article explained that "a different America . . . confronted the world after its Western experience," that "the Western spirit . . . altered that progression. Changed it. Redefined it" (36). From Warhol and Schlesinger, through *Marvel, Brokeback*, and the IGRA rodeo participants, gay cowboys have confronted the West, and with it the whole mythic weight of American identity; changed it, redefined it, offered their own cowboy code, and a vision of the cowboy that might complicate Frederick Jackson Turner's famous "connected and unified account of the progress of civilization across the continent" (71). Beck, pausing to watch the gay cowboys in Texas, had insisted: "We've come a long way." Harley had proposed that the Stonewall rioters had changed the country and were "giants" on whose backs the gay cowboy now stood: "what I did for Pride was to stand on the backs of those giants that were at the Stonewall riots," he said; "those people did an incredible job to get us to where we are today." But the pantheon of the West remains seemingly unchanged. In spite of his eulogy to the Stonewall "giants," Harley concluded that, after all, "we've still got a long way to go."

That "long way to go," from straight-shooting cowboy code to queer frontier, was evident when one cowboy story finally met another, on January 23, 2006. An audience member at a Kansas State University forum asked President Bush: "You're a rancher, a lot of us here in Kansas are ranchers. I was just wanting to get your opinion on *Brokeback Mountain*, if you'd seen it yet?" Visibly embarrassed, Bush replied: "I haven't seen it . . . I hope you go back to the ranch and the farm" (Bush, "President"). The success of Lee's film, for all its equivocations, suggests there is *no* going back, at least for the post-1960s Western. The *New Yorker* soon published its February 27, 2006, cover image "Watch Your Back Mountain," by Mark Ulriksen, depicting Bush and Cheney as Lee's gay cowboys. Willie Nelson soon released his song "Cowboys Are Frequently, Secretly (Fond of Each Other)," written in 1981 and first aired on Valentine's Day, 2006. "The song's been in the closet for 20 years. The timing's right for it to come out . . . I'm just opening the door," explained Nelson, who also contributed to the *Brokeback* soundtrack (qtd. in "Nelson"). But the president turned a blind eye to the gay cowboy, vanquished the queer frontier, and slammed shut that closet door. Anticipating Robert Knight's assertion of February 2006 that "the Western image doesn't include gay cowboys" ("Willie"), or echoing Jim-Bob's insistence that "I ain't never met no gay cowboy," Bush repeated: "I haven't seen it."

NOTES

1. For gay nationalism see Wittman's "Refugees from Amerika" (577–83), Schoonmaker's suggestion that gays take over Manhattan's 19th and 20th Congressional Districts (cited in Teal 292) and Jackson's call for a "Stonewall Nation," in the *Los Angeles Free Press*, Aug. 14, 1970 (cited in Teal, 292–94). For clones, see Cole.

2. Critics still debate whether Joe and Rizzo's relationship is homosexual, for it resists a conclusive label. But the true significance of Schlesinger's 1969 film lies in this debate itself. *Midnight Cowboy* marks a tentative yet clear turning-point in the history of the Hollywood Western. Latent homoerotic subcurrents that had flowed within the genre for so long here rise closer to the surface. Counter-Westerns did exist prior to the more blatant and visible expressions of gay identity in the Stonewall era: arguably, *The Outlaw, Red River* and

The Left-Handed Gun are charged with homoeroticism, and the ambiguous sexuality surrounding Billy the Kid prompted gay author Gore Vidal to explore the homosexual subtext of the legend in a teleplay and two Hollywood films. But while the gay subcurrents of these films occasionally bubble up in moments of release, up-swellings are usually mitigated, subdued or window-dressed. The full emergence of homoerotic subcurrents in Westerns, and the shift beyond this newly apparent liminal space of 1969 would continue through to *Brokeback Mountain*.

3. Though both films were released in 1969, *Lonesome Cowboys* finished production in 1967. During the early 1970s, the FBI seized the film during showings, and Warhol's hopes of releasing the film to a wide audience died under the weight of government censorship. After its initial theatrical release, the film's distribution was limited to one small run of VHS tapes in Britain. Its cultural currency dropped rapidly during the 1970s, and it had to be recovered and archived in a mid-1980s joint project by the Museum of Modern Art and the Whitney Museum.

4. The original story was written by Annie Proulx in 1997, well before America's new cowboy president was on the horizon, but Hollywood's decision to take up the story under Bush's presidency remains significant.

5. Strains of this tragic narrative are evident in films like *The Outlaw*, *The Left-Handed Gun* and *Red River*, which variously kill off the queer cowboy, control latent subversiveness within the trappings of heterosexuality, or banish him to Mexico.

WORKS CITED

The Alamo. Dir. John Wayne. United Artists, 1960.

Aubrey. Personal interview with Christopher Le Coney. 13 Nov. 2005.

Autrey, Gene. Baard, 27–30.

Baard, Erik. "George W. Bush Ain't No Cowboy." *Village Voice*. 29 Sept. 2004: 26–30.

Beck, John. Personal interview with Christopher Le Coney. 11 Nov. 2005.

Bederman, Gail. *Manliness and Civilization: A Cultural History of Gender and Race in the United States, 1880–1917*. Chicago: Chicago UP, 1995.

Bird, Isabella L. *A Lady's Life in Rocky Mountains* [1880]. London: J. Murray, 1910.

Brokeback Mountain. Dir. Ang Lee. Focus, 2005.

Bush, George W. "Guard and Reserves 'Define Spirit of America.'" Remarks by the President to Employees at the Pentagon. Pentagon. 17 Sept. 2001. 26 Mar. 2006<whitehouse.gov/news/releases/2001/09>.

———. "President Discusses Global War on Terror at Kansas State University." Manhattan, KS 23 Jan. 2006. 26 Mar. 2006 <http://www.whitehouse.gov/news/releases/2006/01/print/20060123-4.html>.

Cole, Shaun. "'Macho Man': Clones and the Development of a Masculine Stereotype." *Fashion Theory* 4.2 (2003): 124–40.

Dionne, E.J. "Kicking The 'Vietnam Syndrome': Victory Sweeps Away U.S. Doomed-To-Failure Feeling." *The Washington Post* 4 Mar. 1991: A1+.

Don. Personal interview with Christopher Le Coney. 13 Nov. 2005.

"Five Westerners." *American Cowboy*, Nov./Dec. 2004: 34–41.

Hardy, Cameron. "SRES 138 ATS." Senate Resolution. 12 May 2005 <http://www. nationaldayofthecowboy.com/senate.aspx>.

Harley. Personal interview with Christopher Le Coney. 13 Nov. 2005.

Harrison, Jim. "Poem of War." *Poets Against the War*. Ed. Sam Hamill. New York: Thunder's Mouth, 2003. 98.

Huston, Johnny Ray. "Love, Lee: Behind *Brokeback Mountain* You'll Find a River of Tears." *San Francisco Bay Guardian*, 7–13 Dec. 2005. 20 Mar. 2006 <http:// www.sfbg.com/40/10/art_brokeback.html>.

Ken. Personal interview with Christopher Le Coney. 12 Nov. 2005.

Kevin. Personal interview with Christopher Le Coney. 13 Nov. 2005.

Kifner, John. "John Wayne Plays a New Role: The Invader of Harvard Square." *The New York Times* 16 Jan. 1974: 41.

Kittredge, William. "Outgrowing Myths: Writer Says Good-bye to the Old West." Interview with NEH Chairman William R. Ferris. *Humanities* 22.5 (2001): 6.

Knight, Robert. Interview with ABC News. 5 Feb. 2003. "Not-So-Straight Shooter; Marvel Comics' Rawhide Kid Comes Out."

Kovic, Ron. *Born on the Fourth of July*. New York: McGraw, 1976.

———. "Introduction." *Born on the Fourth of July*. New York: Akashic, 2005.

Law and Order. Dir. Nathan Juran. Universal International, 1953.

Lee, Ang, dir. *Brokeback Mountain*. Focus, 2005.

Left-Handed Gun. Dir. Arthur Penn. Harroll, 1958.

LeHoot, Pussy. Personal interview with Christopher Le Coney. 13 Nov. 2005.

Missing in Action. Dir. Joseph Zito. MGM/UA, 1984.

"Nelson Releases Gay Cowboy Song." *BBC News*. 15 Feb. 2006. 26 Mar. 2006 <http://www.news.bbc.co.uk/2/hi/entertainment/4715822.stm>.

Nelson, Willie. "Cowboys are Frequently, Secretly (Fond of Each Other)." iTunes. Rec. 2005. Lost Highway, 2006.

Oscar. Personal interview with Christopher Le Coney. 13 Nov. 2005.

The Outlaw. Dir. Howard Hughes. Hughes, 1943.

Proulx, Annie. "Brokeback Mountain." *New Yorker*. 13 Oct. 1997: 74–85.

Pumphrey, Martin. "Why Do Cowboys Wear Hats in the Bath?: Style Politics for the Older Man." *Critical Quarterly* 31.3 (1989): 78–100.

Quesada, Joe. Interview. *CNN Live on Location*. CNN. 12 Dec. 2002.

———. "Week 36." *Joe Fridays*. 3 Feb. 2006. *Newsarama*. 26 Mar. 2006 <http:// www.newsarama.com/JoeFridays/JoeFridays36.html>.

———. "Week 37." *Joe Fridays*. 10 Feb. 2006. *Newsarama*. 26 Mar. 2006 <http:// www.newsarama.com/JoeFridays/JoeFridays37.html>.

Rambo: First Blood Part II. Dir. George P. Cosnatus. TriStar, 1985.

Randy. Personal interview with Christopher Le Coney. 13 Nov. 2005.

Reagan, Ronald. "Remarks to 1988 Republican National Convention." New Orleans, LA. 15 Aug. 1988.

———. "Unforgettable John Wayne." *Reader's Digest* Oct. 1979: 114–19.

Red River. Dir. Howard Hawks and Arthur Rosson. United Artists, 1948.

Russo, Vito. *The Celluloid Closet: Homosexuality in the Movies.* New York: Harper, 1987.

Schlesinger, John, dir. *Midnight Cowboy.* United Artists, 1969.

S. Res. 138. 109th Congress, 1st Session. 12 May 2005. "Designating July 23, 2005, as 'National Day of the American Cowboy.' " <nationaldayofthecowboy.com/senate.aspx>.

Sherwell, Phillip. " 'John Wayne Made Real Movies. There Ain't No Queer in Cowboy.' " *Telegraph.* 1 Jan. 2006. 20 Mar. 2006 <http://www.telegraph.co.uk/news/main.jhtml?xml=/news/2006/01/01/wbroke01.xml>.

Shiels, Maggie. "Rawhide Comes Out of the Closet." *BBC News.* 21 Dec. 2002. 24 Mar. 2006 <http://news.bbc.co.uk/1/hi/entertainment/arts/2595301.stm>.

Slotkin, Richard. *Gunfighter Nation.* New York: Atheneum, 1992.

Taylor, Quintard. *In Search of the Racial Frontier: African Americans in the American West, 1528–1990.* New York: Norton, 1998.

Teal, Donn. *The Gay Militants: How Gay Liberation Began in America, 1969–1971.* New York: Stonewall Inn, 1971.

T.J. Personal interview with Christopher Le Coney. 12 Nov. 2005.

Turner, Frederick Jackson. Rev. of Theodore Roosevelt's *The Winning of the West. The Dial.* 10 Aug. 1889: 71.

Ulriksen, Mark. "Watch Your Back Mountain." Cover. *New Yorker.* 27 Feb. 2006.

Uncommon Valor. Dir. Ted Kotcheff. Paramount, 1983.

Warhol, Andy, dir. *Lonesome Cowboys.* Sherpix, 1969.

Wayne, John. "Candid Conversation." *Playboy.* May 1971: 75–92.

Will and Grace. 21 Sept. 1998–18 May 2006.

"Willie Lauds 'Gay' Cowboys in Song." Concerned Women for America radio broadcast with Robert Knight. 14 Feb. 2006 <http://www.cwfa.org/radio.asp?broadcastID=1194>.

Wittman, Carl. "Refugees from Amerika: A Gay Manifesto." *The Radical Reader.* Ed. Timothy Patrick McCarthy and John McMillian. New York: New Press, 2003.

Zimmerman, Ron, and John Severin. *Rawhide Kid: Slap Leather* Vol. 1, issues 1–5. New York: Marvel Comics, 2003.

CHAPTER 11

NEW QUEER WHITE TRASH CINEMA

DANIEL MUDIE CUNNINGHAM

Abstract: *This chapter examines the whiteness and white trashness of the 1990s new queer cinema. Using* My Own Private Idaho *(Gus Van Sant, 1991), Postcards from America* *(Steve McLean, 1994), and* Boys Don't Cry *(Kimberly Peirce, 1999) I discuss the cinematic confluence of queerness with white trash identity, detailing the frequent representation of white trash drifters and hustlers who use the road to move across and through the romanticized American landscape. That these films are road movies featuring white trash hustlers is certainly not accidental— the persistence of the road motif demonstrates how such new queer characters were restless identities that could not be anchored to any one place. New queer cinema recognized that queerness is characterized by a multiplicity of conflicting voices and visions, acknowledging how white trash identity can be a rather queer thing.*

THIS CHAPTER EXAMINES THE WHITE TRASHNESS of the new queer cinema of the 1990s. Little has been made of the cinematic confluence of queerness with white trash identity, despite the fact that new queer cinema abounds with white trash images. According to B. Ruby Rich, new queer cinema refers to the "flock of films that were doing something new, renegotiating subjectivities, annexing whole genres, revising histories in their image" (15). New queer cinema was acclaimed during the 1990s for the way it gave agency to queer subjectivity, recognizing queerness as characterized by a multiplicity of conflicting voices and visions. The category of white trash also renegotiates subjectivities, genres, and histories, specifically through the nexus of race and class. The representations of white trash in new queer cinema explicitly acknowledge how white trash identity is a rather queer thing.

Queer lends itself to white trash, and vice versa, because both categories decenter and destabilize, prompting constant flux. Queer's conceptual ability to move or *pass across* things is comparable to the anchorlessness of many new queer characters; they keep moving *across* the landscape, forever passing *through* and *between* places, identities, things. A working definition of queer I often use is informed by queer theory figurehead, Eve Kosofsky Sedgwick. In *Tendencies*, Sedgwick frames queer as a *movement*, not only in the sense that it refers to a community, collective, or even a cinematic movement, but also because it moves in the literal sense: "The word 'queer' itself means across—it comes from the Indo-European root—*twerkw*, which also yields the German *quer* (traverse), Latin *torquere* (to twist), English *athwart*. . . . The immemorial current that *queer* represents is antiseparatist as it is anti-assimilationist. Keenly, it is relational, and strange" (xii). Sedgwick's definition suggests that queer refers to being in flux, to be passing across sexualities, genders, desires, and practices. The benefit of queer is that it does not allude to the specificity of sex and gender, as gay and lesbian categories do. Queer refers to both the subject (whether individual or collective) and subjectivity (the practices and performances that may be queer).

Sedgwick's emphasis on the relational character of queer is important to the way I conceive of the *queer* relationship between whiteness and white trash. The destabilization of whiteness as a privileged concept occurs when people are forced to examine the incongruity of its supposed supremacy and its ongoing nothingness. Whiteness is an unmarked category because it is both invisible and invincible. As Richard Dyer writes:

> White power none the less reproduces itself regardless of intention, power differences and goodwill, and overwhelmingly because it is not seen as whiteness, but as normal. White people need to learn to see themselves as white, to see their particularity. In other words, whiteness needs to be made strange (10).

White trash dirties whiteness, making it strange, unstable, and decentered primarily because of the relational proximity of white trash to privileged whiteness in racial terms. In a sense, the nothingness of whiteness cannot exist if forced into a relation with white trash. Annalee Newitz and Matt Wray suggest that "white trash is, for whites, the most visible and clearly marked form of whiteness" (4). This useful definition identifies the way white trash is seen as radically different from those who are just white. When something white is marked, it loses its whiteness and can no longer call itself white—it must acknowledge its off-whiteness, its white trashness. To be both white and marked in this sense is to be dirtied, defiled, and decentered. Conversely, to be white is to occupy a neutral and unmarked position of normativity. Labeling people white trash then is to *queer* whiteness, rendering it relational and strange, by marking class-based shortcomings in racial terms. White trash makes whiteness visible. White trash is the film on whiteness.

A kind of scum marking the naturalized claims of whiteness to cleanliness, virtue, luminosity, and privilege. I have conceived white trash *as* film primarily because my broader project is concerned with representations of white trash *in* film.

Using *My Own Private Idaho*, directed by Gus Van Sant; *Postcards from America*, directed by Steve McLean; and *Boys Don't Cry*, directed by Kimberly Peirce, this chapter discusses the way new queer cinema frequently represents white trash drifters and hustlers who use the road to move across and through the romanticized and mythical American landscape. The ability to move and a resistance against standing still informs their thematic content. That predominant films of the new queer cinema are road movies featuring white trash hustlers is certainly not accidental—the persistence of the road motif demonstrates how these queer characters are restless identities that can not be anchored in any one place.

THE TASTE OF ROADS

Dispossessed of home and family, the queer white trash marginality of Mike Waters (River Phoenix) is shaded by a melancholic longing. *My Own Private Idaho* lays bare how queer white trashness refuses the resolved narrative closure favored by much mainstream cinema. Inspired by the novels of William Burroughs, whose fragmented narratives are cutup and random, the film queers narrative logic and makes meaning at intersecting levels of consciousness. Oneiric in structure, *My Own Private Idaho* unfolds from Mike's narcoleptic point of view. Mostly triggered when reminded of his long-absent mother, Mike's narcoleptic seizures blur the edges of waking and sleeping states. In the opening sequence, Mike is asleep on an Idaho road. The scene abruptly cuts to a shot of Mike, a hustler by trade, being blown by a john. A title card interrupts, announcing Portland as the setting. As Mike reaches orgasm, a wooden barn falls from the sky, landing on one of the lost highways of his unconscious. Referencing the tornado that transports Dorothy home in *The Wizard of Oz*, the yellow brick road of Mike's road-trip is wracked instead with looming heartbreak because the home of his fantasy does not exist.

The figure of a hustler rarely lends itself to narrative closure because of his drifting affinity with the road and the street, reinforcing queerness as a perpetual state of movement, longing, and searching. Zigzagging aimlessly around the streets of Portland, Seattle, rural Idaho, and (in a bizarre twist) Rome, Mike exists on the margins of society, outside of conventional employment, and beyond the social institutions of marriage and family. As the film is modeled on Shakespeare's *Henry IV*, the Prince Hal figure, Scott Favor (Keanu Reeves) is Mike's closest friend. Scott is coded as queer for cash, while Mike is queer white trash. Mike's ultimate declaration of love for Scott is unrequited because for Scott, hustling is a temporary measure meant to upset his socially prominent father. Scott knows he will eventually abandon the street life, and his Falstaff-like father figure Bob Pigeon, and return to a life of privilege and unwavering heterosexuality when he inherits his dying father's estate. Frequent references to Scott's wealth buttress the divergent character of the film's social sets, polarizing him along class lines from the street trash hustling world.

When Scott finally returns home, he puts to bed a streak of adolescent rebellion. In contrast, Mike's fantasy of home infantilizes him, rendering him liminal in that he oscillates between childhood reverie and the tough adult world of turning tricks.[1] Dennis Cooper, in his obituary for River Phoenix, writes: "His best recent work found him playing overgrown kids who clung for [their] lives to youthful notions of a perfect romantic and/or familial love" (131). Mike's quest for family takes him out on the open road: a key space used to represent queer white trashness in new queer cinema. The road is the perfect place for queerness to emerge because it is analogous to the always thwarted promise of freedom attending such expansive spaces. The rhetoric of post-Stonewall gay liberation can be paralleled to the road's freedom and visibility because it is an antidote to the interior, restrictive, and demonized space of the closet.

It goes without saying that roads are used for movement, be it for a journey where one's intentions are met, or a trip hindered. Queerness, likewise, stands for movement. In *My Own Private Idaho*, the road is a motif of queerness and white trash marginality. White trash is found on the road and on the run. In much of the new queer cinema, white trash characters move through the landscape, on roads leading nowhere. The road reinforces the placelessness of Mike's queer white trash identity. Alluring in its promise of a destination and resolution, the road ultimately leads to a stretch of road already traveled. Mike uses his fingers to frame the road ahead, revealing its "fucked-up face"—its taunting ability to withhold resolution.

For Mike, the road traps him in a perpetual circuit of searching for something that does not exist. Regardless of whether the road lives up to its promise of something more, the queer white trash characters of the new queer cinema resist being anchored by any one place. Whether it is urban streetscapes lined with queer hustlers or the cross-country highways symbolizing freedom and hope, the possibilities of the road are one of the most enduring representations of society's margins. The road, however, is not always marginal because it frames, in much the same way that it passes through, the landscape. It can be central or distant, intersecting with other roads or none—a limitless romanticized passage or a frustrating series of dead ends. As Steven Cohan and Ina Hark write, although "the road has always functioned in movies as an alternative space where isolation from the mainstream permits various transformative experiences, the majority of road films made before the 1960s more successfully imagined an ultimate reintegration of road travelers into the dominant culture" (5). For the new queer cinema of the 1990s, the road functions as an alternative space and is potentially transformative, but its travelers never integrate into dominant social institutions, forging instead their own queer white trash models of family, marriage, and community.

In *My Own Private Idaho*, the immediacy of the open road and the urban inner-city street functions in opposition to Mike's ideal of home. The closest Mike gets to being home is upon reuniting with his violent and alcoholic brother Richard. Sadly, Mike's idealized notion of family is shattered when Richard reveals he is Mike's brother *and* father—there is no home on the range.[2] Richard shows Mike the last postcard their mother sent, revealing she stayed at a hotel called The Family Tree. A culturally familiar white trash trope, incest ruptures familial ideals, explaining in essentialist terms origins for white trash identity. For film critic Amy Taubin, Mike's back-story of incest and abandonment is "just an extra Oedipal wrinkle in an already disenfranchised existence" (79). Spiked with potential danger, the road with its dark destinations ultimately represents a lesser threat than the contaminated fantasy of the home.[3]

The seamy urban streets of Portland and Seattle emphasize the homelessness and marginality of its queer white trash hustlers, contrasting with the expansive Idaho roads. In the final scene, Mike stands on a sun-bleached Idaho road and says, "I'm a connoisseur of roads. I've been tasting roads my whole life. This road will never end. It probably goes all around the world." The road is certainly cyclical because it features in the opening and closing scenes, connecting Mike's past memories and peripatetic present.

While Idaho is located in the northwest United States, it is represented less in real terms, and more as a symbol of home and family.[4] Van Sant claims the location is "both the literal Idaho of his early years and the utopian Idaho of rooted love" (qtd. in Lafrance). Idaho is the stuff of dreams and childhood for Mike, so it is unsurprising that Idaho triggers narcoleptic dreamscapes of vivid, romanticized imagery. Super 8 footage is used to signify memory, while Mike's dream sequences often focus on the landscape in lush 35-mm, time-lapse cinematography. These techniques beautifully illustrate how wide open spaces cradle Mike, often at the expense of time, which is always evaporating.

Ultimately, a resolved happy ending is shirked because of its melancholic weight. A long shot, the final scene sees Mike asleep on the road, dreaming. He is picked up by a stranger and driven away. Ambiguously, a title card announces "Have a nice day." Elizabeth Pincus claims: "Better to embrace marginality and its possibilities, harrowing and otherwise, for informing a cinema that resonates with more than just the facile palliative of happily-ever-after." But as Robert Lang notes, the "queer road movies of the 1990s, more often than not, don't have conventionally happy endings, but something has certainly changed, for they cannot be called *un*happy endings either" (333). In a collection on new queer cinema, Michele Aaron writes: "No longer does popular culture have to seem to render queer configurations safe—through, for example, humour, homophobia (or other memos of heterosexuality) and, especially, closure" ("Introduction" 10). It is because the melancholic desire of longing is emphasized over closure that it cannot be simplified in happy or unhappy terms; melancholy is neither sad nor happy. The fragmented, oneiric narrative of unfulfilled longing makes *My Own Private Idaho* a queer white trash affair, less interested in sealing identity than providing room for limitless, unresolvable meanings.

THE DISINTEGRATING OUTSIDE

The opening shot of *My Own Private Idaho* focuses on an illuminated dictionary definition of "narcolepsy." Steve McLean appropriates this shot when, fifteen minutes into *Postcards from America*, a dictionary definition of "fag" is depicted, similarly framed by a shaft of light. An intertextual road links both films, analogous to the way actual roads connect their various characters and narrative fragments. Like Van Sant, McLean employs a nonlinear, cutup narrative to heighten its themes of alienation, loss, and fragmentation. In this sense, the narrative style reflects the fragmented biographical remains of David Wojnarowicz, the artist and writer on whom the movie is based.[5] Wojnarowicz is remembered particularly for the way his work always commented directly on his own life.[6] When he was diagnosed with AIDS in 1988, Wojnarowicz's work became increasingly political, fusing shards of his own biography with an ongoing commentary of rage directed at government and religious structures that silence marginal identities. *Postcards from America* evades portraying Wojnarowicz as an artist and activist, representing instead his existential road-trips across the southwestern American desert. Depicted as an alienating and empty wasteland, the vast landscape is a perfect match for a figure whose all-consuming emptiness produces his inevitable disintegration. McLean constructs a stylized version of real events, though importantly, Wojnarowicz's surname is never uttered, transforming the historical figure of David Wojnarowicz into an anonymous queer white trash archetype.

Narrative fragmentation is achieved as three stages of the protagonist's life are interweaved, using three different actors to play each role. In the first, young David (Olmo Tighe) is an overweight boy, growing up in an abusive New Jersey home during the early 1960s. Secondly, teenage David (Michael Tighe) is a petty thief and hustler, living in New York City during the 1970s.

Lastly, adult David (James Lyons) is HIV positive and adrift in the American desert during the late 1980s. Both *My Own Private Idaho* and *Postcards from America* are bookended by scenes where their protagonists inhabit roads that intersect expansive landscapes, reinforcing queer white trash as alienated, homeless, and searching for things located more in memory than in physical reality.

As in the case of Mike—whose narcolepsy is signified through *My Own Private Idaho*'s oneiric structure—dreams, fantasies, and memories punctuate David's identity. Childhood reminiscences signify the tenuous link between beauty and pain through the melancholic nostalgia of country music. At one point in the film, a Connie Francis song extradiegetically bridges childhood and teen memories. In the former (childhood) scene, having escaped the confines of his oppressive house, David is swimming alone in a lake. The song continues into the next scene, where David is a teenager, hustling in Times Square. One line from the chorus, "I find a broken heart among my souvenirs," adds pathos and suggests that David is a tourist in his own life, collecting experiences like souvenirs. The film's title also implies that his experiences are postcards enclosing information narrated in the past tense of memory. As I argue elsewhere, filmmakers often rely on country music to aurally signify white trashness.[7] In *Postcards from America*, David's white trash upbringing is remembered with a degree of bittersweet affection when framed by the songs of Connie Francis.[8]

Despite this use of music, it is the road that most closely aligns it with a white trash aesthetic. The open road is often represented in road movies as a space for marginal identities because it appeals to the myth that one can exist outside of culture. To be *outside* of something, however, inevitably invokes that which lies *inside*. Diana Fuss challenges this dichotomy and its relation to the hetero/homo binary in *Inside/Out*. Fuss argues that homosexuality is always figured as the outside term because it is excluded or marginalized by heterosexuality. The supposed outsider status generated by being queer white trash does not then guarantee radicality because it is perhaps impossible to fully inhabit the excluded domain of outsiderness.

David is represented in *Postcards from America* as an outsider, in keeping with the way the real David Wojnarowicz's work was paradigmatic of an outsider aesthetic. In McLean's film, it is not necessarily queer white trashness that guarantees outsider status. Instead, it is David's engagement with the road that renders him exterior to the dominant culture. The very act of passing or speeding through the landscape becomes the key metaphor for his attempts for a sexually charged transcendence. Narrated in the opening scene's voice-over, David says: "Speeding: It's the only emotion that makes the heart unravel. I don't like highways very much but I love to speed. It makes me think of men's bodies, and driving, and drifting; the sway; the dance of sex; like a dream." What follows is an image of David standing in the desert landscape, screaming. The camera pirouettes around him, gaining speed and painting the landscape a dizzy blur. Speeding, driving, drifting, swaying, dancing, and fucking help him transcend the disintegrating interiority of his body. Of course, the body is utilized in the acts described, but it is through speed-induced abandon, emphasized by the swirling movement of the camera, that David comes to exist outside of himself. Disembodiment is also suggested when David's anonymous sexual encounters trigger painful childhood memories.

More than simply traversing three stages of David's life, *Postcards from America* intersects three identity categories: sexuality, class, and race. In writings on new queer films, little attention is paid to how issues of class and race (and a related term such as white trash) function in relation to the constitution of its predominating queerness. While Wojnarowicz's confessional memoirs detailed the politics and poetics of his queerness, these experiences are grounded in an upbringing of working class struggle that led to his life as a homeless teenage hustler on the streets of New York City. In her essay on Dorothy Allison's queer white trash stories, Jillian Sandell argues that confessional storytelling is a popular and sometimes powerful tool in contemporary culture because these stories, "when told, are presumed to enable and foster the creation of social and political communities" (211). While a proliferation of confessional stories continues to emerge, Sandell notes that "there are still certain stories which *cannot* be told—either because we have no language with which to articulate them or because there is no interpretive community to hear and understand them" (212). One story that cannot be told, for Sandell, is the story of class struggle in white American culture. The existence of white trashness through representations or lived realities does not always entail an awareness of complex class issues. These white trash tropes often flourish within the fabric of American cultural consciousness as a stereotype lacking autonomy and subjectivity (this occurs when white trash is sexualized as raw, uncivilized, and uncultivated). Conversely, depictions of white trash are often exoticized for their outsiderness, and accordingly commodified on romantic and mystified terms.

Representations of whiteness rarely acknowledge or challenge the privileged meanings embedded in the very constitution of white identity. Yet white trash cannot exist without forever acknowledging its class status as trash. When white trash is categorized as a collective cultural experience, through the accumulation of representations and stories, it risks being rendered an empty commodity. Sandell writes, "issues of economic marginality can be tolerated and articulated within the logic of liberal pluralism, so long as they can be circulated as cultural, rather than economic issues" (213). When the markers of identity become cultural signs, they are inevitably commodified.

Class narratives are sidelined because other identity markers better lend themselves to commodification. Paradoxical as it seems, considering that queer resists categorization, new queer cinema is culturally intelligible because of its convenient categorization and commodification as queer pop culture. White trash stories are similarly commodified, but often with lashings of cynical humor or grotesquery, making it difficult to contemplate the complexity of white trash narratives, however fractured and displaced they appear in *My Own Private Idaho* and *Postcards from America*.

THE DUSTLESS DREAM

A key aspect of this chapter has been identifying the alignment of queer white trash with the road. The internal contradictions of white trash—being a marked form of whiteness—parallel the contradictions of the road. Roads signify freedom and escape because they offer (although they can withhold) self-transformation. Conversely, alienation and danger emerge when its ongoing cycle of transformation traps the white trash subject in an inescapable loop. *Boys Don't Cry* shows, like *My Own Private Idaho* and *Postcards from America*, that Brandon Teena's attempts at transformation and longing for love always beget dangerous situations. Importantly, all three films establish the road as a key motif by featuring memorable images of the road in the opening scenes.

Xan Brooks notes that *Boys Don't Cry* "filters its true crime material through the prism of New Queer Cinema." It is the film's representation of crime—invited by comparisons to films such as *Badlands, In Cold Blood*, and *The Executioner's Song* that are about white trash criminals that makes it a white trash text. Like these films (but unlike *My Own Private Idaho* and *Postcards from America*), *Boys Don't Cry* employs conventional narrative structure to detail how Brandon (Hilary Swank) meets a tragic death because the real crime committed, in the eyes of "his" peers, was a crime of performance: the crime of passing as male. While *Boys Don't Cry* is based on a true crime account of Brandon Teena, who was brutally raped and shot dead after "his" female anatomy was exposed on December 31, 1993 in Falls City, Nebraska, I am more concerned here with Peirce's screen depiction of Brandon than with the complex ruminations that unravel around the real-life case. For a reading of the ethics of "biographical temporality" see Judith Halberstam's lucid analysis of the voluminous media "archive" circulating around the figure of Brandon Teena.

Boys Don't Cry demonstrates that gender and sex are forever unstable, inauthentic, disruptive, and capable of generating social division. Such division is represented through the metaphor of the wall. Most of its characters are wall people: bored white trash kids who congregate at night against the

Qwik Stop convenience store wall. Based on a real-life subculture in Falls City, Nebraska, wall people hung out together in such locations because they could consume alcohol and get high on glue and aerosol cans stolen from the convenience store. The sense of small town entrapment is underlined by the wall people and especially evident in Lana (Chloë Sevigny), a disaffected factory worker who, once smitten by Brandon's charms, abandons the wall.[9] Halberstam argues: "While Brandon continues to romanticize small-town life, his girlfriend, Lana, sees him as a symbol of a much-desired elsewhere" (77).

When Brandon arrives in town, he represents freedom and potential escape from small town entrapment, symbolized by the wall. Brandon adopts an exaggerated cowboy masculinity that is assertive and fearless, sensitive and romantic. One of Brandon's killers, Tom, sees through Brandon's cowboy visage, claiming he rode into town on a "pussy-whipped faggot horse." Represented as white trash, but possessing the qualities of "a little movie star" from "some place beautiful," Brandon's overstated masculinity becomes aligned with the Western genre where cowboys proliferate. Westerns mainly consist of white, rural characters whose sense of the landscape defines their identity. Brandon is very much represented as a cowboy traveling throughout a heartland setting of the American West: "a place of renewal and reinvention, a land where pioneers could throw off the shackles of the past and live the life they always dreamed of " (Brooks). Brandon blends cowboy and frontiersman archetypes because such figures embody the performance and, by implication, passing of maleness. For Brandon, this passing is about movement between places as much as it is about passing (or the failure to pass) as a man invested in cowboy signifiers. Aaron argues, "in the spectator's constant awareness of Brandon's ambiguous identity—in the simultaneity of he and she—passing *is* failing: the reassuring distance between these 'events' (and the spectator's experience of them) dissolves" ("Queer Spectator" 190). Ang Lee's more recent *Brokeback Mountain*—which also contains white trash tropes—shows how such heightened constructions of masculinity inevitably engender failed performances of heterosexuality because of barely contained queer investments in those very signifiers of masculinity.

Lana is more identifiable as a white trash archetype. When Brandon returns to Lincoln for a court appearance, he tells cousin Lonny that he will be returning to Falls City because of a girl. Brandishing a photo of Lana, Brandon remarks, "Isn't she beautiful," to which Lonny replies, "If you like white trash." Brandon offers Lana the dream of a future together in a trailer: "The thing about the trailer park is we'll have picnic tables, people playing music . . . . And best of all, we'll have our own Airstream." When Brandon's "airstream" is severed in death, Lana leaves Falls City, following Brandon's fantasy of freedom. In these final scenes, the road is reflected on Lana's face, suggesting she now recognizes the road's limitless possibilities. When, earlier in the film, Brandon and his peers drive recklessly across the "dustless highway," the enveloping and dreamlike experiences of the road contain an element of danger and risk:

> The dustless highway is a real place in Falls City where the kids go; it's a stretch of highway where, if you turn off the main road, this huge cloud of dust rolls up behind you, hides you and you just disappear. . . . It's like driving into a dream, and that's exactly what the experience of going to Falls City was like for Brandon. (qtd. in "Synopsis")

The American dream for the white trash characters of much new queer cinema similarly acts like a car-induced dust storm that "rolls up behind you," erasing the white trash subject. Such a dream is linked to a desire to be in places that are forever held at arm's length and inevitably short-circuited by the road. Marginality renders white trash incapable of experiencing the trans-formative characteristics of the great American road trip. Queerness, with its relational stress on movement, ensures that passing (or the failure to pass) is enacted along literal and metaphoric lines. It is their white trashness that often lures them out onto the road in search of that elusive something more. Whiteness, then, is always at the risk of being trashed when visibly marked by queerness and class, and once marked, it can no longer claim to be white. Queer white trash remains marginal because the *drive* to be transformed above and beyond one's class origins is not a central concern. The key characters discussed inhabit and traverse the road, but the things that they long for remain unresolved, open-ended, and removed from the dominant culture. If anything, their queer white trash marginality is reinforced by the concluding moments of these films. That is, if they make it out alive.

ACKNOWLEDGMENTS

This chapter is adapted from *The "Film" on Whiteness: Depicting "White Trash" in US Film, 1972–2002* (Ph.D. Dissertation, University of Western Sydney, 2004). An earlier version of the *Boys Don't Cry* section was published as "Driving into the 'Dustless Highway' of Queer Cinema." *The Film Journal* 5 (2003): <http://www.thefilmjournal.com/issue5/highway.html>.

The author dedicates this chapter to the memory of his friend and doctoral supervisor, Dr. Phillip Kent, who died from an AIDS-related illness in June 2003. Thanks also to cosupervisor Dr. David McInnes, for providing invaluable insights then and now.

NOTES

1. Coming to terms with childhood experience and its impact on a queer hustler's adulthood is the theme of *Mysterious Skin*, where new queer director Gregg Araki stages the experiences of pedophilia within a queer white trash milieu. Like Van Sant who uses road movie tropes to draw out its white trashness, Araki's earlier film *The Living End* satirizes the romance of the American road trip. In one scene, a hitchhiking character played by Mary Woronov exclaims: "Oh my, a nomadic drifter, a lonesome cowboy hitching across the country like Jack Kerouac. How romantic. Isn't that just fucking romantic."

2. An instrumental arrangement of the iconic song "Home on the Range" appears throughout. In an ironic turn, the phrase "Homo on the Range" appears early in the film as a caption on a porn magazine cover showing a photo of Scott wearing a cowboy hat.

3. Oedipal queer white trash drama is also played out in *Tarnation*, directed by Caouette, an experimental documentary exploring the relationship of the filmmaker to his mother.

4. Idaho has been represented in popular music before as a symbol of home. Van Sant was inspired by The B-52s "Private Idaho," a song whose lyrics speak of a menacing Idaho: "You're out of control/The rivers that roll/You fell into the water and down to Idaho/Get out of that state you're in." In white trash country music classic *Nashville, directed by* Altman, Ronee Blakely sings "My Idaho Home," a song containing the line, "I still love mom and dad best, my Idaho."

5. It is based on Wojnarowicz's biographical books *Close to the Knives: A Memoir of Disintegration* and *Memories that Smell like Gasoline*.

6. See Kuspit "David Wojnarowicz" and Guattari "David Wojnarowicz."

7. See Cunningham "Authenticating."

8. On 11 March 2002, eight years after the film was released, Connie Francis filed a $40-million lawsuit against Universal Music Corporation, who licensed her songs for allegedly pornographic films. "She particularly objected to the use of four of her songs in the unrated film *Postcards from America* . . . Francis describe [*sic*] it as a 'vile, pornographic' movie in her lawsuit. Francis's attorney said that when she learned of the use of her songs in such films, she became particularly distressed given her fragile mental health resulting from a 1974 incident in which she was raped and tortured in a hotel room." See "Connie."

9. Another transgender film of the period, *Hedwig and the Angry Inch*, directed by Mitchell, represents social and sexual division through the figure of the wall. Hedwig's divided sense of self draws out a search for "her" other half. The division metaphor begins by comparing Hedwig's fractured gender identity to the Berlin Wall, which was still intact, oppressively dividing East and West Germany.

WORKS CITED

Aaron, Michele, ed. *New Queer Cinema: A Critical Reader*. Edinburgh: Edinburgh UP, 2004.

————. "New Queer Cinema: An Introduction." Aaron, 2–14.

―――. "The New Queer Spectator." Aaron, 187–200.

The B-52s. "Private Idaho." *Wild Planet*. Reprise, 1980.

Badlands. Dir. Terrence Malick. Warner Brothers, 1973.

Boys Don't Cry. Dir. Kimberly Peirce. Fox Searchlight Pictures, 1999.

Brokeback Mountain. Dir. Ang Lee. Focus Features, 2005.

Brooks, Xan. Rev. of *Boys Don't Cry*, dir. Kimberly Peirce. *Sight and Sound* Apr. 2000. 9 Feb. 2006 <http://www.bfi.org.uk/sightandsound/review/317>.

Cohan, Steven, and Ina Rae Hark. "Introduction." *The Road Movie Book*. Ed. Steven Cohan and Ina Rae Hark. New York: Routledge, 1997. 1–14.

"Connie Francis Sues Universal Music Over Movie Licenses." *Internet Movie Database*. 12 Mar. 2002. 3 Mar. 2006 <http://us.imdb.com/SB?20020312#3>.

Cooper, Dennis. "Beauty and Sadness." *All Ears. Cultural Criticism, Essays and Obituaries*. Ed. Dennis Cooper. New York: Soft Skull, 1999. 129–31.

Cunningham, Daniel M. "Authenticating White Trash: The Performance of Country Music in *O Brother, Where Art Thou?*" *Refractory: A Journal of Entertainment Media* 4 (2003). 12 Mar. 2006 <http://www.refractory.unimelb.edu.au/journalissues/vol4/cunningham.html>.

Dyer, Richard. *White*. New York: Routledge, 1997.

The Executioner's Song. Dir. Lawrence Schiller. NBC. 1982.

Fuss, Diana, ed. *Inside/Out: Lesbian Theories, Gay Theories*. New York: Routledge, 1994.

Guattari, Félix. "David Wojnarowicz." *GlobeE Online Journal*. 12 Mar. 2006 <http://pandora.nla.gov.au/nph-arch/1999/Z1999-Jul-14/http://www.arts.monash.edu.au/visarts/globe/issue6/davwoj.html>.

Halberstam, Judith. *In a Queer Time and Place: Transgender Bodies, Subcultural Lives*. New York: New York UP, 2005.

Hedwig and the Angry Inch. Dir. John Cameron Mitchell. Fine Line, 2001.

In Cold Blood. Dir. Richard Brooks. Columbia, 1967.

Kuspit, David. "David Wojnarowicz: The Last Rimbaud." *Queer Cultural Center Online*. 18 Mar. 2006 <http://www.queerculturalcenter.org/Pages/DavidW/DW_Kuspit.html>.

Lafrance, J.D. "Fringes of Society." *My Own Private Idaho*. 4 Mar. 2006. 9 Feb. 2006 <http://www.myownprivateidaho.com>. Path: Links/News/Misc; Essay from J.D. Lafrance. Lang, Robert. "*My Own Private Idaho* and the New Queer Road Movies." *The Road Movie Book*. Cohan and Hark, 330–48.

Living End. Dir. Gregg Araki. October Films, 1992.

My Own Private Idaho. Dir. Gus Van Sant. New Line Cinema, 1991.

Mysterious Skin. Dir. Gregg Araki. Independent Artists, 2004.

Nashville. Dir. Robert Altman. Paramount, 1975.

Newitz, Annalee, and Matt Wray. "Introduction." Newitz and Wray, 1–12.

―――. *White Trash: Race and Class in America*. New York: Routledge, 1997.

Pincus, Elizabeth. Rev. of *My Own Private Idaho*, dir. Gus Van Sant. *Popcorn Q Movies*. 9 Feb. 2006. <http://www.planetout.com/popcornq/db/getfilm.html?1895>.

Postcards from America. Dir. Steve McLean. Strand Releasing, 1994.

Rich, B. Ruby. "New Queer Cinema." Aaron, 15–22.

Sandell, Jillian. "Telling Stories of 'Queer White Trash': Race, Class, and Sexuality in the Work of Dorothy Allison." Newitz and Wray, 211–30.

Sedgwick, Eve Kosofsky. *Tendencies*. Durham: Duke UP, 1993.

"Synopsis." *Fox Searchlight Boys Don't Cry Official Site*. 1999. 9 Feb. 2006. <http://www2.foxsearchlight.com/boysdontcry/prod.html>.

Tarnation. Dir. Jonathan Caouette. Wellspring Media, 2003.

Taubin, Amy. "Objects of Desire" *American Independent Cinema: A Sight and Sound Reader*. Ed. Jim Hillier. London: British Film Institute, 2001. 79–86.

Wizard of Oz. Dir. Victor Fleming. MGM, 1939.

Wojnarowicz, David. *Close to the Knives: A Memoir of Disintegration*. New York: Vintage, 1991.

———. *Memories That Smell Like Gasoline*. New York: Artspace, 1992.

CHAPTER 12

IDENTITY UNMOORED: YAOI IN THE WEST

MARK MCHARRY

Abstract: *Yaoi describes homoerotic works created by fans, mostly girls and women, of young male characters in Japanese* manga *(comics) and* anime *(animation). Long established in Japan, yaoi has become popular in the West. Some same-sex attracted males in both regions have criticized yaoi's representations as unrealistic and oppressive yet others enjoy them. Reading a Western yaoi story with the ideas of gender theorists Judith Butler, Elizabeth Grosz, and Eve Kosofsky Sedgwick as a frame of reference, I show how yaoi troubles conventional notions of identity and gender to the point where it may be considered a form of resistance to them.*

IN MOST WORLD REGIONS, more women than men publish erotica about male-male sexuality. The stories and drawings they create are usually about media characters. The relationships in which sex takes place may be among multiple partners, between a minor and an older person, among siblings, or with authority figures or foes. Often the sex acts are nonconsensual, violent and/or performed in public spaces. Although these representations may lie beyond real-world cultural boundaries, the theme of almost all of these works is the characters' surmounting of obstacles to connect or bond.

Called *yaoi, shōnen-ai*, boys' love, and slash, the first three of these genres originated in Japan, the fourth in the West. Of them yaoi is the largest and perhaps fastest-growing worldwide. It describes homoerotic literature and art-work based on young male characters in Japanese *manga* (comics) and *anime* (animation). In Japan, yaoi is comprised of noncommercial, fan-created *dōjinshi* (manga) and artwork, and in the West, of fan stories and artwork. *Shōnen-ai* (lit., boys' love) and boys' love describe similarly themed works that are based on original characters and disseminated in English- and Japanese-language markets. *Shōnen-ai* and boys' love products are usually commercial and take the form of anime, video games, and audio CDs in addition to manga. Slash describes the homoerotic works Western women and some men create about male characters from TV programs, movies, and books. Although all four forms are consumed by a much smaller number of men in the West and Asia, most participants are women, many of them young, who identify themselves as straight or as someone whose sexuality is not nameable.[1]

Yaoi, on which I focus here, and the two other Japanese-derived forms play at the intersections of identity and gender.[2] Bodies in yaoi move fluidly past constructions of identity, gender, and sex, seemingly ignorant of cultural boundaries set around them. Judith Butler's work in gender theory, Elizabeth Grosz's on corporeality, and Eve Kosofsky Sedgwick's on homosociality have become influential for conceptualizing gender and sexual identity in English. I will use some of their ideas as a frame of reference in reading a Western yaoi story and to show how yaoi troubles conventional notions of identity and gender to the point where it may be considered a form of resistance to them.

POPULARITY AND PRESENCE

In Japan, the popularity of boys' love and yaoi gives them a presence in mainstream culture, visible in manga and other products sold in bookstores and on magazine racks in small towns as well as cities. Tokyo's largest bookstore, Kinokuniya, held a boys' love manga fair on its main floor in March 2002. Wim Lunsing estimates there are 500,000 "core" Japanese yaoi readers.[3] In the West, yaoi is an activity seen mostly on the Internet. Authors post stories to Web sites and LiveJournals, as well as to fan-fiction archives. One archive, FanFiction.Net, had more than 1.3 million works in May 2006, many of them yaoi stories, up from more than 997,000 in February 2005 and 200,000 in July 2002. Yaoi stories and artwork are the object of reviews on archive sites, commentary on LiveJournals, posts to discussion groups, and comments to Web sites' guest books. A work in one form, such as a story, can stimulate works in another, such as illustration (figures 12.1 and 12.2).

A Google search on 29 April 2006 returned 5,620,000 Web pages with the word "yaoi," up from approximately 770,000 on 16 November 2003 and 135,000 on 4 May 2003.[4] Google searches for an anime title plus a neutral word such as "description" may return yaoi pages in the first ten results. To a much smaller extent English translations of commercial *shōnen-ai* works are sold in stores in some major U.S. cities. In early-to-mid 2006, *shōnen-ai* titles were visible in the window of Tower Records in San Francisco's gay-lesbian oriented Castro district and prominently displayed at the front counter or in the young-adult section in bookstores in other cities, such as Borders and Barnes and Noble in Washington DC's Dupont Circle neighborhood and in Honolulu.

Figure 12.1   Dou Hong, *Freeport*. Mako (far right), a killer on the anarchist space colony Freeport, restraining Preventer agent Wufei Chang. Wufei's lover Duo Maxwell is behind them. 2004, <http://farfie-kins.deviantart.com/>.

Those unaware of yaoi may encounter it when searching the Web for anime or manga. An example is a young male's e-mail to the English-language yaoi Web site *Gundam Wing Addiction* (Tyr). Daniel described himself as "an avid fan" of the popular anime *Gundam Wing*, whose protagonists are a quintet of fifteen-year-old male space pilots.[5] He wrote that he was "quite disturbed" upon being told by people in his school that the *Gundam Wing* characters depicted on a shirt he wore were gay: "So my question for you is—if any characters were actually gay in the original story line, and if so—who?" (Tyr).

The site owner, Tyr, an adult, responded that none of the characters were, and then qualified this with, "or if they are, it is not explicitly stated in the show itself" (Tyr). She reproduced a canonical illustration from the Japanese monthly anime/manga magazine *Animage* showing one of the pilots, Duo, in an embrace with another, Heero (figure 12.3). Even as she noted that "all [other] official GW illustrations have no yaoi content whatsoever," she wrote that "Japanese producers are very open-minded about the idea of yaoi" and that the owners of the anime encouraged fans to interpret their work in ways other than those promulgated canonically (Tyr). Tyr's response and its ambiguity to a question demanding a "yes" or "no" answer mark a discourse between the young and adults around same-sex erotics in the young.

Figure 12.2   Randi Smith, *The Call*. Duo watches Wufei take a call on Freeport from the Earth-based law enforcement organization Preventer. May 2005, <http://www.gwaddiction.com/gallery/album53/call_randiSmith>.

IDENTITY: CONTROVERSY AND CONTESTATION

Some same-sex attracted men have welcomed yaoi's representations as potentially liberatory. Others have expressed opposition to their sexuality's representational custody being in the hands of those who are neither homosexual nor male. From 1992 to 1997, a debate about yaoi took place in the Japanese feminist magazine *Choisir*. Satō Masaki, whom Lunsing identifies as "a gay activist/civil servant/drag queen" (Lunsing 14), complained that yaoi's characters had nothing to do with "real gay men" (14). Satō touched off a yaoi *ronsō* (controversy). For Satō, writes Keith Vincent, "yaoi and its readers were violently co-opting the reality of gay men and transforming it into their own masturbatory fantasy" (3). According to Satō,

> The more confused images of gay men circulate among the general public the harder it is for gay men to reconcile these images with their own lives and the more extreme their oppression becomes. . . . When you're spying on gay sex, girls, take a look at yourself in the mirror. Just look at the expression on your faces! [You look just like those dirty old men salivating over images of lesbian sex.] You can all go to hell for all I care.

新 機 動 戦 記 ガ ン ダ ム W
E n d l e s s   W a l t z ／ 特 別 篇

Figure 12.3 *Endless Waltz.* Duo Maxwell (left) and Heero Yuy. A Nippon Telegraph and Telephone Corporation telephone card offered to readers by the magazine アニメージュ (*Animēju*; in English, *Animage*) (Tokyo) in 1998 to mark its twentieth anniversary. That year the movie *Endless Waltz* featuring Duo, Heero, and other characters from the 1995–1996 TV series *Gundam Wing* was released in Japan.

In the United States, some gay-identified men have expressed unease about or opposition to yaoi. The widely published gay male porn writer Simon Sheppard, speaking on a Yaoi-Con panel, called yaoi "a minstrel show" that "puts gay male sex out there for straight people." A yaoi artist told me that some gay-identified men have complained to her that males portrayed in yaoi are not representative of them or of gay males in general, and that they felt uneasy at being objectified by women (Anonymous). Matt Thorn reports that some slash fans "seem to feel the need to justify slash to the gay community, or even to reform slash in such a way as to make it more palatable or 'politically correct' " (173). Other men, some gay-identified, create and consume yaoi. They attend events such as Yaoi-Con, held annually in the United States since 2001, for similar reasons to those of women: to socialize with other fans, purchase *dōjinshi* and commercial products, engage in *kospure* (costumed play, abbreviated in English as "cosplay"), exhibit artwork, find out more about fandoms, share knowledge, and meet prominent yaoi and boys' love artists.

Identity is essential to our conception of self and it is at the center of the trouble some have with yaoi. Although a personal identity denotes one's sameness to some thing(s) over time, it implies his or her difference from others. A subject's identity is not his or hers alone. Constellations of attributes comprising an identity may become contestable, as they have for identities characterized by "race" or as "queer."[6]

Notions of identity posited by Judith Butler's gender theory maintain that an identity becomes linked to a subject by being interpellated by another and iterated time and again by the subject and others. Identity categories are unstable and elastic, needing continual reinforcement in order to maintain their integrity. Like the imitative effect of gay identities that "works . . . to expose heterosexuality as an incessant and *panicked* imitation of its own naturalized idealization" ("Imitation" 129), yaoi works to destabilize not only anime and manga's canonical primacy but also fixed conceptions of gay identity.

Yaoi's expression engages gender at what Butler terms the "lived experience" of gender differentiation: the body's boundaries ("Lesbian" 150). In a view that has gained currency in the critical theory community, Butler characterizes gender as performative, "*produc[ing]* on the skin, through the gesture, the move, the gait (that array of corporeal theatrics understood as gender presentation), the illusion of an inner depth" ("Imitation" 134). The desires of the subject as well as others are imprinted as signs on the subject's body for others to see as presumed easily readable identities. Yaoi creators, by publishing works depicting nominally heterosexual characters engaging in non-homonormative scenarios and acts, blur the signs that signify contemporary hetero/homosexual identity. One way in which the fluidity of yaoi may be seen is in how the characters in yaoi stories look at one another.

FRAMING DESIRE

In *Chasing the Crown*, a story in the series *Mission: Arcadia and Beyond*,[7] based on characters and events in the commercial anime *Gundam Wing*,

Duo Maxwell introduces his lover Heero Yuy to the idea of a ménage à trois with fellow pilot Wufei Chang:

> Heero's Prussian blue eyes widened momentarily then blinked at the sudden pictures in his mind. "I . . . Is that . . . Have you talked to him about this?" he finally managed, as the Perfect Soldier felt his face suddenly flush with heat. (RavynFyre et al., "Part Twenty-five")

Later, walking a few paces behind Duo, Wufei asks Heero,

> "Why is your lover flirting with me? He is doing that, correct?"
>
> "Wufei, have you ever looked into a mirror?" Heero asked. "And yes, Duo is flirting with you. He thinks you're handsome and so do I, but have you done the mirror thing? [. . .] [It's] where Duo and . . . well he did it with me, so I guess it could be all three of us or something. Anyway, you stand naked in front of the mirror and Duo points out your good points. The objective is to get yourself looking at you in a different way. I found it effective." [. . .] (RavynFyre et al., "Part Thirty-two")

> Wufei watched [Duo's] face intently, noting the momentary hesitance, and the glance. The Chinese pilot found that he was breathing very deeply. He turned, leaning his shoulder against the wall to face Duo more directly. "So you want to make up new rules, Duo?" he said softly, his dark eyes focused on Duo's face.
>
> "Why have rules at all?" Duo asked quietly before turning his head to peer at Wufei from under his bangs. "Why not just live, Wufei?" [. . .]
>
> "Just . . . live . . ." Wufei repeated, as if the idea was just beyond the edge of his comprehension. Suddenly he reached up, and placed his hand alongside Duo's cheek, leaned forward and pressed his lips to the other boy's. (RavynFyre et al., "Part Thirty-three")

There may be no more fundamental way to show the presence of eros in desire than the gaze. Erotic desire is at the heart of yaoi and accordingly the gaze is probably the most common device in Western yaoi fiction. *Chasing the Crown*'s authors use the mirror to stress the link between erotic desire and the gaze.

In psychoanalytic theory, Jacques Lacan's idea of the infant's first seeing a reflection of itself in a mirror signifies the beginning of notions of corporeal self-awareness and hence the possibility for a subject's symbolic and linguistic exchange with others. In her discussion of Lacan, Elizabeth Grosz theorizes that the mirror is key to the infant's learning to place his or her body in space. An adult's notion of his or her surroundings, dominated as it is by "a spatiality of hierarchized perspective" (44), is only gradually realized by the child, who learns to "understand perspectives or the relations between figure and ground, which require oppositions that the child has not yet acquired" (219).

Duo uses the mirror to frame the three pilots' bodies in the same space, collapsing the distance between them, and to show Heero and Wufei that they exist as erotic objects. In this, Duo's technique echoes the idea of the infant's learning from the specular image of itself that others can take a viewpoint on him (93).

A theme common in *Gundam Wing* yaoi stories is portraying Duo with an intense need for love because of his fending for himself on the streets of a ramshackle space colony during childhood. The authors' use in *Chasing the Crown* of a device prominent in psychoanalytic theory indicates the great importance they place on the gaze as a way to stress the urgency of Duo's desire.

Seeing also connotes apprehension of the seen. It is about the seer's autonomy and self-affirmation. The action in *Chasing the Crown* and other yaoi stories frequently brings the characters together in ways that facilitate their looking at one another. Several times in *Chasing the Crown* we watch characters interrogate each other's gaze as they talk or shift their gazes from one to the other during sex, in the latter case, a character framing what he sees as if it were a tableau to be committed to memory. In another story, Maldoror's *Freeport*, in several scenes, Wufei watches Duo's retreating form, seeing it as a challenge and an invitation to follow. In these and many Western yaoi stories, as the narrative moves between characters' points of view, our gaze moves with it. The effect of this constantly shifting gazing fits with the fluidity of yaoi's bodies and it produces a power equilibrium among the characters.

RESISTING IDENTITY

Central to *Chasing the Crown* and to Western yaoi fiction in general is a discursive frame that allows little in the way of conceptions of sexuality that operate to force an either/or identity division. Although most or all of the male characters in a yaoi story prefer sex with males, in almost all of the several hundred yaoi stories I have read, there is little or no sense of a homonormative environment established in opposition to a prevailing heteronormative one, little or no need for same-sex desiring males to form an identity or to, in support of it, allow or prohibit conduct and viewpoints. This is in contrast with the representations of queers in English-language comic strips, where, according to Edward Sewell, queer cartoonists focus "on the creation of a thoroughly queer culture that often is in opposition, if not direct conflict, with the dominant heterosexual culture."[8]

The bodies of the three principal protagonists in *Chasing the Crown* move freely between being subject and object, fucking and being fucked, narcissistic identification and voyeuristic objectification, sometimes encompassing all of these states simultaneously. This is a characteristic of many yaoi stories and it is enhanced by yaoi's being a form that recreates canonical texts. Media characters seen first in canon, inscribed therein with a relatively fixed set of traits, are seen again and again in each new yaoi work, each time with their needs reimagined and their desires newly enacted. These continually evolving representations occur in a field of free-floating homoeroticism that lacks an oppositional context that might obstruct them. This fluidity is unlike the real-world construction of gender qualities into a state of opposing masculine and feminine sexual identities.

Eve Kosofsky Sedgwick describes the calculus of sexual identity in the West on a scale of masculine to feminine. She enumerates sixteen paired traits for sexual identity, showing how the elements of each masculine-feminine pair are constructed as binary opposites. They form a set shielding Western masculinity from things deemed nonmasculine ("Queer" 7). Yaoi disrupts this panoply. It does so acutely in works featuring young children.

Chasing the Crown has five six-year-old boys living with Duo and Heero, mirror images, as it were, of the older characters in terms of both appearance and personalities (figure 12.4). The pilots took in two of the children, Kenny and Duan, when they destroyed the base on which the children were living. The authors portray them in ways that maintain some stereotypically male attributes for fighters, such as their easy skill at using explosives to destroy military targets, while more often showing them tenderly touching each other, holding on to one another, as Kenny holds on to Duan's braid. This sign of their intense friendship and mutual need is a nonsexual echo of the relationship between Heero and Duo. The young boys' deep affection for each other is validated in their minds by that between the older pilots. The protection and love that the boys derive from the pilots' custody contrast starkly with Western culture, where, writes Sedgwick, not-masculine-enough boys and youth are effaced from the discourse of same-sex attracted adults, leaving them even more vulnerable to homophobic predation than they might otherwise be.[9]

Yaoi recalls Sedgwick's conception of queer as "a continuing moment, movement, motive—recurrent, eddying, *troublant*" ("Forward" xii). Western yaoi may have elements of queer, but as a genre it is not queer, if for no other reason than most of the yaoi creators with whom I have talked expressed disparate motives for their activities. Most refused to label what they did under any one rubric, including "queer."

Part of what might account for the intensity of the criticism of yaoi by some men who identify as gay is the importance of seeing. Whether in illustrations created by yaoi artists or in descriptions of yaoi characters gazing at each other, seeing is vital to yaoi's purpose of expressing erotic desire. Seeing is as important to many gay-identified males who cruise other males for sex

Figure 12.4   Kitsune, *Mite, mite!* Heero Yuy carrying a younger Duo Maxwell. April 2000, <http://www.silvertales.com>.

and/or use visual pornography. These activities can be a way of affirming their individual sexual interests and linking them to their identity as gay men. Yaoi resists static conceptions of gender and the construction of identities. Yaoi's images may appear "confused" to Satō because they refuse position or definition beyond that of a wide-ranging homoeroticism, one which may not fit his or others' conceptions of "gay."

Yaoi, *shōnen-ai*, boys' love, and slash are widespread. Yaoi allows the imagination free rein to queer the idea that gender boundaries should be fixed or that they should exist at all. It not only troubles culturally dominant notions of identity and gender, it also empowers people—notably youth, who have little power—to resist them. As such it represents a critical nexus in the theory and praxis of gender.

NOTES

1. For Japanese yaoi and boys' love generally, see McLelland and Suzuki. For a description of Western fans reading a Japanese boys' love text, see Sabucco. For slash, see Decarnin. For Western yaoi, see McHarry, "Yaoi: Redrawing" and "Yaoi."

2. Yaoi is a type of play, as its sardonic name implies, the acronym for *yamanashi, ochinashi, iminashi*, or "no climax, no point, no meaning." In talking with yaoi fans in Canada, Mexico, the United Kingdom and the United States, the only common denominator I found as to why they like yaoi is because it is fun.

3. Lunsing, 9. In 2002 almost 400,000 people, many of them young women and teenage girls, attended Comiket, a biannual fan-organized event in Tokyo (the largest of several held in Japanese cities), to buy or sell *dōjinshi*, much of it yaoi-themed and created by individual artists or small circles of friends. See Iawamoto, editor of *Biblos*.

4. The search criterion for the Google searches was "yaoi." Returns were Web pages with the word in roman characters. Google searches are subject to large fluctuations for searches with a high number of returns, but the trend of steady and rapid growth between 2003 and 2006 is clear.

5. *Gundam* (War Story) began as an anime on Japanese TV in 1979 (Simmons 7). It follows a genre of super-robot anime popular in the 1970s, the story lines of which typically describe a male child or youth put in charge of a giant robot that must defend the world under threat from an external menace (Snyder 2000). *Gundam* was unsuccessful in its only season on Japanese TV, but gained popularity in reruns, spawning a large number of follow-on products. *Gundam Wing*, the anime canonical for the yaoi story discussed in this chapter, was first shown on Japanese TV in 1995 and in North America via the Cartoon Network in 2000 (Simmons 8).

6. John Russell discusses the effects of racialization in Japanese constructions of blackness, which he terms "simulations," that have been contested by some living in Japan who identify as black (6, 12). Jagose (101–26) and Sullivan (43–52) provide several examples of the contestation of "queer," including antithetical definitions by those publishing for a nonheterosexual audience: the editors of the Toronto queerzine *Bimbox* and the editor-in-chief of the gay and lesbian magazine *OutWeek* (44–45).

7. The series, by RavynFyre et al., is comprised of six stories totaling 116 chapters. The age given for the Gundam Wing pilots in *Mission: Arcadia and Beyond* is seventeen, not fifteen as it is canonically.

8. Sewell is writing about publications such as *XY Magazine*. Queer characters in comic strips drawn by heterosexual cartoonists for mainstream newspapers, on the other hand, do "not have any clear distinguishing characteristics to differentiate [them] from the dominant culture" (268). Sewell defines "queer" in part as "a sexual orientation different from heterosexual or straight" (271).

9. Sedgwick characterizes this erasure as "annihilating homophobic, gynephobic, and pedophobic hatred" ("How" 158). Piontek extends Sedgwick's analysis in arguing that the rationale presented by the American Psychiatric Association for its pathologization of effeminacy in male children is paradoxical (60).

WORKS CITED

Anonymous. Interview with Mark McHarry. 9 Feb. 2006.

Butler, Judith. "Imitation and Gender Insubordination." Salih, 119–37.

————. "The Lesbian Phallus and the Morphological Imaginary." Salih, 138–80.

Decarnin, C.M. "Slash Fiction." *Encyclopedia of Erotic Literature.* Ed. Gaëtan Brulotte and John Phillips. New York: Routledge, 2006. 1233–35.

FanFiction.Net. 15 May 2006 <www.fanfiction.net>.

Grosz, Elizabeth. *Volatile Bodies: Toward a Corporeal Feminism.* Bloomington: Indiana UP, 1994.

Iawamoto. Press conference. Yaoi-Con. San Francisco. 19 Oct. 2002.

Jagose, Annamarie. *Queer Theory: An Introduction.* New York: New York UP, 1996.

Lunsing, Wim. "*Yaoi Ronsō*: Discussing Depictions of Male Homosexuality in Japanese Girls' Comics, Gay Comics and Gay Pornography." *Intersections: Gender, History and Culture in the Asian Context,* 12 Jan. 2006. 15 May 2006 <http://wwwsshe.murdoch.edu.au/intersections/issue12_contents.html>.

Maldoror. *Freeport.* 2004–2006. *Gundam Wing Addiction.* 13 May 2006 <http://gwaddiction.com/Maldoror.shtml>.

McHarry, Mark. "Yaoi: Redrawing Male Love." *The Guide* 23 (2003): 29–34. 13 May 2006 <www.guidemag.com/content/index.cfm?id=225>.

————. "Yaoi." *Encyclopedia of Erotic Literature.* 1445–47.

McLelland, Mark. "No Climax, No Point, No Meaning? Japanese Women's Boy-Love Sites on the Internet." *Journal of Communication Inquiry* 24 (2000): 274–91.

Piontek, Thomas. *Queering Gay and Lesbian Studies.* Urbana: U of Illinois P, 2006.

RavynFyre et al. *Chasing the Crown.* The Extended Family Fics Index. *Gundam Wing Addiction.* 10 Mar. 2006 <http://www.gwaddiction.com/bonnevon/exfam.htm>.

————. "Part Twenty-five."

————. "Part Thirty-two."

————. "Part Thirty-three."

Russell, John G. "Playing (with) Race: Authenticity, Mimesis, and Racial Performance in the Transcultural Diaspora—Or How Black Has Become the New Black." Race in Japan: Changes and Challenges. Sophia University, Tokyo. 4 Mar. 2006.

Sabucco, Veruska. "Guided Fan Fiction: Western 'Readings' of Japanese Homosexual-Themed Texts." *Mobile Cultures: New Media in Queer Asia.* Ed. Chris Berry, Fran Martin, and Audrey Yue. Durham: Duke UP, 2003. 70–86.

Salih, Sara, ed. *The Judith Butler Reader.* Malden, MA: Blackwell, 2004.

Sedgwick, Eve Kosofsky. "Forward: T Times." Sedgwick, *Tendencies* xi–xvi.

————. "How to Bring Your Kids Up Gay: The War on Effeminate Boys." Sedgwick, *Tendencies,* 154–64.

————. "Queer and Now." Sedgwick, *Tendencies,* 1–20.

————. "Paranoid Reading and Reparative Reading; or, You're So Paranoid, You Probably Think This Introduction Is about You." Introduction. *Novel Gazing: Queer Readings in Fiction.* Ed. Eve Kosofsky Sedgwick. Durham: Duke UP, 1997. 1–40.

————. *Tendencies.* Durham: Duke UP, 1993.

Sewell, Edward H., Jr. "Queer Characters in Comic Strips." *Comics and Ideology.* Ed. Matthew P. McAllister, Edward H. Sewell, Jr., and Ian Gordon. New York: Lang, 2006. 251–74.

Sheppard, Simon. Gay Porn vs. Yaoi Panel. Yaoi-Con. San Francisco. 18 Oct. 2002.

Simmons, Mark. Introduction. *Mobile Suit Gundam: Awakening, Escalation, Confrontation.* By Tomino Yoshiyuki. Trans. Frederik L. Schodt. Berkeley: Stone Bridge Press, 2004. 7–11.

Snyder, Stephen B. "Giant Robots/Distant Fathers: Size and Anxiety in Japanese Animation." Session, Entertaining Passions: Amusement and Obsession in Japanese Popular Culture. Association for Asian Studies Annual Meeting, San Diego, 9–12 Mar. 2000.

Sullivan, Nikki. *A Critical Introduction to Queer Theory.* New York: New York UP, 2003.

Suzuki, Kazuko. "Pornography or Therapy? Japanese Girls Creating the Yaoi Phenomenon." *Millennium Girls: Today's Girls Around the World.* Ed. Sherrie A. Inness. London: Rowman, 1998. 243–67.

Thorn, Matt. "Girls and Women Getting Out of Hand: The Pleasure and Politics of Japan's Amateur Comics Community." *Fanning the Flames: Fans and Consumer Culture in Contemporary Japan.* Ed. William W. Kelly. Albany: State U of New York P, 2004. 169–87.

Tyr. "Why Yaoi?" 2000. *Gundam Wing Addiction.* 13 May 2006 <http://gwaddiction.com/yaoi1.shtml>.

Vincent, Keith J. "Envisioning the Homosexual in Yaoi." Conceptualising Gender in Different Cultural Contexts Conference. The School of Oriental and African Studies, U of London. 2–3 May 2002.

CHAPTER 13

WHY (NOT) QUEER?: AMBIVALENCE ABOUT "POLITICS" AND QUEER IDENTIFICATION IN AN ONLINE COMMUNITY IN TAIWAN

TERRI HE

Abstract: *It is perhaps not widely recognized that queer travels across the traditional boundaries of time, language, culture, geography, and history, as a coping strategy for LGBT people around the world to find a point of departure in dealing with their experiences of social oppression or marginalization. Considering specifically queer's translingual and transnational aspect, I set out in this chapter some discussions of queer/*tongzhi/tonxinglian *in contemporary Taiwan society, where the traveling of queer is simultaneously framed in the dialectics of "the East and West" as well as of "China and Taiwan." Giving an example to illustrate my arguments, I focus on participants in an online community named Spiteful Tots, where people collectively keep away from the politics of naming, such as* tongzhi *and* queer. *By looking into some of the problematics of queer's traveling in this chapter, I hope to shed light upon the many faces of queer in a socioculturally glocalized context.*

THE CENTRAL ISSUE THIS CHAPTER EXPLORES is how queer as a political identity is negotiated in Taiwan.[1] This research question will be put in the context of an online community in which, among the participants' different sexualities, the majority are self-identified gay men. Participants in this online community, named Spiteful Tots, have been part of the lesbian, gay, bisexual, and transgender (LGBT) pride parades for three years from 2003 to 2005, and they would not have marched on these occasions had they not gone online and got to know and talk to each other.[2] Participants in Spiteful Tots come from places all over Taiwan, and yet most of them have now moved to or around the capital city Taipei. Almost all of them, born in or after the 1970s, had previously received education in colleges and universities in Taiwan, where they familiarized themselves with networked computers.[3] These online subjects are, then, well-educated, capable of using technology, and live in an urban area, but despite their limited social range, they are interesting to investigate as they represent in Taiwan a specific group or generation that rose after public discussions and social discourses were enabled by the lifting of martial law and were informed by feminism and queer studies.[4] The Spiteful Tots participants and their community are therefore intricately bound to the backdrop of the lifting of martial law and the social immersion in Western discourses in Taiwan, through which their sexual identifications become a problematic site.

My discussion of this topic inevitably starts from a number of perspectives that are informed by current political, social, and cultural situations in Taiwan, to and by which Spiteful Tots as a whole is connected and influenced. In this in-depth exploration, I hope to set up some initial theorization and critical investigation revolving around the traveling of queer from the so-called West to, in this case, the islands of Taiwan.[5] I start with a brief overview of sexuality studies undertaken by local researchers, then move to discuss analyses of feminist movements, the rapid developments in information and communication technology (ICT), and the political roles that China and the West/the United States each play in Taiwan. I will argue that the three politicoanalytic subject matters—sexuality, technology, and political affairs with China—are ultimately intertwined and mutually informing to one another within this specific context. I use Spiteful Tots as an example in order to concretize and foreground the arguments I try to make in this chapter. I would like to make it clear, however, that the representation of Spiteful Tots, while based on my observations and participations in this online community since the year 2000, is not meant to be exhaustive but instead illustrative of the changing and multilayered sociopolitical manifestations in the society of Taiwan. The discussion and illustration of Spiteful Tots community is understood from the perspective of the sexual dissidents in the said community embedded in a specific time and space, enabled by the invention of Internet technology and impacted by contestation of contemporary ideas.

A Brief Overview

Anxieties and Technological/Social Developments

A country with very limited land, space, and natural resources, Taiwan has long depended on its people's hard work and devotion to its economy. In the early days, the major lifeblood of the economy came from labor-intensive industry such as textile and bicycle production; nowadays, it is the technicians, laboratory researchers, and engineers who have proliferated and dominate the job market. Basically, fast development of ICT—Internet technology included—is a significant driving force for Taiwan's economic well-being and its heightened international status. Accompanied by these substantial changes in Taiwanese economic and social structures is the challenge of its own position amongst foreign partners and counterparts (Howe; Simon). Taiwan, as small islands, cannot but endeavor to build both collaborative and competitive relations with the outside world, but its de facto status almost always hinders its access to international visibility. For Taiwanese people, as a result, the pain of not being recognized as a country in spite of its for-all-intents independence has permanently marked its national identity.[6]

A fact that can be seen as related to this wounded psyche of not being officially recognized as a country is that Taiwan spared no efforts in developing its capacity for high-tech industries in response to the restructuring global economy. The building of infrastructure for ICT and the implementation of the Taiwan Academic Network throughout colleges and universities island-wide were in the 1990s completed with the intention of helping Taiwan catch up with its Western counterparts. This idea of catching up is common to most of the East-Asian countries, as they tend to run parallel in terms of economic development. What distinguishes Taiwan in the familiar catching-up scenarios, though, is this anxiety of mirroring Taiwan in the eye of the West. Technological development so often and so readily lends itself as a criteria determining a country's state of development, a concept that has itself been defined by Western models. Consequently, in order to make the islands known to other peoples and countries, it is considered essential to throw ourselves into the technology race and strive to take the lead. Behind this drive is again the concern about being a country not understood by the West in particular and by the world in general, a concern that originates from the scant international attention paid to Taiwan because of its marginal and illegitimate national status.

On a different and yet related track, Taiwan, as part of the Chinese-speaking world, manages to become impressively much more liberal about nonnormative sexuality than all the others in the area, which in turn allows more space for queer expressions in public and thus catches attention from the West. This liberal attitude, in my opinion, has much to do with the historical timing of the lifting of martial law, as well as with Taiwan's willingness to tacitly accept "Western imports" at the time. Toward the end of the twentieth century, to be sure, Taiwan started to find itself more and more deeply caught in a transnational phase, and in the last decade, witnessed drastic changes in its notions of gender and sexuality. With the rise of gay/lesbian/queer movements in the 1990s, male homosexuality, lesbianism, and queer sexuality, which used to be understood as unspeakable in public, have become one of the hottest matters in Taiwan. This is evident in popular culture (TV soaps, variety shows, and movies) and operates alongside new Western expressions of sexuality— queer, feminism, translated novels, and imported art works.[7]

While one may argue that this phenomenon is in part brought about by globalization, something quite readily mated with capitalism and Western influence, it is also acknowledged as having much to do with the lifting of martial law in 1987.[8] In that year, governmental control of printed matters, TV programs, radio broadcasting, and electronic media relaxed, and Taiwan was immediately saturated with Western feminist, lesbian, and gay theories and discourses. When the term queer was coined and utilized as a political articulation in the West, queer discourse also found its way to Taiwan. As Tze-lan D. Sang writes:

> The rise in Taiwan during the last decade of novels and whole collections dealing with the subject of lesbian eroticism and lesbian subjectivity—which occurred amid a burgeoning lesbian and gay identity politics and the general proliferation of queer discourses—distinguished the cultural scene of Taiwan not only from that of the PRC [People's Republic of China, commonly known as China] but also from that of the former British colony Hong Kong or any other Chinese-speaking society. (256–57)

The proliferation of nonnormative sexual discourses and liberalism found in this period of time in Taiwan, although inspiring, opened up a complex and dialectical process of negotiations between globalization and localization in aspects of sexuality.

POLITICAL DEBATES AND SOCIAL DISCOURSE IN THE PAST DECADES

The all-at-once exposure to feminist, gay and lesbian, and queer movements involves a multifaceted and interactive course of translation that is still going on. But first, before proceeding with discussions on the translationality and transnationality, let us return to the time and historical background of 1987 with a view to contextualizing this time period. The decade between 1979 and 1989 saw competition between two contending discourses of democratization, which are, for one, the demand of appreciating the land and culture of Taiwan, and, for the other, an insistence on the belief that Kuomingtang (Nationalists from Mainland China in 1949) would eventually beat down Communism and recapture China.[9] These discourses are represented by the earlier inhabitants of Taiwan who regarded themselves as Taiwanese (though previously under Japanese colonization) and the later settlers from Mainland China in the 1950s (roughly identified as Kuomingtang-related). This conflict in interpreting and understanding Taiwan is demonstrated by people's current self-identifications: no one can escape from the ambiguity of being both Chinese and Taiwanese. For example, I grew up in the 1980s and was educated in my childhood to consider myself one of the little freedom fighters who wished to rescue those suffering fellow nationals in the Communist mainland; I thought of myself as an "authentic" Chinese from Taiwan, the Republic of China—not the People's Republic of China.[10] Then in my teenage years, there was the shift, demonstrated in sites as diverse as textbooks and the yearly presidential speeches on TV; instead of asserting this Chinese identity, the argument was for building up a democratic nation-state in Taiwan. Such a political shift was an embarrassment for the then in-power Kuomingtang, a move that also contributed to its later failure in securing the majority in the congress in March 2000.

At this time, the feminist movement, as a landmark social movement in Taiwan coming from the West, flourished after the end of martial law. The success of feminism was focused on the initial accomplishment of the first presidential election and the political democratization process from 1987 to 1989 and was enabled by a public need for respite from the deadlock between independence and unification camps over the eternal question of national identity.[11] Lesbian and queer movements, around the same period, also started out as branches within the feminist movement. The first Internet group, Women Zhijian (a name that comes from the French film *Entre Nous* [Between Us] with lesbian themes) was initiated in 1990, populated by both white American researchers and Taiwanese lesbian women, each taking up a half of the group.[12] In the Internet group, at least half of the participants were Western. The first sign of queer movement was fashioned in the Queer Special Issue of the new, left journal *The Isle's Margin* in 1994, with articles such as Ta-wei Chi and Tang-mo's "Ku'er Xiaoxiao Baike" ["Queer Mini-Encyclopedia"] and "Zhizhunü zh Wen—Rus zi Shiren de Gangmen Yanshen Baozhang" ["Kiss of the Spider Woman—Milky Thin Thread Extends and Grows from Wet Anus"], and Lucifer Hung's "Kashanzhuola de Kuoqiang Yu Gaochao" ["Kashanzhuola's Mouth and Orgasm"]. These works showed that the authors were very familiar with Western theoretical terms and ideas. The queer movement during this time was significantly influenced by Western sexual and theoretical discourses.

As feminist, gay, lesbian, and queer discourses were introduced to Taiwan during the same period of time, the trajectory of these movements was quite different from those generated in the Western society. Whereas the queer movement in the West was preceded by the successful strategy of resorting to identity politics, Taiwan's feminist, gay, lesbian, and queer movements launched simultaneously, with a good number of the activists and participants taking part in more than one movement. Under such circumstances, I argue that queer was not granted the opportunity to be comprehended or utilized in the way the West had theorized it. Queer, rather, was juxtaposed with other terms such as gay and lesbian, and indiscriminately thought of as yet another term coming from the West referring to homosexuality.

TRANSLATION AND HYBRIDITY

At this point, to approach the local understanding and employment of feminism, lesbian and gay movements, and queer studies means to, first of all, return to the translational and translingual practices. In her Translingual Practice, Lydia Liu argues that she is

> interested in theoretical problems that lead up to an investigation of the condition of translation and of discursive practices that ensue from initial interlingual contracts between languages. Broadly defined, the study of translinguial practice examines the process by which new words, meanings, discourses, and modes of representation arise, circulate, and acquire legitimacy within the host language due to, or in spite of, the latter's contract/collision with the guest language. Meanings, therefore, are not so much "transformed" when concepts pass from the guest language to the host language as invented within the local environment of the latter. In that sense, translation is no longer a neutral event untouched by the contending interests of political and ideological struggles. Instead, it becomes the very site of such struggles where the guest language is forced to encounter the host language . . . until new words and meanings emerge in the host language itself. (26)

Liu articulates that various translingual practices simply must include the efforts of adaptation, domestication, and negotiation. In the process of translating "identifying with queer," for instance, the focus and concern may therefore have to be changed, revised, and deflected. In between issues of translingual practices, therefore, speech acts and power dynamics/interplay should be viewed as deserving most of the attention and should always be carefully examined.

In terms of the popular reception, there have been numerous disagreements among gay and lesbian people interested in academic theories. Sometimes for them to adopt a feminist stance seems like conforming to the Western norms and mores, which reflects that some notions of gender and sexuality are considered far-fetched and unrelated to the Taiwanese context (Sang 261). Sometimes, too, the poor public reception of these "new" identities seemed like an inherent translational failure or difficulty. If closely examined, however, what determines the similar and the different is profoundly about the willingness to understand and attend to the local specificities. The translational practice between the West and Taiwan, then, is not at all about producing or importing something completely new, but rather about finding the most effective signifier to connect with the local culture, ideology, and phenomena that already exist.

The issue of translation, moreover, can be understood from yet another perspective. The seemingly imported terms and discourses simultaneously put Taiwan in a difficult situation due to its long-term protecting and nurturing relationship with the United States: that is, everything that is already Americanized does not feel so much new and foreign to Taiwanese people but simply normal, familiar, or at times even mundane.[13] This every day Americanizedness further exposes a hybrid Taiwanese culture that in many ways has not only integrated the foreign but has also made it home. Hybridity as a way of life creates an ambivalent relationship to people's general reactions to various ideas derived from feminist theories and gender studies because, although symbolizing something modern and advanced, they are at the same time also taken as being banal.

AN ANALYSIS OF QUEER/TONGZHI AND THE ONLINE COMMUNITY OF SPITEFUL TOTS

LOCAL TRANSLATIONS OF QUEER

The first time queer was seen in public was when some Western movies produced in the late 1980s were introduced to Taiwan under the name New Queer Cinema. This was a small-scale film festival organized by the same group of people who had previously organized Hong Kong's Lesbian and Gay Film Festival. Later, in 1992, in Taipei, New Queer Cinema was translated into traditional Chinese by these organizers from Hong Kong as "Tongzhi Film Festival." Tongzhi was an appropriation from "comrade" in the Communist context in China.[14] Queer's first presence in Taiwan was thus simultaneously both an ironic and a political appropriation of Communism.

Tongzhi has now become the popular way of addressing homosexual people in Taiwan, and this kind of appropriation has also resulted in the usage of tongzhi, queer, gay, and lesbian becoming interchangeable, with tongzhi being the ultimate all-inclusive term. The term "tongzhi" thus neglects the many levels of politics and meanings of different identities—gay, lesbian, and queer—to the extent of losing these identities' originally intended political objective, while simultaneously neglecting to include other sexualities such as those of trans people and sadomasochists. Extensively used as a euphemism for homosexual, tongzhi has so far been limited to sexual identities such as gay and lesbian and is somehow a kind of equivalent of queer, although it does not demonstrate the politics of queer. In its daily and conversational presences, then, tongzhi has become a term specific to Taiwan, offering specific boundaries to its inclusiveness, boundaries that are different from those pertaining to the Anglophone homosexual.

But, as it turns out, tongzhi does have its own politics in the Taiwanese context. Due to China's military threats, Tongzhi as an identity is steeply embedded in the marginality of the country and its society. As an ironic appropriation of Communist comradeship, then, the term criticizes China's pseudo-Communism and homophobia. Through satire, consequently, tongzhi resonates with the peripheral's status of being constantly haunted by the vast shadow of China, which in this situation embodies both authoritarianism that objects to democracy and heterosexism that bans homosexuality. Tongzhi thus encapsulates a spirit of relentless resistance as well as a state of living with the enemy in that tongzhi people resist as well as identify with the enemy's language. By identifying with tongzhi and recognizing the political power endowed with this term, the irony of this simultaneous refusal and acceptance is indeed an infinitely rich and subtly intricate one.

However, the translation from queer to tongzhi, which had happened as a result of some sense of mocking humor in the film festival in 1992 in Taipei, was done not without some risks. Tongzhi, as an all-inclusive term for gays, lesbians, and queers in Taiwan suggests one arbitrary way of dealing with various facets of identity politics in relation to nonnormative sexuality. The underlying danger of doing this is of overlooking many important nuances and differences in alternative expressions of sexuality that, in addition, render the use of tongzhi as a political term as potentially counterproductive as it might risk reiterating the sexual alternatives as deviants of norms, instead of allowing multiplicity, traversing boundaries of identities, and exposing these identities' arbitrariness. Thus, what might follow could be further social discrimination (e.g., tongzhi as associated with AIDS and drugs) as well as the burdening of sexuality issues with the unsettled business between China and Taiwan to reassert validity and urgency in their own right. In fact, tongzhi has already started to show a tendency of being reclaimed due to negative mainstream media representations. Although tongzhi is still widely employed as a political term in Taiwan, the public finds it closely associated with controversial issues such as promiscuity and drug use—as if tongzhi has been duped and corrupted by the West and global sexuality imperialism. This tendency toward social disciplines along with emergent concerns about Western corruption bespeaks the strong affinity between agency and globalization. Globalization and Western discourse empower the local sexual dissidents, although they also put these subjects in difficult situations because of their non-Western locations.

Another parallel development of sexual terminology in Taiwan occurred when "queer" was introduced as *ku'er* in 1994. Different from tongzhi, ku'er is a transliteration that means "cool kid" provided in 1994 by Ta wei Chi, a then graduate student in the English Department in National Taiwan University, in the special queer issue of Isle's Margin. As the academic version of queer, Ku'er is imbued with a much more Western academic and intellectual genealogy and is thus in a problematic way even more positive and thus empowering. Rather than finding the equivalent of freak, pervert, or abnormal in traditional Chinese, ku'er as a term does not go into the strategy of preemptively transforming a historically stained slur into empowerment.[15] Instead, it asserts that to be queer is to be a cool kid, which conveys that at the time going for a popular image was easier to embrace for sexual alternatives— despite the implication of subsequently losing its edge.

On the other hand, as queer came to Taiwan almost the same time as in the West, it was literally impossible for the society to formulate discussions and create similar argumentative momentums for queer studies. For one, Taiwan had not had many years of groundwork of social movements fighting for women and LGBT people's rights. And for the other, the repression of women and LGBT people is still rooted in the patrilineal society of Taiwan, which narrows down the possibility of a preemptive attempt to proudly assume an identity such as queer in the West. In order to make queer survive in Taiwan, ku'er simply has to be something quite different from queer, and the meaning-making/negotiating will be a long path in which selection, adaptation, domestication, and reinvention ceaselessly take place.

To start with, ku'er was perhaps best re-imagined and redefined in a playful tone in *Ku'er qishilu: Taiwan Dangdai Queer Lunshu Duben* [Queer Archipelago: A Reader of the Queer Discourse in Taiwan] edited by Chi. Chi's *Ku'er qishilu* is a collection of scholarly essays. These essays are written in a creative, resourceful, and ironic way. This collection is enjoyable to read and such writings cause one to feel optimistic about the future of ku'er people in Taiwan; it also testifies to their privilege of being urban citizens, well-educated, and usually more from the middle class than the lower class, in short, people more at the social center than on the margins of the island. This implication of ku'er as an identity that is readily stratified and unavailable to those who are not familiar with the manipulation of knowledge has been one of the most important critiques of ku'er culture and identity in Taiwan.

Inasmuch as it is less accessible, ku'er remains largely strange and unheard of by the general public in Taiwan. Especially after a new drink called "Qoo" was introduced into the market by Japanese Coca Cola company in 1999, ku'er as a term is much more likely to be related to the cute and blue cartoon-like character whose name in traditional Chinese is also "ku'er," with exactly the same Chinese characters.[16] In this respect, how ku'er can be effectively reintroduced and perhaps metaphorically recreated so as to be made available for political assertions becomes an immediate issue. At this point, I would like to direct the discussion threads to Spiteful Tots for a contextualized examination of queer—both in the sense of tongzhi and ku'er—in Taiwan.

REJECTION OF QUEER

Spiteful Tots' rejection of the identity of tongzhi, primarily expressed online, has been going on right from its instigation.[17] As explained, queer is—first and foremost—understood by the Taiwanese as tongzhi, and its status as "an equivalent" of queer is necessarily a problematic one. But in this rejection of identifying the online community of Spiteful Tots as a tongzhi community, there is something significantly similar about these online participants' concerns for tongzhi as well as for queer, which is the suggested political implication of these terms. Instead of believing in the political empowerment of "tongzhi" or Western-imported and locally-transformed "ku'er" in the Taiwanese context, the online community of Spiteful Tots chose to veer away from it without hesitation. This choice results from a wish to be treated as one of the ordinary and common crowd, instead of being politically active or Westernized. As tongzhi, queer, and Internet technology have always been associated with the West, their rejection, despite coming from this specific time and social climate, manifests a break away from the complicated politics, globally and locally. However, they did call themselves Spiteful Tots, as the central idea was to self-mock their existence as "somewhat different" from the "normal and ordinary crowd" in that "they were simply more spiteful than the kind of people one usually knows."[18] As a frequent visitor and quasi-member of Spiteful Tots for more than five years, I tend to think that it had more to do with the rejection of "the heterosexual majority" as well as their distrust in "politics," rather than with some wishful naming strategy that was meant to enable themselves to become "spiteful and proud."[19]

At this point, the implications of "politics" might need some more exploration. Politics in Taiwan, ranging from personal beliefs to group dynamics and then to the country's unsettled business with China, has been in some sense stigmatized into being nothing but helplessly complex, if hopeless and deadlocked, because of the China-Taiwan issue. Incidentally, as from the late nineteenth century Taiwan has not been self-determining for a hundred years but has rather been continuously under the rule of Ching Dynasty China (which lost Taiwan to Japan), Colonial Japan, and Nationalist Mainlanders. Politics on a national and social level has been something that people in Taiwan have little say about. The society of Taiwan, as if developing a corresponding strategy, has evolved into being a gregarious, communal, and collective one, with the intention of helping each other survive different regimes without resorting to political acts that might induce juridical sentences or possible danger to oneself or the family. In this situation, then, championing the political in the coinage of tongzhi and queer is recognized as undesirable for people, and interpersonal relations are likely to become fragile as diverse viewpoints cause disharmony, disputes, or verbal conflicts. The best way to elude this kind of predicament, perhaps, is to be neither specific nor absolute when it comes to politics; elusion and flexibility provide the basis of a smooth and ingratiating manner. The least painful and troubling coping method, following this line of thought, is to downplay or ignore politics.

But, on the other hand, these participants' rejection of tongzhi does not keep them from joining in the annual pride parades in Taipei. I thus wonder what it might be that connects members of Spiteful Tots community and makes them willing to come together and march in the LGBT parades. While the LGBT pride cannot but be labeled as yet another political counter to maintain Taiwan's democracy and progression vis-à-vis China, participants in the Spiteful Tots community who joined pride events seem to be drawn in despite their rejection of both Taiwanese tongzhi and Western queer. I would therefore like to offer a brief history based on ethnographic research, with a view to probe into some ideas in relation to this seeming contradiction.

Spiteful Tots was started by a group of gay and heterosexual people who knew each other as friends in a university. At the moment of establishment, it was quickly agreed that this online community, in spite of its members' sexuality and their preferred topics of discussions, would not be a tongzhi community. Messages on the discussion board either directly criticize tongzhi as an identity or express members' discomfort with this term. This is partly because of tongzhi's ready links to its excessive media exposure, and partly because homosexual (*tongxinglian* in Mandarin) as a term seems to be the more realistic term for them.[20]

As variants of *tongxinglian* (homosexual), *tongnan* (homo-man/men) and *tongnü* (homo-woman/women) were frequently applied in the online community of Spiteful Tots. Tongnan and tongnü are the combinations of tongxinglian (homosexual) and *nanren* (male person) or *nüren* (female person). These terms were considered neutral and realistic, without much intended political implications. Before tongzhi became the popular form of address, tongnan and tongnü were used only inside gay and lesbian circles, not readily understood outside these groups, and did not, in themselves, communicate much objection to heteronormativity. Tongzhi, after achieving its common parlance in public and media in Taiwan, appeared fashionable and modern, charged with political strength and a hint of progression in the society.[21] Tongnan and tongnü are thus either not in use anymore or simply, if mistakenly, thought of as derivatives of tongzhi.

While at present the term homosexual has been largely replaced by tongzhi in Taiwan, the participants in Spiteful Tots are still uncomfortable using tongzhi and occasionally challenge the term as a fad that people in general pick up in order to feel fashionable and in. In their mind, they prefer whatever seems to convey "what it simply is" rather than "what it has to be politically or publicly." Forum board messages that deal with naming either avoid self-naming or simply fall back to the now-rarely-used-elsewhere terms of tongnan and tongnü without obvious fuss about such terms and their meanings. At any rate, the community of Spiteful Tots moves away from the political regardless of the social shifts outside of their community from homosexual to tongzhi. The circumstances, however, have changed gradually. After Spiteful Tots took part in the annual pride parade three times, and after the creation of greater awareness as a result of media coverage of tongzhi, members feel less awkward and more comfortable using tongzhi—at times tongzhi can even be a way of self-naming, though, again, not completely without some doubt and trepidation. It is never a flat name, like tongnan or tongnü.

The Spiteful Tots members' strategy of dealing with the various names serves as cues that may validate my focus on politics. To start with, regular members of Spiteful Tots, or online participants who have been in the community for more than three years, tend in general to downplay the political aspects of their sexuality. There is something ordinary about "who we are" that seems too precious to cast away although they would also like to assert a kind of spitefulness as difference. They are very aware of their desire to be seen as ordinary. This preference to ordinariness, as I conceive of it, might have to do with the kind of collectivism prevalent in Taiwanese society, in the sense that one is neither better nor worse than the other, but simply the same. In maintaining a kind of sameness, whose concern is not so much equality but rather a sign of friendliness, participants in the Spiteful Tots community have always strived for a harmonious atmosphere during the online exchanges and dialogues, where ordinariness functions as a key to the funny, sharp, and yet congenial tone throughout the textuality in the community as a whole.

The ordinariness that is so necessary in their preferred way of seeing themselves as a community does at times make them shy away from exposure, which is perhaps why for the past three pride parades they have always been masked, fully clothed, and covered, instead of showing off their bodies— something groups in Western prides parades would do. Explaining their choice of being ordinary over political, I do not want to suggest that they are then necessarily placid and content with the current situation, but simply that they favor a kind of companionship that is free of conflicts and troubles, perhaps at some level as an escape from the overwhelming and looming political imbroglios of China-Taiwan issues.

Since their avoidance of politics may be potentially similar to being indifferent and hypocritical, it is perhaps appropriate to infer that the participants in the Spiteful Tots community have a more privileged social status in spite of their underprivileged sexuality, and that they are therefore able to afford their choice of being nonpolitical. On the other hand, to understand the non-West again proves to be the process of understanding the local ecology, where, in this case, politics did not seem an integral part of life for most of the people in Taiwan, as the Taiwanese had been under the government of mainlanders for at least forty years, without having their say in concrete and political matters. Under such circumstances, interpersonal relations among one another really become a primary concern, whose politics functions in a radically different way and yet is much more accessible and negotiable than the politics over unification and independence.

Although members of the Spiteful Tots community made a point of staying clear of politics, their lives as separate from the mainstream sexual and social norms are indeed readily political and their online self-representation in the community is also about nothing but the politics of transnationality. The intentional avoidance of the political does not change the complicated nature of such matters, but simply underlines the difficulties in being who they are in the society where everyday experiences can all be seen related to the nation's anxieties and worries about China's threats. At this point I want to tie these experienced difficulties together with the idea of the online texts as vehicles that so readily and easily carry emotions, sensitivity, and feelings. The online community texts of Spiteful Tots are revelations of struggles, strengths, and escapes lived and experienced by these members in both online and offline scenarios, and are definitely not void of political force per se, no matter how much they prefer to downplay this specific dimension of their textual production. Their status as gay and lesbian people in everyday life is inevitably considered Western, and meanwhile their textual representations of their feelings and experiences are really evidence of negotiations between the global and the local. Through their collective wish to refuse queer/tongzhi and their willingness to join in the pride parades pleading for sexual citizenship, a necessary rupture between the name and deed can hence be witnessed, validated, and theorized as yet another path for understanding the politics of sexuality in the particular context of Taiwan.

NOTES

1. This chapter is an adaptation of some parts of my work-in-progress Ph.D. thesis at Centre for Women's Studies, University of York, U.K. Some of the materials have been presented in the panel discussion "Sexuality, Community and Cyberspace" in Not Just Sexuality, held by Centre for Women's Studies,

University of York in association with Feminist and Women's Studies Association in the United Kingdom and Ireland on 25 February 2005, and in my individual paper "The Traumatically Effected: Studies on a Haunted Online Community in Taiwan" in CongressCATH 2005 on The Ethics and Politics of Virtuality and Indexicality held by School of Fine Arts, History of Arts and Cultural Studies, University of Leeds on 3 July 2005. Additionally, I would like to thank Dr. Ann Kaloski-Naylor and Dr. Thomas Peele for having read it through and given me some advice for the betterment of this chapter.

2. Spiteful Tots is a pseudonym.

3. To protect the privacy of Spiteful Tots, I will not give their Web site. But it is based on one of the largest BBS sites named KKCity, where many online communities of all topics are sustained and visited daily by more than 200,000 people in Taiwan. Spiteful Tots was initiated in the year 2000, and was a private BBS site for almost a year. I was invited as a participant from the beginning, but did not start to take on a researcher's identity until 2003. Thus much of the observation will inevitably come from my knowledge gained from reading posted messages there as well as going back to the archived discussions; both to a certain extent are necessarily never "perfectly complete."

4. The privilege of living in the urban area of a country is a concept informed by Gayle S. Rubin, who writes: "Dissident sexuality is rarer and more closely monitored in small towns and rural areas. Consequently, metropolitan life continually beckons to young perverts. Sexual migration creates concentrated pools of potential partners, friends, and associates. It enables individuals to create adult, kin-like networks in which to live" (295).

5. Taiwan is composed of several islands, but in this chapter I will focus only on the main island of Taiwan, and most of the time on the metropolitan city of Taipei.

6. For more information please consult many monographs that deal with the multilayered reality of the people in Taiwan, a reality that has made an impact on the island's national identity; see Brown; Ching; Corcuff; and Roy.

7. Please refer to Chang; Chi.

8. See for example Champagne.

9. Please consult Roy, especially chapter three, for more detailed information about this part of history in Taiwan.

10. The many country names of Taiwan, Formosa, Taiwan and Republic of China, are witness of its complex historical and political past and present. Formosa was given in 1542 by Portuguese sailors on their way to Japan. Coming across an island not identified on their maps, they were amazed at the forest-cloaked land, and thus they shouted, "Ilha Formosa," meaning "Beautiful Island." Formosan, as a result, became the name for the early settlers in Taiwan during the Japanese occupation in nineteenth century. Taiwan was a name that has to do with the Dutch occupation in 1624–1662, a variant from how the Dutch called the peninsula "Tayouan," meaning terrace bay. After the Second World War, Taiwan was taken over by the Mainlander

Chinese government led by Chiang Kai-shek, and was the Republic of China (ROC) in the United Nations before March, 1979. After March, 1979, People's Republic of China (PRC), what we know as Mainland China nowadays, replaced ROC in the UN. However, in legal and official documents, ROC is still widely used despite the fact that it causes confusion. This intended confusion in the earlier times was done to assume the legitimacy of being the authentic China. But, of course, as I have explained, the display of authenticity now has been outdated and also quite undesirable since it goes against the current pursuit of independence. More information on this part of Taiwanese history can be found on Web sites such as 228 Incident Memorial Foundation; A Collection of Famous Paintings; and Taiwan History.

11. The debates over Taiwan either as an integral part of Mainland China or as an independent nation-state can be followed in academic publications. See Brown; Zagoria; Copper *Nation-State* and *Taiwan*; and Shambaugh. For other related monographs on this part of history and continuing complication see Wang; and Lu and Yueh-yu Yeh.

12. Regarding the setting-up history of "Between Us," please see Zhuang, 16–26.

13. The American protectorate approximately starts from 1949, after the National army led by Chiang Kai-shek retreated to Taiwan—an island that has never before received so much attention from the mainland Chinese. The United States then provided life-sustaining support to Chiang's regime as part of the deployment to block the advance of world communism, and thus, Taiwan developed a strong American orientation in many cultural, societal and political aspects. Even though in 1979, Nixon's normalization of diplomatic relations between the United States and China was carried out at the expense of ties with Taiwan, American influences continued both in popular and elite dimensions, such as the import of American sitcoms, higher education systems and academic practices as well as Taiwan's oppositional politics. For more references on Taiwan studies, see Roy; Edmonds.

14. Tongzhi, a term still used widely in China nowadays to mean comrade, was originally derived from "toshi" in Japanese in the beginning of 1900s. "Tong" means "the same" and "zhi" is "will."

15. Chao points out that queer was translated as, for one, "guaitai" (freak) by Hsiaohung Chang and, for the other, "ku'er" by Tawei Chi (85). But "ku'er" has a higher exposure than "freak" and because "ku'er" has been more extensively discussed and theorized by scholars such as Chu; and Kaweipo. and I thus choose to omit the less popular translation by Chang.

16. Instead of offering a link to the Qoo company itself, I give a link to the Wikipedia entry. Qoo as a character has been quite popular in Taiwan and in other East-Asian countries as it is cute-looking in the TV commercial. Due to Japanese Kawaii culture (cuteness culture), cuteness has proved to be a selling point that almost always works well in, at least, Taiwan and Japan.

17. In the period of its initial establishment in the year 2000, Spiteful Tots community has stated in the welcome page that "this community is not a tongzhi community."

18. This point was made in a series of online messages that were posted and replied by the members of Spiteful Tots in the first few weeks of starting the online community.

19. Although I am a board master of Spiteful Tots' discussion board "ChickenRIB," I do not own a private board there, which has been the only defining criterion of being a full member of Spiteful Tots. But this is not to say that I am not welcome in Spiteful Tots, though it might add to my somewhat marginalized status that I am a woman who did not know many people at Spiteful Tots' initial period, and who has studied and lived abroad since 2003 and has been familiarized with the West.

20. A member of Spiteful Tots comments: "I really hate this term tongzhi, as if to hide something. It doesn't make any sense. Who invented tongzhi to replace tonxinglian? They both start with 'tong' but its creation is really alienating. Tongxinglian is a sexual orientation and a behaviour, but tongzhi is an identity of a group. People easily say 'you tongzhi,' 'your circle'—'you.' "

21. Having made this observation, I am of course aware that the change of meaning and implication of tongzhi depends on people's continuous use of it. The positive and negative implications of tongzhi are thus the focus of observation in an evolutionary process in contemporary Taiwanese society and should not be regarded as final in any way.

WORKS CITED

228 Incident Memorial Foundation. 15 June 2006 <http://www.228.org.tw/history228_general.php>.

Brown, Melissa J. *Is Taiwan Chinese?: The Impact of Culture, Power, and Migration on Changing Identities.* Berkeley Series in Interdisciplinary Studies of China 2. Berkeley: U of California P, 2004.

Champagne, John. "Transnationally Queer?: A Promlegomenon." *Socialist Review* 27.1–2 (1999): 143–64.

Chang, Hsiaohung. "Queer Politics of Desire." *Chung-wai Literary Monthly* 29.4 (1996): 6–25.

Chao, Antonia. "Taiwan Tongzhi Yanjiu de Huigu u Zhanwan" ["Review and Prospect of Tongzhi Studies in Taiwan"]. *Daizhe Caomao qu Luxing: Xingbie, Quanli, Guojia [Travelling Everywhere with a Straw Hat: Gender, Power and the State].* Taipei: Juliu, 2001. 85–124.

Chi, Ta-wei, ed. *Ku'er Qishilu: Taiwan Dangdai Queer Lunshu Duben [Queer Archipelago: A Reader of the Queer Discourse in Taiwan].* Taipei: Yuanzun Wenhua, 1997.

Chi, Ta-wei, and Tang-mo. "Ku'er Xiaoxiao Baike" ["Queer Mini Encyclopedia"]. *Isle's Margin: Queer Special Issue* 10 (1994): 47–71.

———. "Zhizhunü zh Wen—Rus zi Shiren de Gangmen Yanshen Baozhang" ["Kiss of the Spider Woman—Milky Thin Thread Extends and Grows from Wet Anus"]. *Isle's Margin: Queer Special Issue* 10 (1994): 26–44.

Ching, Leo T.S. *Becoming Japanese: Colonial Taiwan and the Politics of Identity Formation.* Berkeley: U of California P, 2001.

Chu, Yuan-Horng. "Cong Binli dao Zhenglue: Kaowai yige Shehuixue Dianfan" ["From Pathology to Strategy: A Sociology Paradigm with a Twist"]. *Taiwan: A Radical Quarterly in Social Studies* 24.11 (1996): 109–41.

A Collection of Famous Paintings. 15 June 2006 <http://www.npm.gov.tw/en/home.htm>. Path: English; Search: Famous Paintings.

Copper, John F. *Taiwan: Nation-State or Province?* 3rd ed. Boulder, CO: Westview, 1999.

———, ed. *Taiwan in Troubled Times: Essays on Chen Shui-bian Presidency.* 2002. River Edge, NJ: World Scientific, 2002.

Corcuff, Stéphane, ed. *Memories of the Future: National Identity Issues and the Search for a New Taiwan.* Armonk, NY: Sharpe, 2002.

Edmonds, Richard Louis, and Steven M. Goldstein, eds. *Taiwan in the Twentieth Century: A Retrospective View.* Cambridge, Eng.: Cambridge UP, 2001.

Howe, Christopher. "The Taiwan Economy: The Transition to Maturity and the Political Economy of Its Changing International Status." *Contemporary Taiwan.* Ed. David Shambaugh. Oxford: Oxford UP, 1998. 127–51.

Hung, Lucifer. "Kashanzhuola de Kuoqiang yu Gaochao" ["Kashanzhuola's Mouth and Orgasm"]. *Isle's Margin: Queer Special Issue* 10 (1994): 6.

Kaweipo, Yingbin Ning. "Shemeshi Ku'er Yianjiu?" ["What is Queer Studies?"] *Gender Studies* 3.4 (1998): 32–46.

Liu, Lydia. *Translingual Practice: Literature, National Culture, and Translated Modernity—China, 1900–1937.* Stanford, CA: Stanford UP, 1995.

Lu, Sheldon H., and Emilie Yueh-yu Yeh, eds. *Chinese-Language Film: Historiography, Poetics, Politics.* Honolulu: U of Hawaii P, 2005.

Ning, YinBin. "Shemeshi Ku'er Yianjiu?" ["What is Queer Studies?"]. *Gender Studies* 3.4 (1998): 32–46.

"Qoo." Wikipedia. 13 Mar. 2006 <http://en.wikipedia.org/wiki/Qoo>.

Roy, Denny. *Taiwan: A Political History.* Ithaca: Cornell UP, 2003.

Rubin, Gayle S. "Thinking Sex: Notes for a Radical Theory of the Politics of Sexuality." *Pleasure and Danger: Exploring Female Sexuality.* Ed. Carol Vance. London: Routledge, 1984. 267–319.

Sang, Tze-lan D. *The Emerging Lesbian: Female Same-Sex Desire in Modern China.* Chicago: Chicago UP, 2003.

Shambaugh, David, ed. *Contemporary Taiwan.* Oxford: Oxford UP, 1998.

Simon, Denis Fred. "Technology Transfer and National Autonomy." *Contending Approaches to the Political Economy of Taiwan.* Ed. Edwin A. Winckler and Susan Granhalgh. Armonk, NY: Sharpe, 1988. 152–79.

Taiwan History. 15 June 2006 <http://members.shaw.ca/leksu>.

Wang, Dewei. *The Monster That Is History: History, Violence, and Fictional Writing in Twentieth-Century China.* Berkeley: U of California P, 2004.

Wang, Hao-wei, ed. *Isle's Margin: Queer Special Issue* 10 (1994).

Zagoria, Donald S., ed. *Breaking the China-Taiwan Impasse.* Westport, CT: Praeger, 2003.

Zhuang, Huichiu. *Yangqi Caihong Qi: Wuo de Tongzhi Yudong Qinyian 1990–2001* [When the Rainbow Flag Raises: My Experiences with Tongzhi Movements 1990–2001]. Taipei: PsyGarden, 2002.

CHAPTER 14

RECONFIGURING DIFFERENCES: RADICALIZING POPULAR CULTURE PEDAGOGY

LAURA GRAY-ROSENDALE AND KENDRA BIRNLEY

Abstract: *Drawing from postcolonial studies, feminist scholarship, and queer theory, the authors reveal how the S.T.A.R. Summer Writing Program at Northern Arizona University created by Gray-Rosendale (and built around the course "Rhetoric in the Media") addresses issues of identity. In order to build community across differences, they argue for examining and fostering moments of theoretical, curricular, and pedagogical hybridity and intersectionality. The chapter presents detailed information about the curriculum, the writing and reading assignments, and specific pedagogical exercises to foster discussion about complexities surrounding identity. The chapter closes with suggestions for ways to teach popular culture that reconfigure how we understand difference.*

FOR NEARLY TEN YEARS, Laura has built and revised the curriculum, directed, as well as taught in the S.T.A.R. (Successful Transition and Academic Retention) Summer Writing Bridge program in conjunction with the Multicultural Student Center at Northern Arizona University. For three years Kendra has been a teacher in the program. While Arizona is a politically conservative state, the aims of this program are themselves quite politically progressive, providing extra liberal studies credit and writing experience to students from Arizona and from those tribal lands that extend from Arizona into the neighboring states of Utah and New Mexico. In order to qualify for this program, students have to fulfill at least one of the following criteria (though many fulfill all three): first generation college, racial or ethnic minorities, and/or in economic need. Fortunately over the last several years, the number of students in the program has nearly doubled in size. This has occurred largely due to the fact that longitudinal studies have proven this program to be more successful in retaining such students than any other such on-campus programs as well as comparable programs nationwide.

The curriculum centers around one key course, "Rhetoric in the Media," that teaches critical reading, writing and thinking skills, rhetorical analysis, and argumentation. These skills are practiced primarily by examining issues of identity in various texts of popular culture, including advertising, television, film, cyberculture, sports, and music.

Many arrive with tribal scholarships, others with state funding, and still others with monetary support from Northern Arizona University—and all of the students elect to be a part of the program. A number of the students are basic writers. Interestingly, while the vast majority of the students identify as people of color (Native American, Chicana/o, African American), more still identify as mixed-race (attributing their heritage to three or more races, ethnic heritages, or tribal groups as well as to three or more linguistic communities). Likewise, every year a small group of these students also identify as Gay, Lesbian, Bisexual, Transgender, or Queer (GLBTQ). During the program, all of the students often become increasingly articulate about the complex intersections of their various racial, ethnic, class, and gender identities.

While the structure of the course is certainly informed by studies in postcolonialism, gender studies, and queer theory, these theories also shed important light on the nontransparent identities our students adopt. Since much contemporary identity theory can inadvertently force a separation between various identity categories in order to foster critical analyses (Moya; Scott), our curriculum attempts to draw from multiple perspectives that foreground agency within differences. In doing so, we hope to encourage speaking across and between issues of difference rather than about identity categories in isolation. Doing so is also critical since, as Margaret L. Andersen contends in "The Fiction of 'Diversity Without Oppression': Race, Ethnicity, Identity, and Power," multiculturalism will become mere cultural pluralism if we do not "dissect the institutional arrangements by which systems of group privilege and disadvantage are created and sustained through group oppression" (16).

Importantly, postcolonial theory has examined the ways in which colonizing cultural influences distort the realities of colonized peoples as well as construct them as inferior. Focusing on disrupting such marginalizing positions of otherness, postcolonial studies argue that identity and difference operate in conjunction, often utilizing the concept of resistance as subversion, opposition, or mimicry and rethinking the values and meaning of the colonizing culture so as to undermine it. Scholar Homi K. Bhabha among others calls specific attention to the contradictions within colonizing discourses themselves and to the need to examine "hybrid identities," those instances that represent the multiple "overlap and displacement of domains of difference," since they are inherently deconstructive of binary oppositions (2).

Taking a similar tack, feminist theorists have referenced the importance of understanding identity in terms of "intersectionality," investigating the dynamic effects that race, gender, class, colonialism, age, and bodily ability have on the constitution of identities (Mohanty; Minh-ha; Mills; Gunn Allen). Arguing that it is unreasonable to try to separate or compartmentalize the different subject positions that women occupy, they contend that to do so is to erase the fact that these subject positions are mutually influential. Therefore, identities should be understood not just as socially, culturally, and historically instantiated (Butler *Gender* and "Imitation"; Kennedy and Davis)—but also, as Linda Scholl asserts, as "multidimensional, mobile, hybrid, and never complete" (144).

Queer theory has also attempted to complicate what William Spurlin terms "(hetero) normative" sexual identity "as it is imbricated within a range of social norms, categories, and institutions, including but not limited to, the family, child care, the body, censorship, health care, reproductive politics, citizenship, national affiliation, and (neo)imperialism" ("Theorizing" 10). As Spurlin contends, sexual identity cannot be easily separated from other forms of cultural marginalization since it is always "already mediated by race, gender, class, and geopolitical spacialization" ("Introduction" xx). In particular, the use of the term "queer" has become crucial since it "purposefully disrupts the notion that identity is fixed or immutable. It includes a move to highlight the existence of and interrupt silent assumptions about heterosexuality as normal and homosexuality as Other" (Loutzenheiser and McIntosh 152). As Amy E. Winans asserts, queer pedagogy itself reconfigures difference, "decentering dominant cultural assumptions, exploring the facets of the geography of normalization, and interrogating the self and the implications of affiliation" (107). Inherently resistant, queer theory rethinks the "very grounds of knowledge and pedagogy in education," examining the production of normalization as a system of thought while also disrupting it (Britzman 151). As a result, queer theory's transgressive practice of deconstructing normalcy is "obviously not confined to teaching *as, for,* or *about* queer subject(s)" (Luhmann 151) but has critical relevance for examining all identities' shifting boundaries and junctions.

Similarly, our students' dynamic identities-in-progress often show movement as well as dissonance and conflict within, between, and among the various groups with whom they identify. Their hybridized identities are complex mixtures in which selves and others oftentimes scrape up against each other. As such, our students represent not just separate and distinct differences, but also differences that intersect and thereby reshape one another constantly, accounting for complex interconnections between racial, ethnic, class, and gender identities as well as white supremacy, bigotry, class privilege, and heterosexism. Acknowledging this phenomenon is important since, if we do not do so, we risk including one of these students' marginalized identities at the expense of others. As Kevin K. Kumashiro maintains, "Ironically, our efforts to challenge one form of oppression often unintentionally contribute to other forms of oppression, and our efforts to embrace one form of difference often exclude and silence others" (1). We may also fail to investigate how power/knowledge relations can simultaneously produce and reinforce these same students' oppressive identities. Likewise, self-reflective approaches to teaching academic discourse to these students are critical since the unified version of the self present in much academic discourse undermines the plurality of these students' selves, posing a "significant threat to critical agency residing in a student's multiple subjectivities" (LeCourt 151).

In effect, confronting our students' multiple identities means not only utilizing a combination of theories to make sense of their positionalities, but also constantly wrestling with a series of complex questions that our students articulate as well as embody: How can we recognize and find a language to speak about multiple conceptions of difference productively rather than reinforce negative potentialities? How can we support the multiplicity of identities and allow for hybrid potentialities while also teaching students about the tenets of academic discourse? What happens to the concept of otherness when students might embody several different others at the same time—some of which may be battling with one another?

As we struggle with these issues, related pragmatic concerns also emerge. Popular culture texts are notoriously one-dimensional, oftentimes silencing or even erasing the complexity of identity, and with it, the realities of many, if not all, of our students. In pop culture media, identities can appear as little more than static characters that regurgitate fixed, stereotypical notions of who we are: *this* is a straight black man, *this* is a gay white male, *this* is a straight Latina woman. While it can be relatively easy to encourage our students to focus on an analysis of these stereotypes, the real difficulty comes when we try to move beyond these discussions to analyses that tease out the complex notion of identities-in-process, while allowing them the freedom and safety to explore these complexities in their own identities—and deal with some of the discomforts of doing so. Our curricular and pedagogical goals involve moving beyond an analysis of pop culture at face value and toward inviting more thoughtful exploration of self and other. Many of our students struggle with these and other issues of identity, even if they, and we, may not feel as though our vocabularies or theories are always able to articulate our confusions or frustrations. Helping to extract and validate our students' feelings and argumentative claims about their identities is part of the challenge and the satisfaction of teaching a diverse group of students such as those we teach in the Summer Bridge program. Our students provide the very means by which we are able to bridge the gap between a fragmented examination of shallow pop-culture identities and a substantial dialogue about the fluidity and motion of hybrid identities.

THE S.T.A.R. SUMMER WRITING
PROGRAM CURRICULUM

The five-week curriculum involves both informal and formal writing assignments. The informal assignments encourage students to respond to the cultural criticisms they read in class, to consider the personal and societal effects of popular culture images, as well as to reflect on their own writing processes. These assignments provide spaces where students can learn to formulate their opinions in all their complexities as well as get experience supporting them with close textual readings. The formal writing assignments include (1) a close rhetorical analysis of a piece of cultural criticism, (2) an argumentative paper that is itself a piece of cultural criticism—examining texts from popular culture such as advertising, television, film, cyberculture, sports, music, and constructions of identity, and (3) a group-created spoof of a print or commercial advertising campaign (using media such as hard copy, computer programs, radio, and live performance).[1]

In the course students notice and question what *is* represented in the media as well as what *is not*. Many of our students are already aware of how the groups with whom they identify are represented, even if infrequently, in mainstream American media. They know the stereotypes by heart. Since a large majority of them are marginalized by society in general, they tend to look more questioningly at the media and their perspectives as outsiders are typically more acute than your average, white, middle-class American consumer. By the same token, many of them are very much struggling with the effects of identity marginalization and can sometimes understandably resort to rather conservative responses in an attempt to reconcile those internal differences. At times we have witnessed students of color disparaging first generation and lower-income students' concerns, first generation and lower-income students overlooking GLBTQ concerns, and GLBTQ students ignoring oppression based on race and ethnicity. Though we have sometimes intervened when such questions of identity become rigidified, more often other students themselves openly challenge these positions.

Over the years, the students' written work in the course—particularly their cultural criticisms—have been varied and very intriguing for what they reveal about the ways in which students explore their hybrid identities through analyses of popular culture. We have received papers on African American lesbian communities and popular sports; rave culture and transgender identities within Native American communities; advertising, gender identity, and homoeroticism; issues of gender, ethnicity, and race: Apple's iPod ads; the benefits and dangers of online gender switching in chat rooms; representations of gay identity in film; and challenges to gender norms in Latin music among many others. These projects—and many more we cannot list here—have been attempts to engage multiple marginalized identities simultaneously, to view when and how identities marked by difference intersect each other, speak to each other, and silence each other.

TEACHING MOMENTS IN HYBRIDIZATION

Rather than investigating one single identity at a time in our classrooms, we try to look at intersectionality or hybrid identities, taking on a particular type of media and analyzing several examples specifically from it. One theme that these students consistently overlook in their analyses is (hetero)normativity and its connections with gender, race, ethnicity, and class issues. Even some of our gay students who identify as minorities from first generation and lower-class backgrounds have been so conditioned to their own erasure in the mainstream media and have internalized dominant media images that they sometimes do not notice and/or feel comfortable pointing out the lack of GLBTQ characters or relationships in the media.[2]

Laura chooses to foreground such complex relationships—intersectionalities and hybrids—between identity and popular culture in her discussion of sports rituals among other media forms. In conjunction with reading the Michael Messner essay on gay politics, sports, and masculinity, and watching a video on femininity, gay culture, and Title IX, students bring in media images of men and women engaged in sport (including print ads, commercials, and other representations in magazines and on television shows). Already armed with a list of rhetorical issues to examine (such as audience, purpose, ethos, pathos, logos, exigence, arrangement and composition, intertextuality, social myths and narratives, use of color, font and style, and constraints), the students produce close analyses of the ads and then share those ads and their analyses with the rest of the class.

As the discussion unfolds, inevitably comments emerge about the objectification of female bodies in sports and the question of how female athletes from various cultural backgrounds are rarely represented as having real agency in action arises. Laura's students note that images of the female body as strong and muscular appear infrequently since the fear is that such appearance would signify masculinity. Gradually, Laura and her students arrive at the fact that by failing to admit to the real work of female athletes, advertisers also erase the presence of GLTBQ athletes by reinforcing a specifically (hetero)normative gaze, securing a view of femininity and masculinity as innate rather than socially constructed. Once the discussion has moved to this level, Laura then tries to push the discussion one step further: What else does the gaze's (hetero)normativity depend upon? Typically, unless the sport depends upon class privilege for its signification (golf, for instance), students remark that class is also erased, as if the viewer has no class affiliations or interests except as consumers. Likewise, a positive focus on diverse populations in sports, students note, is too often mitigated by placing the athlete of color only in stereotypical arenas, by elevating the athlete to the role of individual celebrity (and oftentimes known only for one-raced identity), or by placing the athlete of color amongst a group of other white athletes.

These kinds of discussions lead students to assert that the objectification of women, (hetero)normativity of the gaze, absence of class status, and inadequate representation of athletes of color in media representations of sports are forms of marginalization that are all intricately interconnected. By causing viewers to fail to interrogate this, ads often produce anxieties, beliefs, desires, and needs in the viewer (often implying that the viewer is in danger of social ostracism because s/he does not adequately conform to a particular social norm) so as to offer the product as a solution for these lacks. As such, students are investigating the ways in which "heterosexuality, and the gender roles it underwrites, in its need to proclaim its own naturalness and normality, can only produce an anxiety at never actually being natural and normal" (Dyer 271). They come to see that the "anxiety reflected in the discourse designed to stabilize rigid definitions" of identity is in fact "not inherent, essential, or stable. Identity might be better understood as something that is performed, with the goal being to replicate some prior performance, which is itself illusive and unstable" (Winans 113).

Next students consider what sorts of argumentative claims they might make about how social and cultural issues such as race, class, gender identity, and ethnicity operate simultaneously within these representations, drawing connections between them. How are people of color represented? How are masculinity and femininity being depicted differently? How is class status operating in the representation and to what ends? How are ability and disability represented? How does (hetero)normativity shape the choices of the text? Invariably students discuss the manipulative ploys that are operating within the texts and how they, as viewers, are being strategically positioned as consumers.[3]

One specific exercise that Kendra employs to encourage more discussion around the complicated notion of hybrid identities begins with an examination of gender and then moves to a self-reflective exploration of the students' own complex identities. Prior to embarking on this exercise, Kendra shows her students parts of the second season premier of *The Bachelor*. Those who have seen the show know that it lends itself well to an analysis of gender roles and (hetero)normativity. With *The Bachelor* fresh in her students' minds, Kendra writes the words "masculine" and "feminine" on the board, drawing a large box around each of them. Students then brainstorm qualities and character-istics that they associate with these two words. Answers that she receives reveal how entrenched (hetero)normativity is: men are tough, brave, strong, rational, and successful, while women are emotional, nurturing, mothers, passive, and beautiful. Once the class has collected a fairly substantial list, Kendra asks her students how people refer to men or women who don not fit these descriptions. She places these adjectives—words such as "fag," "bitch," "sissy," "butch," "dyke," or "whore"—outside the box. This leads to a very compelling discussion on gender, sexuality, queer identities, and (hetero)normativity.

From here, Kendra tries to move the discussion from an examination of gender to an exploration of hybrid identities. To accomplish this, Kendra takes this exercise yet one step further by completing boxes for different men and women of color. The lists inside the boxes tend to be slightly different from the first ones and sometimes the characteristics are harder to define or categorize. Members of each group often have conflicting ideas concerning what words should be listed. Complicating things even more, Kendra encourages her students to consider how socioeconomic status and disability can also shape which characteristics are associated with the identities.

Once Kendra's students are struggling with the limitations of the boxes and the categories, she asks them what a person is to do if s/he identifies with several boxes at once or if s/he identifies with the inside *and* the outside of the boxes. Responses usually echo the same idea: the boxes have to go. Kendra erases the boxes from the board and invites students to help her create a new visual representation of identities. She encourages volunteers to come up to the board to play a version of connect-the-dots, asking them to draw lines between and amongst the characteristics that *they* claim as a part of their identities. Kendra allows them to add terms to the board that they feel are missing. Lines often zigzag all over the board, constructing a messy but intri-cate web of characteristics emphasizing students' complex selves. To make the exercise beneficial to all, she encourages those who do not come up to the board to map out their own identities on a piece of paper at their desks.

Discussion resulting from this exercise is lively, complicated, confusing, elusive, and rewarding, providing a framework for the students to talk about their own hybrid identities. Since this pedagogical tactic provides a more accurate and positive dialogue about the potentialities of identities, it also affords students agency. Breaking down the isolating categories that cause conflict for many of them, it affords a proactive and self-reflective opportunity for students to determine their own senses of who they are. Such agency is critical, making our students central to the curriculum's goal of addressing the complexity and promise of hybrid identities.

MOVING BEYOND THE GAP: TOWARD A RADICAL POPULAR CULTURE PEDAGOGY

Increasingly we must utilize the multiple understandings of difference proffered by connections between postcolonial studies, feminism, and queer theory to create writing curricula using pop culture that better accommodate entering first-year writers. We need to better address the many issues associated with hybrid identity constructions that take issues of race, ethnicity, class, and gender identity as central. As we too continue to work toward a radical popular culture pedagogy, one that begins to "articulate an appealing and coherent shared agenda for social change across disciplinary, identity, and issue-domain boundaries," we close with a few suggestions (Rosendale xix):

• Offer diverse in-class lessons, writing assignments, and curricula that focus directly on issues of hybrid identities, intersectionality, and queer deconstructions of difference, combating race, ethnicity, class, and gender stereotyping. In doing so, we can disrupt the implicit privileging of some identities as normative as opposed to others, instead acknowledging the complex social oppression of marginalized students (Peele and Ryder 34; Broldo 349).

• Make the convergence of discourses about race, ethnicity, class, sexuality, and gender identities central to the writing classroom. This causes all course participants to not only rethink how popular culture functions in the perpetuation of racist, classist, sexist, and (hetero)normative gender and other stereotypes but also, as Harriet Malinowitz argues, "demands that we think about identity and power" structures altogether while it "jolts us into rhetorical considerations of voice, position, audience, perspective, relation, and authority" (114).

• Invite students to speak about complex identity issues, but only when they are willing and feel comfortable doing so. Demanding students speak on behalf of one or many of the groups with which they identify can put them in uncomfortable positions, leading to a kind of tokenism that defeats the purposes of thorough discussions concerning the fluidity and complexity of hybrid identities. Students' emotional responses to material that encourages self-reflection and a critical analysis of power structures can be intense. Understanding that emotional responses to shifts in the dominant paradigms that structure our thinking are productive, constructive, and important intellectual responses in and of themselves (enabling us to theorize the personal and personalize the theoretical) is imperative to undermining and ultimately transforming students' marginalization (Alcoff and Gray-Rosendale; hooks 43).

• Realize that students' challenges to static identity constructions norms are critical, political, and personal acts, part of the continual process of hybrid identity construction itself. In teaching about identity and popular culture, we must recognize and actively resist the ways in which oppositional assumptions about race, ethnicity, class, gender, and sexuality operate, the false dualistic thinking that pits some identities against others, instead always acknowledging our own participation in and perpetuation of them (Malinowitz 42; Von Destinon, Evans, and Wall 372). Including postcoloniality, feminism, and queer theory as part of multiple identity perspectives allows both teachers and students to see how various discourses about sexuality and gender are always operating simultaneously with discourses about class, ethnicity, and race as well as the ways in which they come into conflict with one another.

Reconfiguring differences and working toward a radical popular culture pedagogy for our students will entail building bridges between theoretical modes and identity categories—not examining race, ethnicity, class, sexuality, and gender issues in isolation from one another. It will mean working between and amidst issues of difference as a way to combat approaches to identity politics in isolation from communal action and interaction. Foregrounding the complex nature of hybridized identities, intersectionality, and queer theory may provide a pedagogical path toward valuing differences while accounting for the ever more insidious intersections of identities and racism, bigotry, class privilege, gender discrimination, and heterosexism, and other forms of discrimination.

NOTES

1. In recent years Laura has added a Web-enhanced component to the course, providing various clips of cultural texts alongside the assignments. Though the readings have varied from year to year, typically the course moves from advertising to television and film to cyberculture to sports to music to identity and culture. Laura's forthcoming textbook with McGraw-Hill, tentatively titled *Pop Perspectives: Readings to Critique Contemporary Culture*, offers these readings as well as many others—along with the pedagogical apparatus for the program's curriculum. Please consult that book if you are interested in the pedagogy, curriculum, and readings. We offer a few particularly relevant citations that lend themselves to discussions of differences across identity categories in the Selected Bibliography.

2. The reasons we see for this silence around homosexuality could easily comprise a separate chapter. In short, though, the silence is indicative of a larger social

attitude that unfortunately continues to surround the issue. Homosexuality is still fairly taboo when compared to race and class and even gender, especially in a conservative state such as Arizona, where homosexuality is too often framed as a moral issue rather than a social one.

3. Another way to initiate such a discussion is by pointing to how popular cultural images themselves can reveal the complexity of identities as well as force premature closure on such discussions. *Chappelle's Show* among others has offered a number of skits including "Race Draft 2004," "Frontline" (featuring the black white supremacist), and "Ask a Gay Dude" with *Sex and the City* star Mario Cantone. Such episodes have both raised critical political issues concerning hybrid and multiple identities as well as revealed the specific ways in which such concerns have not yet been examined adequately by mass media.

SELECTED BIBLIOGRAPHY

Berger, Arthur Asa. "Checklist for Analyzing Print Advertisements." *Seeing is Believing: An Introduction to Visual Communication.* Mountain View, CA: Mayfield, 1998. 65.

Blood, Rebecca. "Weblogs: A History and Perspective." *Rebecca's Pocket.* 7 Sept. 2000. 17 Feb. 2005 <http://www.rebeccablood.net/essays/weblog_history.html>.

Chung, Olivia. "Finding My Eye-Dentity." *Yell-Oh Girls! Emerging Voices Explore Culture, Identity, and Growing Up Asian American.* Ed. Vicky Nam. New York: Harper, 2001. 137–39.

Cornford, Adam. " 'Colorless All-Color': Notes on White Culture." *Bad Subjects* 33. 1997. 13 July 2006 <http://bad.eserver.org/>.

DeRose, Justin, Elfried Fürsich, and Ekaterina V. Haskins. "Pop (Up) Goes the Blind Date: Supertextual Constraints on 'Reality' Television." *Journal of Communication Inquiry* 27 (2003): 171–89.

Eck, Lindsey. "Defining Country Music." *Bad Subjects* 56. 2002. 13 July 2006 <http://bad.eserver.org/>.

Hicks, Gary R. "Media at the Margins: Homoerotic Appeals to the Gay and Lesbian Community." *Sex in Advertising: Perspectives on the Erotic Appeal.* Ed. Tom Reichert and Jacqueline Lambiase. Mahwah, NJ: Erlbaum, 2003. 229–47.

Lambiase, Jacqueline J. "Sex—Online and in Internet Advertising." *Sex in Advertising: Perspectives on the Erotic Appeal.* Ed. Tom Reichert and Jacqueline Lambiase. Mahwah, NJ: Erlbaum, 2003. 247–72.

Lasn, Kalle. "The Cult You're In." *Culture Jam: How to Reverse America's Suicidal Consumer Binge—and Why We Must.* New York: Quill, 2000. 51–57.

Marr, John. "Confessions of an eBay Addict." *Bad Subjects* 42. Mar. 1999. 15 June 2006 <http://bad.eserver.org/>.

McKissack, Frederick C., Jr. "Cyberghetto: Blacks Are falling Through the Net." *The Progressive* 62.6 (1998): 20–22.

Messner, Michael A. *Power at Play: Sports and the Problem of Masculinity.* Boston: Beacon, 1995.

Rubio, Chris. "Throws Like the Girl She Is." *Bad Subjects* 35. 1997. 15 June 2006 <http://bad.eserver.org/>.

Sandoval, Tomás F., Jr. "On the Merits of Racial Identity." *Bad Subjects* 33. 1997. <http://bad.eserver.org/>.
Valdes-Rodriguez, Alissa. "Crossing Pop Lines: Attention to Latinos Is Overdue, But Sometimes Off-Target." *Los Angeles Times* 11 June 1999, Orange County ed.: F2.

WORKS CITED

Alcoff, Linda Martin, and Laura Gray-Rosendale. "Survivor Discourse: Transgression or Recuperation?" *Getting a Life: Everyday Uses of Autobiography.* Ed. Sidonie Smith and Julia Watson. Minneapolis: Minnesota UP, 1996. 198–226.
Andersen, Margaret L. "The Fiction of 'Diversity Without Oppression': Race, Ethncity, Identity, and Power." *Critical Ethnicity: Countering the Waves of Identity Politics.* Ed. Robert H. Tai and Mary L. Kenyatta. Lanham: Rowman, 1999. 5–20.
The Bachelor. ABC. 25 Mar. 2002–Present.
Bhabha, Homi K. *Location of Culture.* London: Routledge, 1994.
Britzman, Deborah. "Is There a Queer Pedagogy? Or, Stop Reading Straight." *Educational Theory* 45.2 (1995): 151–65.
Broido, Ellen M. "Ways of Being an Ally to Lesbian, Gay, and Bisexual Students." *Toward Acceptance: Sexual Orientation Issues on Campus.* Wall and Evans 345–71.
Butler, Judith. *Gender Trouble: Feminism and the Subversion of Identity.* New York: Routledge, 1990.
———. "Imitation and Gender Subordination." *Inside/Out: Lesbian Theories, Gay Theories.* Ed. Diana Fuss. New York: Routledge, 1991. 13–31.
Chappelle's Show. Comedy Central. 22 Jan. 2003–Present.
Dyer, Richard. "Heterosexuality." *Lesbian and Gay Studies: A Critical Introduction.* Ed. Andy Medhurst and Sally R. Munt. London: Cassell, 1997. 261–73.
Gray-Rosendale, Laura. *Pop Perspectives: Readings to Critique Contemporary Culture.* New York: McGraw-Hill, 2007/8. Forthcoming.
Gunn Allen, Paula. "Angry Women Are Building: Issues and Struggles Facing American Indian Women Today." *Race, Class, and Gender: An Anthology.* Ed. Margaret L. Andersen and Patricia Hill Collins. 5th ed. Belmont, CA: Wadsworth, 2004. 44–48.
hooks, bell. *Teaching to Transgress: Education as the Practice of Freedom.* New York: Routledge, 1994.
Kennedy, Elizabeth Lapovsky, and Madeline D. Davis. *Boots of Leather, Slippers of Gold: The History of a Lesbian Community.* New York: Penguin, 1994.
Kumashiro, Kevin K., ed. *Troubling Intersections of Race and Sexuality: Queer Students of Color and Anti-Oppressive Education.* Lanham, MD: Rowman, 2001.
———. "Queer Students of Color and Antiracist, Antiheterosexist Education: Paradoxes of Identity and Activism." Kumashiro. 1–26.
LeCourt, Donna. *Identity Matters: Schooling the Student Body in Academic Discourse.* Albany: State U of New York P, 2004.
Loutzenheiser, Lisa W., and Lori B. McIntosh. "Citizenships, Sexualities, and Education." *Theory Into Practice* 43.2 (2004): 151–58.

Luhmann, Susanne. "Queering/Querying Pedagogy? Or, Pedagogy Is a Pretty Queer Thing." *Queer Theory in Education*. Ed. William F. Pinar. Mahwah, NJ: Erlbaum, 1998. 141–55.

Malinowitz, Harriet. *Textual Orientations: Lesbian and Gay Students and the Making of Discourse Communities*. New York: Heinemann, 1995.

Mills, Sara. "Gender and Colonial Space." *Feminist Postcolonial Theory: A Reader*. Ed. Reina Lewis and Sara Mills. New York: Routledge, 2003. 692–719.

Minh-ha, Trinh T. *Woman, Native, Other: Writing Postcoloniality and Feminism*. Bloomington, IN: Indiana UP, 1989.

Mohanty, Chandra Talpade. "Under Western Eyes: Feminist Scholarship and Colonial Discourses." *Feminist Review* 30 (1988): 61–88.

Moya, Paula M.L., and Michael R. Hames-Garcia, eds. *Reclaiming Identity: Realist Theory and the Predicament of Postmodernism*. Berkeley: U of California P, 2000.

Nagel, Joane. "Ethnicity and Sexuality." *Annual Review of Sociology* 26.1 (2000): 107–33.

Peele, Thomas, and Mary Ellen Ryder. "Belief Spaces and the Resistant Writer: Queer Space in the Contact Zone." *Journal of Basic Writing* 22.2 (2003): 27–46.

Rosendale, Steven. "Introduction." *Radical Relevance: Toward a Scholarship of the Whole Left*. Ed. Laura Gray-Rosendale and Steven Rosendale. New York: State U of New York P, 2005.

Scholl, Linda. "Narratives of Hybridity and the Challenge to Multicultural Education." Kumashiro 141–62.

Scott, Joan W. "Fantasy Echo: History and the Construction of Identity." *Critical Inquiry* 27.2 (2001): 284–304.

Sex and the City. HBO. 6 June 1998–22 Feb. 2004.

Spurlin, William. "Introduction: Queer Studies/English Studies." *Lesbian and Gay Studies and the Teaching of English: Positions, Pedagogies, and Cultural Politics*. Urbana, IL: National Council of Teachers of English, 2000. xiii–xxxiii.

———. "Theorizing Queer Pedagogy in English Studies after the 1990s." *College English* 65 (2002): 9–16.

Von Destinon, Mark, Nancy Evans, and Vernon A. Wall. "Navigating the Minefield: Sexual Orientation Issues and Campus Politics." Wall and Evans 371–88.

Wall, Vernon A., and Nancy J. Evans, eds. *Toward Acceptance: Sexual Orientation Issues on Campus*. Lanham, MD: UP of America, 2000.

Winans, Amy E. "Queering Pedagogy in the English Classroom: Engaging With Places Where Thinking Stops." *Pedagogy* 6.1 (2006): 103–22.

CHAPTER 15

QUEERING *HARRY POTTER*

JILL R. EHNENN

HARRY POTTER LOOKS LIKE A LESBIAN.

It can't be denied. He's got *that* look—just like scores of young dykes with their short spiky haircuts and dorky-cute glasses. Not the *L-word* look—oh no!—more like Rachel Maddow, like countless butch/boi faces in lesbian indie cinema, like Mo from the renowned lesbian cartoon series, *Dykes To Watch Out For*. In fact, Alison Bechdel, artist-creator of Mo and the gang, noticed it, too. Soon after the fourth Harry book was published, a segment of *Dykes To Watch Out For* featured Mo at work at the Madwimmin Bookstore, promoting Potter-mania, and surrounded by clamoring children who think she is their favorite J.K. Rowling character, magically materialized for the afternoon.[1] Yes indeed, as far as stereotypes of white lesbians in contemporary popular culture go, Harry Potter is a veritable lesbian clone.

Or at least, he *could* be. That's one way to read the books, to queer them, much as many adult lesbians, looking back, now recognize that their childhood fantasy lives included queer identification with cultural icons such as Harriet the Spy, Jo March from *Little Women*, James Dean, David Cassidy, Sporty Spice, and the other Jo—from *Facts of Life*.[2] If, along with theorists such as Alexander Doty and David Halperin, we think of "queer" as a verb, a reception practice, an anti-heteronormative way of reading and seeing the world, then Rowling's texts offer ample opportunity for such queering, for both youth and adult LGBT readers, for fanfiction writers of all orientations, even for those far on the religious right, as this chapter will show. Doty's mode of queering reminds us that reading—whether it be literature, any cultural text, or any experience in the world—is what reader response theorists would call a transactional process. My discussion of Rowling's texts, then, will highlight the importance of individual responses in making meaning, while it also will examine what kinds of readings, meanings, and possibilities the *Harry Potter* books invite its readers to easily imagine.

Here, I will be thinking about both documented and potential responses to J.K. Rowling's *Harry Potter* series. For the most part, my project will target three different yet related audiences: (1) queer and proto-queer-identified youth; (2) queer adults; and (3) those on the religious and political far-right, who fear that reading *Harry Potter* will turn their children to witchcraft and whose disapproval of the series has only increased since Rowling's announcement that she had always thought of Harry's headmaster, Professor Dumbledore, as gay ("JK"). I am interested in how these three groups' responses to *Harry Potter* might intersect, especially regarding the issues of difference and Otherness so aptly addressed in Rowling's treatment of her bespectacled underdog protagonist and his wizarding subculture.

As an enormously popular cultural artifact particular to our historical moment, Potter-mania, both pro and con, I contend, is usefully examined as a repository of many of Western culture's deepest fantasies, anxieties, and political visions including those involving sex, gender and sexuality, and power, difference, and morality. Ultimately, what makes *Harry Potter* of particular interest to queer politics, including LGBT activism, is how these intense and assorted responses, taken together, might help us think about the complex relationship between groups in the center and on the margins. What can we learn from considering how marginalized subjects appropriate and subvert dominant narratives? How might various readings of *Harry Potter* be said to critique, or to reinforce, mainstream conceptions of normalcy? In light of these concerns, this chapter will use the *Harry Potter* texts and their related and varied Potter-manias to investigate some of the ways that subjectivities, bodies, and material products are labeled and/or claimed both by those considered in the mainstream and on the margins; to interrogate instances where supposedly oppositional positions overlap; and to trace, in the context surrounding this popular cultural artifact, how shifts among the categories dominant, marginal, and oppositional, occur.

*   *   *

J.K. Rowling's *Harry Potter and the Sorcerer's Stone*, first published in 1997, is the story of an orphaned boy who discovers on his eleventh birthday that he is a wizard. Harry leaves the abusive home of his Muggle, or non-wizard, aunt and uncle, and attends Hogwarts School of Witchcraft and Wizardry, where he experiences large and small discoveries and trials, both in and out of the classroom. He takes classes such as Potions, Charms, and Transfiguration, and becomes adept at Quidditch, a wizarding team sport played on flying broomsticks. Harry also learns about relationships: making friends for the first time in his young life and dealing with bullies among both students and teachers. Finally, the year at school gives Harry the opportunity to begin to reclaim his origins and to solve a magical mystery; in the process he emerges victorious from a dangerous encounter with the nefarious Lord Voldemort, who, as part of a plot to rule the world, had killed Harry's parents, long ago.

This book and its six sequels (published between 1997 and 2007) have all firmly occupied the New York Times Bestseller List and are avidly consumed by both child and adult readers (Garner).[3] Rowling's website states that the books have appeared in 69 languages and 200 territories, with over 400 million sold (Booth; "Everything").[4] Warner Brothers' film version of the first book grossed $93 million[5] the first weekend of its November 2001 release, and of the six books that have become movies thus far, five are listed among the Top 20 All-time Box Office earnings, worldwide, with all outranking the blockbuster *Twilight* movies ("All-Time;" Grove). The market has responded predictably to the popular texts; Potter-phernalia can be found for sale at every turn: costumes, action figures, board and computer games, furniture, calendars, mugs, clothing, accessories, etc., and even a new theme park in Orlando, Florida. With a net worth of $1 billion, Rowling is now the world's richest author and number 14 on *Forbes's* list of the world's self-made female billionaires (Kroll). Meanwhile, child and adult readers alike already are avidly awaiting the second half of the movie version of the final book, *Harry Potter and the Deathly Hallows*, which is scheduled to appear in July, 2011.

Many, perhaps most, educators and parents are thrilled that J.K. Rowling's books have elicited such an unusually charmed response from children—especially in an era when test scores seem to indicate that kids' reading abilities are declining as their thumbs, trained on remote controls and videogames, are increasing in dexterity. Reading specialists, child educators, and psychologists have lauded *Harry Potter* in a plethora of mainstream venues such as newspapers, TV talk shows, teaching sourcebooks, and popular magazines ranging from *Child* to *Time*.[6] All these seem to agree that *Harry Potter* is so popular (and morally valuable) because children powerfully identify with the novel's marginalized underdog who confronts his fears and overcomes adversity.

In an early analysis of *Harry Potter's* wild and somewhat surprising success, *New York Times* columnist Richard Bernstein similarly theorizes the appeal of the first three books, drawing upon child psychologist Bruno Bettelheim's classic study of children's literature, *The Uses of Enchantment*. Summarizing Bettelheim, Bernstein notes that "children live with greater terrors than most adults can understand, and fairy tales both give uncanny expression to that terror and show a way to a better future." Bernstein draws parallels between the Potter stories and classic fairy tales, focusing on universal fears about parental abandonment, sibling rivalry, and the innate powerlessness of childhood. *Harry Potter* is so popular, Bernstein concludes, because Harry, like the heroes of fairy tales, finds that if he "does not shy away, but steadfastly meets unexpected and often unjust hardships, [he can] master all obstacles and at the end emerge victorious." I agree with Bettelheim that at some level it is likely that all children on the verge of adolescence feel alienated, misunderstood, and Othered; for these children, the pleasure of reading the *Harry Potter* books may well resonate with fantasies of empowerment, mastery, and acceptance gained by "trying hard." When read in this manner, indeed, *Harry Potter* becomes not unlike many fairy tales and other children's fiction: a moral tale that renders the "ugly duckling" a hero in a battle of good and evil, a struggle also ultimately rewarded by social acceptance.

Yet we must not forget that as "universal" childhood terrors are soothed and moral lessons are taught, such children's stories also take on great political utility for Western readers: to reify a progress narrative founded upon individualism, patience and hard work. In short, they create "good subjects" who somewhat paradoxically believe in their personal uniqueness while they practice a Protestant work ethic in order to fit into (and thereby uphold) the status quo. In the case of *Harry Potter*, of course, the stories also create good consumers of Potter paraphernalia. Thus, in this sense, *Harry Potter*'s "virtues" would include indoctrinating child readers in the values necessary for getting ahead in culture—values that reinforce dominant capitalist narratives—assimilationist values that teach that if you work hard (and buy the right toys), difference ceases to be different after all. Children's literature theorist, Jack Zipes, posits, in fact, that *Harry Potter* is a "conventional work of fantasy [that] has been fetishized" (172) and that the reading tastes of the many fans of the series have merely been quite effectively shaped by clever marketing. Zipes, indeed, views the series as fundamentally conservative, assimilationist, and formulaic (175–76). Rachel Falconer glosses Zipes's position: "books that speak to a mass number of people are likely to appeal to more homogenous tastes" (4).

Zipes's view is provocative and has been quite influential in the field. Yet his explanation of *Harry Potter*'s popularity fails to fully account for the far-from-homogenous responses to the series. Even among readers for whom *Harry Potter* has great appeal, there are intensely contradictory views: about the basis of morality in the books; whether they are feminist or sexist; queer or heteronormative; radical or reinscriptive regarding racial prejudice, etc. In her discussion of gender politics in the series, Annette Wannamaker advocates, as I want to as well, an understanding of the text that considers diverse readings as real and meaningful. She writes:

> [T]he contradictory readings by critics of portrayals of gender . . . [they] function in a space between, where dominant ideology is simultaneously re-enforced,

challenged and negotiated. Ultimately, [the *Harry Potter*] books are popular
with so many child and adult readers, not because they didactically advocate
either feminist or patriarchal ideals, but because, through their complex
portrayals of characters, gender, and relationships, they depict the anxieties,
tensions and uncertainties.

In a similar spirit I would like to return—via Bettelheim—to ask: What of
the queer or proto-queer child—he or she who feels even more intensely the
anxieties and uncertainties of not-belonging because of gender identification
or affectional orientation that doesn't "match" his or her biological sex? Or
children who can't even put a finger on why, but only that they are very different in ways they intuitively know they perhaps ought not to mention? I
suggest that *Harry Potter* might provide particularly different pleasures for
such children, pleasures that are usefully understood as stemming from what
an adult would call a queerly resistant reading.

The queer or proto-queer child's reading of *Harry Potter* would indeed
involve identification with an outsider-hero who eventually fits in. However,
a careful reading of the text reveals that *Harry Potter* doesn't follow the precise
model proposed by Bettelheim and praised by the child experts.[7] Harry actually doesn't gain acceptance by mastering obstacles and thereby earning a
place in society. Harry gains acceptance by discovering *another* society, a complex subculture that contains its own obstacles and challenges, but most
importantly for my argument, a society filled with outcasts, in short, people
like him. Harry finds happiness and earns a place for himself, but Harry
never becomes normal—in the Muggle or in the wizarding world; thus, especially for the extremely marginalized child, the Rowling books don't necessarily function to indoctrinate the young reader with the belief that hard work
and perseverance will normalize oneself and thereby guarantee a place among
the status quo. Interestingly, as Christopher Routledge observes, the magical
events Harry's adoptive family find so perverse

> are presented as unusual, but as we later learn, perfectly natural. They seem
> mysterious and strange to Mr. Dursley only because he and his family, and the
> "Muggle" community in general, refuse to acknowledge them as a part of
> life. . . . Perhaps by way of emphasizing this point, Rowling avoids depicting
> Hogwarts . . . as mysterious in any deeper way than that it is unknown to
> Harry. (203)

In other words, *Harry Potter* has the potential to foster and perhaps even
inspire fantasies about a secret culture where no one is "normal," and difference is "natural," as the reader understands normal and natural to be.

In her study of *Harry Potter*'s representations of nonnormative masculinities,
Wannamaker similarly argues that the books' portrayals of the separation

between normal and abnormal "have profound meaning for child readers who feel like freaks" (133). She describes the outcome of a survey of "75 gay male fans of the *Wizard of Oz* stories," the majority of whom had been fans since childhood. Based on the results of the survey, the author postulated that "gay men are attracted to Oz from a very early age because of the escape from the everyday, normal world that the stories represent. . . . that welcomes them and their supposed 'abnormalness' " (133). Wannamaker concludes, "Boys (both heterosexual and homosexual) who do not easily conform to hegemonic versions of masculinity also may find comfort in the 'abnormal' Wizarding world of the *Harry Potter* novels" (133).

Therefore, identifying with Harry may render the novels quite a different book for queer readers than for others. In fact, as the next section will show, quite beyond highlighting a message of tolerating or accepting difference, reading queerly makes possible a pervasive critique of normalcy in these books. Thus, queering *Harry Potter* has the potential to invite readers to imagine a spectrum of strategies and subjectivities, especially queer youth who may have few resources and no role models for anything other than heteronormativity.

*   *   *

What queer or proto-queer child readers of *Harry Potter* may only vaguely yearn for (or desire to escape), the adult queer reader may be able to name more concretely.[8] The book's first chapter, which introduces Harry's relatives, immediately establishes "normal" as unlikable, boring, hypocritical, shallow, and cruel: "Mr. and Mrs. Dursley, of number four, Privet Drive, were proud to say they were perfectly normal, thank you very much" (Rowling *Sorcerer's* 1). Harry's uncle is unimaginative: "Mr. Dursley always sat with his back to the window in his office" (3); judgmental: "Mr. Dursley couldn't bear people who dressed in funny clothes" (3); and suspicious of difference: "Oh, these people's minds work in strange ways, Petunia," Uncle Vernon informs his wife, "they're not like you and me" (40).

Queer readers can feel particularly sympathetic toward Harry because this normal world, the place where Harry doesn't fit, is a wizardphobic world upheld by peer pressure and the rejection of difference, which is feared and believed to be contagious. Most "normal" people know nothing of the wizarding world; it is invisible. Those who do know of it, like the Dursleys, wish they didn't. In fact, the Dursleys force Harry to live in the cupboard, or closet under the stairs, and in social situations they often pretend he, indeed all wizards, doesn't exist. For example:

> Mrs. Dursley pretended she didn't have a sister, because her sister and her good-
> for-nothing husband were as unDursleyish as it was possible to be. The Dursleys

shuddered to think what the neighbors would say if the Potters arrived in the
street. . . . they didn't want Dudley mixing with a child like that. (2)

It is clear in subsequent novels that the Dursleys will never accept Harry: the
first chapter of the second book, *Harry Potter and the Chamber of Secrets*,
states, "as far as they were concerned, having a wizard in the family was a matter of deepest shame" (4); while book three, *Harry Potter and the Prisoner of
Azkaban*, explains early on that because the Dursleys "lived in terror" of anyone discovering that Harry attends a wizarding school, they lock away all his
magic-related possessions, and "forbid him to talk to the neighbors" (2–3).

Moreover, the novels contain frequent examples where perceiving oneself
as normal is marked by self-righteousness and the use of hate speech: Harry's
Aunt says of his mother, "I was the only one who saw her for what she was—
a freak!," and of him, "I knew you'd be just the same, just as strange, just as—
as—*abnormal*" (Rowling *Sorcerer's* 53). The fourth book, *Harry Potter and the
Global of Fire*, explains that because "[the Dursleys] hated and despised magic
in any form. . . . Harry was about as welcome in their house as dry rot" (19).
In language reminiscent of homophobic parental response and aversion therapy, the Dursleys think that Harry's developing self-knowledge apropos
magic might engender "dangerous ideas" (Rowling *Sorcerer's* 26), that it is
simply "dangerous nonsense" (36), and "probably nothing a good beating
wouldn't have cured" (56).

Where magic is not addressed in hate speech, it is unspeakable: both identity
and behavior that dare not speak its name. For example, Harry is not told of
his magical birthright and his uncle can't bring himself to name the practice
of the art, even in an adult-only conversation with his wife, where he blusters
about Harry's mother having magical abilities, "Well, I just thought . . .
maybe . . . it was something to do with . . . you know . . . *her* crowd"
(Rowling *Sorcerer's* 7). Such silencing, in every depiction of Harry's life with
his relatives, attempts to teach Harry the lesson that he should not ask questions about anything, especially where difference, and his parents (the root of
his difference), are concerned. "For years, Aunt Petunia and Uncle Vernon
had hoped that if they kept Harry as downtrodden as possible, they would be
able to squash the magic out of him" (Rowling *Prisoner* 2). Thus Harry is not
allowed to think critically, to question the status quo. One could even stretch
the queer metaphor so far as to argue that for Harry, like for gay men and
women, all men and women in the age of HIV/AIDS, that Silence=Death.
After all, if Harry did not eventually learn about the evil Lord Voldemort, he
would not have known how to protect himself from the dangers of the wizarding world, even as he explored its pleasures. The reader suspects, however,
that this would not have made much difference to his wizardphobic aunt and
uncle. If his parents' unfortunate demise is any indication, had Lord

Voldemort also succeeded in killing Harry, Aunt Petunia and Uncle Vernon would probably have said he deserved to die.

Notably, the *Harry Potter* novels provide the reader with, indeed, *advocate* a subculture that critiques the values and practices of the "normal" world. To begin, the wizarding underworld is complete, and has an understanding of itself as such. Hagrid, the hirsute, oversized groundskeeper at Hogwarts, can't wait to tell Harry "About *our* world, I mean. Your world. My world. *Your parents' world*" (Rowling *Sorcerer's* 50). With its own money, sports, history, ethics, fashion, and food, the world of *Harry Potter* offers a tantalizing package for readers who might fantasize about a comprehensive universe, not just a "lifestyle" that is marginal to an unfriendly "norm." Queering *Harry Potter* becomes, in this sense, part sociopolitical vision.

Furthermore, *Harry Potter* performs an ironic critique of dominant ideology, not only in the creation of a completely self-sufficient subculture, but in its representation of the magical underworld's response to the everyday world. As Judith Butler explains, queer is critically disruptive of an arbitrary yet powerful status quo that "Others" and shames marginalized groups and names them deviant. Thus, "The term 'queer' has operated as one linguistic practice whose purpose has been the shaming of the subject it names, or, rather, the producing of a subject *through* that shaming interpellation" (*BTM* 226). In this spirit, and through the inversion of the self-Other binary that Harry's relatives use to discriminate against wizards and mark them as deviant, the dominant, normative group is derisively nicknamed by the subordinate group. "Muggle. . . it's what we call nonmagic folk like them" Hagrid says (Rowling *Sorcerer's* 53). In fact, in the wizard world, Muggles are often unmentionable, as Harry learns from his new friend, Ron, "I think Mum's got a second cousin who's an accountant, but we never talk about him" (99).

In addition, much like the practice of camp, in which an exaggerated performance of gender denaturalizes assumptions concerning the biological basis of the sex-gender system, the inhabitants of Hogwarts expose the normalcy of the nonmagical world as arbitrarily constructed. Throughout the novels, Harry's friends ask him about Muggle practices and Muggle things like money, washing dishes, and driving cars. Even photography becomes a way to comment on the relationship between and assumptions among the dominant and the marginal; Ron can't believe that in "the Muggle world, people just stay put in photos. 'Do they? What, they don't move at all?' Ron sounded amazed. '*Weird!*' " (Rowling *Sorcerer's* 103). Thus, even while "regular people" like the Dursleys think wizards are abnormal, the somewhat separatist wizard world is not above a little hierarchical discrimination itself in the way it views the (inverted) binaries in which it find itself a part. Such inversions of the normal at the expense of those in the status quo, especially for readers familiar with drag shows and other ironic forms of queer humor, would invite associations between the wizarding subculture on the one hand and LGBT subcultures on the other.

For Harry and the wizarding world, LGBT readers may notice, coming into identity as a wizard in many ways parallels the rhetoric of the closet and the process of coming out. For example, many of the wizards feel their safety would be jeopardized if they don't maintain a low profile. Professor McGonagall, whose surname recalls Britain's long history of marginalizing the Irish, is afraid of wizards being too out: "People are being downright careless, out on the streets in broad daylight," she frets at the beginning of the first book, "not even dressed in Muggle clothes, swapping rumors" (Rowling *Sorcerer's* 10). Meanwhile, Harry's reaction while coming to terms with his nonnormative identity is a mix of fear, of putting together and making new sense of "clues" in his past, and most of all, of relief: "Harry felt a great leap of excitement. He didn't know what he was going to—but it had to be better than what he was leaving behind" (98). He embraces his identity, and the world suddenly looks different, especially the realization that "we are everywhere," that the Muggle world is filled with wizards and wizard things. "This was just an ordinary street full of ordinary people," Harry muses on his first trip to London and the Wizard Bank. "Could there really be piles of wizard gold buried miles beneath them?" (68). Even after he's been training at the school for four years, an outing to The Quidditch World Cup provides Harry with a moment of delight, "It was only just dawning on Harry how many witches and wizards there must be in the world" (Rowling *Goblet* 81).

Harry's first days at school even involve the exchange of coming out narratives—the children discuss who always knew they were a wizard, whose parents are also wizards, who has already experimented with magic, and who has only fantasized about it. Sharing these stories makes Harry feel more at ease with his new identity, and Harry is especially relieved to find that not everyone always knew exactly why and how they were different from other people: "Lots of people were from Muggle families, and like him, didn't have any idea they were witches and wizards" (Rowling *Sorcerer's* 154).

All of these textual events could have particularly poignant resonances for readers who have, themselves, experienced closeting, come to terms with new identities and shared coming out stories. In a particularly amusing turn of events, the queer-ing reader will even discover that Harry, even before he has a name for the source of his difference, has his own wizarding equivalent of gaydar:

> Yet sometimes he thought . . . that strangers in the street seemed to know him. . . . A tiny man in a violet top hat had bowed to him once while out shopping . . . . A wild-looking old woman dressed all in green had waved merrily at him once on a bus. A bald man in a very long purple coat had actually

shaken his hand in the street the other day and then walked away without a word. (Rowling *Sorcerer's* 30)

Thus, *Harry Potter* assures the reader that there are strategies by which those who are Othered can recognize and support one another.

In other words, the *Harry Potter* books can be read as valorizing difference. Notably, the wizarding world of Hogwarts School and related environs can be seen as an apt metaphor for a full spectrum of queer existence; Hogwarts is a diverse place—occupied by students and teachers of many ethnicities and differing physical appearances—where ghosts, animals, giants, half-breeds, and other nonnormative characters co-exist as wizards in relative acceptance of one another. A moment that is exemplary of this diversity occurs after Harry's first Sorting Ceremony, when Dumbledore invites everyone to join in singing the school song. "Everyone pick your favorite tune," he says, "and off we go!" (Rowling *Sorcerer's* 127). The narrator notes that "Everyone finished the song at different times" (128). I might add that the song would always be in flux as well, like queer notions of sex and gender, resisting concrete, absolute definition and form, since each time there might be different participants or singers might pick different songs. Yet the headmaster approves, in fact is moved to tears, "Ah, music," he intones expansively as the diverse symphony draws to a close. "A magic beyond all we do here!" (128). Thus, the books teach that claiming a nonnormative identity is no cause for shame, that power is gained when subordinated persons gather together for collective learning and action, and that diversity can be productive and should not be viewed with fear.

For these and other reasons I disagree with readings that dismiss the *Harry Potter* series as assimilationist in its sexual and gender politics, such as Tison Pugh and David Wallace's critique that "Harry Potter offers itself as a series of queer texts, yet their queerness never fully overcomes their investment in cultural normativity" (261). Pugh and Wallace are not content with Michael Bronski's observations, which, like the ones I have been making, suggest that the books' "celebration of a deviant, nonconformist, renegade identity invite queer readings (in the broadest sense of the term)" (Bronski, in Pugh and Wallace 262). Instead, Pugh and Wallace contend that, in *Harry Potter*, "nonnormative sexual identities are completely absent, possible queer-affirming readings are problematized, women and girls are presented in subservient and sexualized roles, and Harry's own character is forced into a narrow action-hero role that requires the death or removal of any competitors" (275). Pugh and Wallace overstate the case; they dismiss out of hand the kinds of things I have been calling attention to in this section: the series' subtle (and sometimes not-so-subtle) mode of critiquing normalcy, including norms of sexuality and gender.

For instance, the final book of the series (not yet published at the time of Pugh and Wallace's writing) strongly illustrates many of the characters performing acts that complicate traditional representations of gender (while the previous books perhaps do so more subtly).[9] Ginny and Mrs. Weasley, Luna and, especially, Hermione, exhibit great heroism and act on their own agency: standing firm in their convictions, finding solutions others cannot, and dueling with the dark forces in ways that are far from conventional femininity. They do, certainly, serve alongside other characters, but contra to what Pugh and Wallace suggest, they are agents, not objects; they do not act merely in the service of the men. Rather, Hermione and the other unconventional girls and women who stand with Harry, function, like Dumbledore and some of the male characters as well, to promote Rowling's message that being a lone hero is not the way to battle Voldemort, and that justice is best attained when sought through friendship and love. Among Harry's many companions and advisors, he is drawn to courageous women who are intellectual (Hermione), athletic (Ginny), and extremely eccentric (Luna and Tonks); the men in his life include one who wears dresses and heels (Dumbledore), a half-giant wielding a pink umbrella (Hagrid), a werewolf (Remus), a shaggy dog (Sirius), and a nerdy, sensitive boy who relates best to plants (Neville). "You don't have to do everything alone, Harry," Hermione reminds us (Rowling *Deathly* 583). Indeed, gender stereotypes seem, in the novels, most associated with the self-serving men and women who the novel clearly delineates as Harry's enemies and who have no sense of working for justice or the greater good: the narrow minded conventionality of the Dursley family, the violent racism and patriarchal bullying of Lucius and Draco Malfoy, and, despite her pink sweaters and fuzzy kittens, the rigid, self-righteous cruelty of Doris Umbridge.

Finally, no consideration of potentially queer readings of these novels would be complete without considering Harry's relationships with his two best friends, Ron and Hermione. As numerous scholars of queer spectatorship have noted, gay and lesbian consumers of visual and written culture often consciously or subconsciously rewrite the plots of movies, plays, musicals, and books. In queerly resistant readings, same-sex relationships that might, to others, appear secondary to the plot, take precedence over the heterosexual romance and/or adventure narrative. Especially given the many literary representations of homoeroticism within English school boy friendships (Dickens's *David Copperfield* and Hughes's *Tom Brown's Schooldays*, for example), Harry's extremely close relationship with Ron, the friend in whom he confides absolutely everything, even when it gets him in trouble, is easily read as a bromance that could provide opportunities for a reader's queer identification and fantasy. Similarly, a queer reading of the text might focus upon brainy Hermione's relationship with Professor McGonagall, especially in the

240 JILL R. EHNENN

later books, when Hermione enjoys private tutorials with her female mentor,
who teaches her skills that must be kept secret from everyone else.
Alternatively, a lesbian reader's cross-gender identification with Harry opens
space for the kind of imaginative cross-dressing and gender-bender romantic
tension which has its roots in both Shakespeare and Restoration Drama, as
Harry's (or Harriet's?) relationship with Hermione shifts from love-hate banter, to taking turns saving each other, to real and lasting affection.

Such homoerotic readings of *Harry Potter*'s cast of characters have been
suggested to some degree by campy responses to the books, especially early
on, in the queer press (Bronski; Croft; Hari; Mersmann). More recently,
Karin Westman has addressed Rowling's outing of Dumbledore; her analysis
contextualizes Dumbledore's intense youthful passion for the dark wizard,
Grindlewald, vis-à-vis the series' ongoing treatment of the uses and abuses of
the power of love. She concludes, ". . . Rowling's revelation of Dumbledore's
desire prompts us to focus not just on the object of his affection but the type
of affection it represents—and how we can best wield the power of love not
only for ourselves, but for our world" (197).

Surprisingly, although extended analyses of other potentially homoerotic
dynamics within the *Harry Potter* novels are thus far absent from queer scholarship, such queer readings are an extremely diverse and powerful presence within
online fanfiction. In fact, slash fiction—fanfiction that imagines and develops
a romantic or sexual encounter between characters of the same sex—is, according to Catherine Tosenberger, "one of the most popular genres of Potter fanfiction."[10] Slash originated with 1970s *Star Trek* fans (mostly straight women)
creating gay scenarios between Kirk and Spock (K/S); but the form is now practiced by fans of all sexualities. A quick google of Harry Potter fanfiction sites
reveals a virtual explosion of possible pairings, among them Harry/Ron,
Harry/Draco, Remus/Sirius, Hermione/Ginny, Hermione/ McGonagall, and
"Grindledore" (Dumbledore/Grindlewald). Slash is undeniably creative,
reflecting the reader's own fantasies; but especially in the examples defined by
the fans as "canon," slash also often reflects an erotic subtext that is visible to
particular readers. As J.K. Rowling mentioned herself, when pressed during the
Carnegie Hall interview where she outed Dumbledore and Grindlewald, "I
think a child will see a friendship and I think a sensitive adult may well understand that it was an infatuation" (Tosenberger, "Homosexuality" 187). Thus, as
Catherine Tosenberger's meticulous and thoughtful analysis of the phenomenon illustrates, slash is yet another example of the extent to which Pugh and
Wallace's reading of the series as fundamentally heteronormative just does not
seem to reflect many readers' engagement with the texts. Tosenberger observes
that "Potter fandom is an arena in which fans of all ages, genders, and sexual
orientations can tell stories to satisfy their own desires" ("Oh My" 202). The
epilogue of the final book of the series may conclude by cataloging the characters'

heterosexual marriages and children; but between the 4000 or so pages of story, overall, and the reader's own desires and creativity, *Harry Potter* provides ample fodder for queer imaginings.

*   *   *

I don't believe that any of this is necessarily intentional on Rowling's part, of course; I want to be clear that I'm not arguing that Harry is, indeed, a lesbian, or a gay man. But the text definitely invites a host of queer appropriations. And Harry is in grand company: from Dorothy, Peppermint Patty, Laverne and Shirley, and James Dean to the more recent Tinky Winky, Xena, Pee Wee, Buffy, Madonna, Martha Stewart, and of course, Sponge Bob and Lady Gaga. Even with the increased visibility of gay and lesbian characters on television series in the past decade since *Harry Potter* first burst onto the scene—*Queer as Folk*, *The L-Word*, Kurt on *Glee*, Marshall on *The United State of Tara*, and Justin on *Ugly Betty*, to name just a few—it seems unlikely that queers will renounce the pleasures of fantasizing about a world that contains more folks like them, simply because mainstream media has thrown them a few bones. In fact, there's a dazzling array of straight popular culture as queer iconography, if the campy trinkets sold in gay-lesbian bookstores and at Pride Festivals are any indication.

Beyond the provocative theories of Dick Hebdige, and following him, Alexandra Chasin, that such commodities help to assimilate marginalized subcultures into capitalism, thereby watering down their subversive power, these queered artifacts do complex cultural work, I think. They begin to denaturalize hegemonic ways of perceiving identity and identity categories. Simultaneously, they function as markers of and rallying points for identity politics, as a way to laugh in the wake of hatred and pain, and, when detected, as thorns of varying sizes in the sides of the far Christian Right and other homophobes. There's even a series of buttons and bumper stickers that play on Pat Robertson's infamous statement on feminism: "Sorry I missed church. I was busy practicing witchcraft and becoming a lesbian." Well, watch out, Pat. Here comes Harry Potter. And he (or is it she?)'s got a stock of wizarding supplies, a line of action figures, and a whole generation of children behind her!

Which seems precisely to be the problem, as the Religious Right have argued, their strenuous objections to Harry and friends growing louder and more prolific with each new book in the series.[11] The problem, as described by Kimbra Gish, is that witchcraft and sorcery are forbidden by the Bible and "[W]e believe witches are real. . . . witchcraft is as real to us as any religion" (263). Accordingly, the American Library Association reports that requests to censor *Harry Potter* on religious grounds have made it number one on the list of most challenged books of the 2000–2009 decade ("Top"); and the Internet is packed with sites dedicated to anti-Rowling warnings. Some opponents, including the Southern Baptist Convention, Campus Crusade for Christ, and those voicing their opinions on websites belonging to Focus on the Family and TraditionalValues.org, argue, like Gish, that the Rowling series makes children more open-minded and curious about the occult, including Wicca, and thereby should be read with caution and frequent parental intervention.[12] The oft-cited Richard Abanes's *Harry Potter and the Bible: The Menace Behind the Magick* argues against "Potterethics"—a subjective, context-based ethics instead of abiding by Christian ethics stated in the Bible. Abanes objects to the fact that *Harry Potter*'s characters, both students and teachers, frequently break rules; he claims and takes offense that Muggles can be read as Christians (250); and he asserts that allusions to witchcraft could "easily stir a child's curiosity about occultism—perhaps enough for that child to one day dabble in it" (24). Some of these naysayers caution that *Harry Potter* is a giant step in preparing the world for divination and witchcraft, a kind of wizarding John the Baptist primer that will prepare the way for the Antichrist; the following is a representative example: "Without question I believe the Harry Potter series is a creation of hell helping prepare the younger generation to welcome the Biblical prophecies of demons and devils led by Lucifer himself" (Chambers). Meanwhile, a small California-based operation, Jeremiah Films, has even released a documentary video, *Harry Potter: Witchcraft Repackaged*, which asserts that the Potter books promote radical feminism and homosexuality, because, the film argues, these things are integral to the practice of Wicca. I'm sure these assertions come as a big surprise to many Wiccans, homosexuals, and radical feminists; but hey, with this great three-abominations-for-the-price-of-one deal, I'm sure kids will be defecting from the mainstream faster than they can say Quidditch!

Seriously, what is particularly interesting about the anti-Harry movement is that it does invoke the curious yet pervasive discourse that links together all forms of witchcraft (Wicca, paganism, etc.), homosexuality, and feminism. We also saw this discursive association in Jerry Falwell's response to the September 11 terrorist bombing of the World Trade Center when he said,

> I really believe that the pagans, and the abortionists, and the feminists, and the gays and the lesbians . . . the ACLU, People for the American Way, all of them who have tried to secularize America. I point the finger in their face and say, "you helped this happen."

The antidote to the collective sins that Falwell and his ilk believe have and will continue to induce apocalyptic consequences (even though he recanted the above statement) is, of course, Christian fundamentalism. Notably, once Rowling revealed to the Carnegie Hall audience member who had asked about Dumbledore's romantic history that she had always thought of the headmaster as gay, those on the Religious Right who had been trying to censor the series quickly added Dumbledore to the list of reasons why the books are dangerous. Berit Kjos, a Christian author who had taken to task religious institutes who use the series to illustrate Christian allegories writes, "My first response was 'Thank you, Lord,' because this helps us show others that these books should not be used in the churches to illustrate Christianity. Because Dumbledore has been revealed as a homosexual, it helps me communicate my message" (Mudhar). Linda Harvey, president of *Mission America*, which "monitors both the homosexual agenda directed at children as well as paganism among American youth" agrees that Christians should not permit their children to engage in "hero-worship of an 'out' homosexual. . . . An agenda seems to be lurking," she writes, "The link between pagan/occult spirituality and outlaw sexuality has always been strong, one more reason to keep impressionable kids away from the increasingly weird genre of 'fantasy' books and movies" (Harvey).

So, let us probe how *Harry Potter* fuels this association between two marginal positions by a third—this easy coupling of witchcraft (or Wicca or paganism) and homosexuality by Christian fundamentalist discourse.[13] The Religious Right believes the books really will increase interest in the occult, and also asserts that clear associations exist between witches and homosexuals, with a few Rowling critics stating outright (and transitional properties of logic stating implicitly) that *Harry Potter* will tempt readers to both witchcraft *and* homosexuality. (Albeit without observing, with Alison Bechdel, that Harry Potter looks like a lesbian.) So, if LGBT readers find themselves queering *Harry Potter*, thereby recognizing a parallel of some utility between two positions outside of the American mainstream, does this recognition merely acknowledge as I have, above, that a magical underworld could function as an obvious and useful literary metaphor for LGBT subcultures? Or, does this queering reflect and subvert far Right assumptions that Wicca and homosexuality are associated with and/or precursors of one another? These are chicken and egg questions, and largely, I pose them rhetorically. Still, we see that a mainstream cultural artifact has been appropriated simultaneously by two groups on opposite margins: one conservative and one radical. And, we see that both conservative and radical readings of this text rely upon—through a causal claim for the former, and the play of signifiers for the latter—the notion that witches and queers are somehow related—a *real* assertion for the former, and a *metaphorical* one for the latter.

Interestingly, the fundamentalist war on *Harry Potter* doesn't extend to other popular children's stories that feature magic—texts such as L. Frank Baum's *The Wonderful Wizard of Oz*, C.S. Lewis's *The Chronicles of Narnia*, and J.R.R. Tolkien's *Lord of the Rings* trilogy.[14] Both Tolkien and Lewis have been in the public eye this past decade, with *The Lord of the Rings: The*

Fellowship of the Ring opening in movie theaters only a month after *Harry Potter and the Sorcerer's Stone* and *The Chronicles of Narnia: The Lion, the Witch and the Wardrobe* four years later. Thus, it is not surprising that the mainstream press has begun to explore what makes representations of magic in children's fiction threatening in one book but not in another (Weiss; Paulson). Although a very small percentage of fundamentalists do find fault with all these children's stories, those interviewed by the media overwhelmingly stress the fact that Lewis was a theologian and Tolkien a devout convert to Catholicism, and that both series, unlike *Harry Potter*, are filled with strong Christian allegory. Thus, they conclude, these magical tales will not seduce child readers to become pagans . . . or perverts.

Beyond these explanations in the popular press, however, I find other contrasts between the children's books—contrasts that offer cogent suggestions about why Christian fundamentalists denounce Rowling while embracing Lewis and Tolkien. These differences also provide some insight about the discursive linkage of magic and homosexuality so pervasive in Christian fundamentalist rhetoric and appropriated to humorous effect by queers. First, however, I would like to posit, somewhat as a given, that nonthreatening magical tales seem to take on one of two incarnations. Some, like the traditional fairy tales discussed earlier (and addressed by Bruno Bettelheim), take place more or less *in* the real world and feature an outsider who eventually assimilates into the dominant order. Such is the case in the movie *The Wizard of Oz*, where we find that Dorothy's colorful, magical world was a dream, and the doubling of characters in Kansas and in Oz teach her useful lessons, including reinforcing that "there's no place like home." Or, nonthreatening magical tales take place in a world marked completely Other: one with no plot ties to, yet with significant allegorical parallels with, reality, especially the moral tenets of mainstream culture. This is the case in *The Lord of the Rings*, a novel with a setting completely separate from our own; there is no "real world," although there are real parallels to Christian ideology.

Harry Potter's wizarding realm, unlike settings of traditional fairy tales, is a distinct subculture; in essence, it is another world. Yet although *Harry Potter's* world is, for the most part, independent of the dominant culture, at times it does interact with the "real" Muggle world—wizards living secretly among Muggles, and a Ministry of Magic "to keep it from the Muggles that there's still witches an' wizards up an' down the country" (Rowling *Sorcerer's* 65). This interaction with normal life is one of the things that makes *Harry Potter* significantly different from (and more threatening than) the other magical stories like *The Wizard of Oz* or *The Lord of the Rings*. Perhaps "worlding" in Lewis's tales come closest to *Harry Potter*, with Peter, Susan, Edmund, and Lucy's entrance into Narnia through wardrobes, pictures, and train stations bearing similarities to Harry's jumping onto an invisible train platform in order to catch the Hogwarts Express. But, like Tolkien's novels, the Narnia stories are so obviously filled with Christian allegory they create no threat for Christian fundamentalists; indeed, magic in Narnia often resembles miracles in the Bible.

Because *Harry Potter*'s wizarding subculture interacts with dominant culture, it seems more real than worlds like Narnia or Middle Earth. Further, as Routledge asserts, Rowling's representation of Harry's world depends stylistically on realism; therefore, magic in the *Harry Potter* books seems incidental— perfectly natural and normal. And finally, the overwhelming quantities and varieties of Potter-phernalia available for purchase helps to naturalize and normalize Harry's magical world as well, once again following Hebdige and Chasin's assertions that capitalism helps to assimilate subcultures into the mainstream—that commodification minimizes a subculture's subversive power. These three characteristics of *Harry Potter*, taken together, initiate a shift in the way magic is perceived by the reader: (1) Elements in the plot, textual realism, and Pottermania, especially Potter merchandise, concretize and naturalize, through *Harry Potter*, representations of something (magic) that fundamentalist readers believe to be transgressive. (2) As *Harry Potter* is concretized and naturalized, magic moves away from the marginal status automatically conveyed upon things that aren't natural or real, and closer to normal, closer to center. And (3), once closer to the normal, *Harry Potter* and magic become even *more* subject to criteria by which fundamentalists scrutinize other aspects of the "real" world. Of course, it fails the judgment to which "normal" life is subjected, and is viewed by fundamentalists to be even more transgressive, more threatening. *Harry Potter* and Pottermania thus create a dynamic that pushes "magic" closer to normal; but as "magic" becomes more naturalized so does its threat, which fundamentalist readers perceive not as representation or metaphor, but as real. Ironically, this is when the Right renders *their* ideological defense tangible—selling the aforementioned books, videos and TV airtime—creating their own line of anti-Harry commodities.

I believe that Potter-mania in its varied forms can help us to recognize that the question of the natural, and, in particular, *shifts* in the extent to which something is deemed natural may function as the linchpin between the perhaps unlikely bedfellows of magic and homosexuality in Christian fundamentalist rhetoric. Following René Girard's theories of mimetic desire and the monstrous double, or the idea that the more similar something is to you the more you hate and fear it, on a continuum of dominant and marginalized positions, both magic and homosexuality may pose the greatest threat to the Right in contexts where they appear, *not at their most freakish*, as one might expect, but where they appear to have moved closer to normal and natural, such as in the late twentieth-century mainstreaming of various pagan/Wiccan/New Age spiritualities and in recent increased visibility of and civil rights lobbying for LGBT persons. Let us review Girard's framework more closely, as it provides one useful way to theorize the backlash against the *Harry Potter* craze in the name of protecting Christian children against the occult, as well as a thoughtful explanation for the Fundamentalist argument that gay marriage will degrade the sanctity of heterosexual unions.

Girard explains deep-rooted conflict as mimetic desire, or rivalry over a desired object, which may be intangible, such as the notion of "being," especially "superior being," or as we might say in the case of Christians, pagans, and queers, "right being" or "acceptable being." Thus, "[i]n human relationships words like *sameness* and *similarity* evoke an image of harmony. If we have the same tastes and like the same things, surely we are bound to get along. But what will happen when we share the same desires?" (146). According to Girard, the mimetic aspects of desire result in contradictory signals: "Man cannot respond to that universal human injunction 'Imitate me!' without almost immediately encountering an inexplicable counterorder: 'Don't imitate me!' (which really means, 'Do not appropriate *my* object')" (147). Girard continues, "When all differences have been eliminated and the similarity between the two figures has been achieved, we say that the antagonists are *doubles*" (159). For the purposes of my argument, this is the point when magic (or homosexuality) has shifted from the far margin and has made some progress toward mainstream acceptance, thereby intensifying its position as rival to the group on the Right, who similarly have a stake in the definition of "acceptable" or "right" being.

However, Girard observes, to insure that social bonding occurs within a group, the I/Other binary must be reestablished. To this end, the group unanimously reasserts the double as monstrous, and violence against that double, or sacrificial victim, substitutes for and permanently expunges violence from within (among) the group. This, then, correlates to the fundamentalist backlash against anyone who rivals their claim to define "being" yet has taken on the characteristics of the "double" by shifting closer to "normal" or "natural." Notably, in this case, this is also the point where *all doubles*—the various groups that have shifted from the (left) margin toward the norm—coalesce under fundamentalist rhetoric. Girard anticipates this dynamic as well:

> In the collective experience of the *monstrous double* the differences are not eliminated, but muddled and confused. All the doubles are interchangeable, although their basic similarity is never formally acknowledged. They thus occupy the equivocal middle ground between difference and unity that is indispensable to . . . the polarization of violence onto a single victim who substitutes for all the others. . . . The monstrous double, all monstrous doubles in the person of one—the "thousand headed dragon" of *The Bacchae*—becomes the object of unanimous violence. (161)

For those on the Christian Right like Jerry Falwell and Pat Robertson, then, the "thousand-headed dragon" finds its discursive identity in the marriage between magic (Wicca/paganism) and homosexuality (and radical feminism, etc.). And no small wonder, if we consider recent history in light of Girard: the past few decades have seen the most recent wave of Christian fundamentalism emerging and rising right alongside the emergence and gradual mainstreaming of Wiccan/pagan/New Age, LGBT, and feminist movements.

What else can we learn from this curious overlap of two ideologically opposed groups that have each found queerness in a story about magic and that are both simultaneously making their slow way toward the U.S. mainstream? Perhaps the Girardian dynamics that explain this phenomenon suggest we should revisit the notion of mimetic desire when formulating LGBT political action; Girard's theory has implications for some of the assumptions on which civil rights and anti-prejudice strategies are based. More often than not, activism is founded on the premise that if people talk to one another and find a point of commonality, then hate and violence will decrease and coalition building can occur. We are all familiar with the narrative: "I used to be a homophobe (racist, anti-Semite, etc.), but then I talked to a gay person (black person, Jew, etc.) and my attitudes changed when I realized we are not that different, after all." We are also all familiar with injunctions from the more conservative yet perhaps more politically powerful among us to "take small steps," to "work within the system for a place at the table" and to "act *normal.*" Efforts based on these narratives and injunctions can and do have successful outcomes, of course; marginalized groups assimilate, thereby moving into positions closer to dominant norms, or norms change such that those toward the margins are accommodated. Yet, sadly, activism grounded in communication and education does not always work, and one year's political triumphs get overturned the next. The Girardian dynamics traced above suggest these failures and repercussions are inevitable: sooner or later, at least some reassertion of the I/Other binary will occur, most likely in a violent fashion.

Queer theorists such as Gayle Rubin and Michael Warner eschew activism focused on mainstreaming and advocate more systemic change, arguing that as those closest to the norm gradually gain acceptance by virtue of demonstrating certain characteristics (straight behavior and dress, long-term monogamous partnerships, practicing vanilla sex but not talking about it), they actually reinscribe heteronormativity, by reifying its hierarchies and privileges. Meanwhile, Rubin and Warner contend, LGBT persons further toward the margins continue to be demonized and attacked. I agree with their observations, although I think it imperative for future studies and strategists to press the distinctions between "assimilating" and "appropriating." Moreover, following Girard, I'm not convinced that those closer to normal will have it any better in the long run. Harry never does become completely normal, even within the wizarding world; nor does he want to. Similarly, to some in the mainstream, leatherfolk, stone butches, and patrons of gloryholes will be scary; and to others, catered gay marriages and lesbian soccer moms will be scarier. Thus, we need to continue to theorize the varied dynamics that govern *all* forms and targets of queer oppression, even as we imagine new systems of social politics and ethics, and develop multiple and fluid strategies for putting those systems in place.

In order for the imbalances and abuses of power between the dominant and marginal to change in any meaningful and lasting way, neither assimilating into nor changing social norms will be enough. I'm not suggesting that we stop lobbying for legal assurance that our basic civil rights will be protected. But mainstream styles of LGBT politics can only take us so far. How can we reduce the risk of seeing our efforts reversed? What would a multivalent approach to social change entail? What should our priorities be? Can we envision new ways to combine and revamp the approaches that are familiar—assimilation, changing norms, reforming laws, the more radical styles of AIDS activism? Are there modes of activism we haven't tried, or even imagined yet? As many queer theorists have noted, the answers to these questions will be found only by rethinking the paradigms that currently regulate the existing sex/gender system. It will be necessary to rethink how sex/gender systems intersect with other mechanisms of oppression. It will be necessary to work with other groups, especially other groups on the margins.

I think it will also be necessary to realize that the way we conceive of the I/Other binary is one of culture's biggest problems, along with resistance to recognizing that the very concept of normal is arbitrary and dependent upon linear ways of thinking of being that perpetuate the way we think of the I/Other binary. The answer to the question, "What is natural" must become simply, as Harry begins to discover, "Difference is natural;" although *not* the kind of difference that fuels rampant individualism, but the kind of difference that permits multiple and hybrid ways of individual and collective being in the world. As long as our conceptions of human sexuality (indeed, any aspect of human experience) are dependent upon an axis that runs from what Foucault has termed the "limits of intelligibility" on the one end and the convergence of norms on the other, the specter of Girard's monstrous double will always loom large. Thus, LGBT and other marginalized persons need to find new strategies that will challenge the limits of intelligibility, and the regulatory systems that govern those limits, themselves.

*   *   *

I want to end with two very practical and somewhat related observations. First, to reiterate the obvious, queer and proto-queer kids are at risk; and queer youth growing up amid the homophobia of fundamentalist communities are particularly vulnerable. While we labor in the slow process of analyzing and changing the cultural institutions that perpetuate heterosexism and related violence structurally, we must not lose sight of the fact that the hazards our queer youth face are immediate and very real. Traditional family values (values, in fact, held by families like the Dursleys) can render the home a very dangerous place for queer kids—youth who face emotional and physical violence at the hands of their families and "concerned" counselors, clergy, and physicians—youth who may be driven to self-inflicted violence, or face other dangers if they run away. Thus, even while some may question the literary merit of children's fiction in general and *Harry Potter* in particular, and while we theorize the many ways that children's literature is often prescriptive, reinscribing values that uphold the status quo, we should not dismiss or belittle its potential for queer readers. For some, especially queer and proto-queer youth who feel isolated, a text like *Harry Potter* may constitute one of very few outlets for momentary solace amid heterosexist oppression, as well as an opportunity to begin to learn they can resist that oppression. *Harry Potter* is not a panacea for homophobia, but its place among other useful and interesting artifacts should not be underestimated in queer studies of cultural phenomena, especially where children and/or the formation of queer identity and practice are concerned.

Second, it strikes me as more than a little ironic that the fundamentalists' warnings—that reading *Harry Potter* will make children more curious about Othered religions and sexualities—are actually *not* illogical fears, despite the histrionic rhetoric. Personally, I think (and hope) that Rowling's texts, ultimately, *could* be instrumental in teaching children—all readers— to be more accepting of human diversity, and to make the world a more just place, even if it involves thinking outside of the box or breaking some rules. Another project could easily create a detailed resistant reading of *Harry Potter* that argues, alongside the Christian Right although with a different political agenda, that *Harry Potter is* a tool that encourages readers to challenge traditional beliefs about religion, sexuality, and lots of other things. Such a project could probably argue that the evil Lord Voldemort can be seen as a cautionary allegory for what ecofeminist philosopher Karen Warren calls "all isms of domination"—including religious fundamentalism, capitalism, racism, heterosexism, sexism, class-ism, ageism, and species-ism.

I'm not going to pursue this argument here, other than to point to the emergence of The Harry Potter Alliance, a registered nonprofit which appears to be the first ever fan-based philanthropic organization. The tagline on their website reads "The Harry Potter Alliance—The Weapon We Have Is Love" and their mission states:

> The HP Alliance takes a creative, outside of the box approach to activism by taking parallels from the *Harry Potter* books to educate and mobilize over 100,000 young people across the world on issues of social justice and personal empowerment. The result has been the building of a thriving, effective activist community that gets results, media attention, builds chapters, and opens the door to a new kind of activism that uses new media platforms in the most cutting edge ways. (*The HP*)[15]

The Alliance has, among other things, raised funds for the people of Darfur and Burma, donated 13,000 books all over the world, registered voters, made calls for marriage equality, and, most recently, was the recipient of a $250,000 Chase Community Giving Challenge on Facebook. Self-described as "Dumbledore's Army for the real world" the group's specific agenda is to:

—Work with partner NGOs in alerting the world to the dangers of global warming, poverty, and genocide.
—Work with our partners for equal rights regardless of race, gender, and sexuality.
—Encourage our members to hone the magic of their creativity in endeavoring to make the world a better place. (About)

Thus, clearly, the *Harry Potter* novels can encourage readers to keep pursuing strategies that will challenge those regulatory powers, or Foucauldian "politics of truth" that determine who and what we can be, as I concluded we must do at the end of the last section (32). In terms of queer inquiry, *Harry Potter* is most useful and holds the most promise in its potential to inspire readers to think in ways that will challenge, as Butler puts it, not just the "laws that govern our intelligibility, but ways of knowing, modes of truth, that forcibly define intelligibility" ("Doing" 621). Certainly, Rowling doesn't have all the details right; *Harry Potter* is by no means a coherent blueprint for queer political strategy or world vision, whatever that might be. What the book does achieve, however, is to support and fuel our *desire* for another world, not just one where persons on the margins are better tolerated, or even accepted, but a different world, with a more just politics of truth, altogether.

So let's make things perfectly queer. Magic may or may not be afoot in America, but there's definitely something very queer at Hogwarts. At least so far. The extent to which the last two *Harry Potter* movies and further commodification of the series will lend itself to queer reading remains to be seen, especially now that Harry has discovered the magic of adolescence. On the whole, I'm optimistic. If the movies have rendered some of the book's queer charm invisible, at least the Harry action figures still look like lesbians, at least to me. Certainly, The HP Alliance is inspiring. Meanwhile, among those clamoring in favor of or against *Harry Potter*, aside from Alison Bechdel and a few film reviews in the gay press, a large and recognizable queer voice, thus far, is strikingly absent. Here, I have advocated that it should not be. Beyond the simple literary pleasures that might result when the friends of Dorothy become friends of Harry, in these texts there is much to be appropriated with creativity, wit and heart, and useful metaphors to be unpacked. Most importantly perhaps, queer readers will recognize, in *Harry Potter*, the longing to imagine new kinds of worlds and ways of being in those worlds; and they will find assurance—assurance that there are realms of possibility beyond Harry's closet under the stairs.

NOTES

1. Bechdel has even occasionally recycled the successful visual Mo=Harry gag in *DTWOF* segments in subsequent years.
2. See Robin Bernstein.
3. Elizabeth D. Schafer reports, "Rowling's books were the first children's books included on the *New York Times' Bestseller* list since E.B. White's *Charlotte's Web* in 1952. Beginning on November 28, 1999, Rowling's three novels were ranked in the first three positions on the [list]" (14).
4. Although the international popularity of J.K. Rowling's books certainly helps to establish my project as the study of a powerful cultural artifact particular to our historical moment, my queering of *Harry Potter* should be understood solely as an assessment of potential LGBT appropriation in Western, particularly U.S., culture. Without information specific to LGBT experience and cultural politics in other areas of the world, I would not presume to extend my observations elsewhere, since the particularities of the relationship between dominant and marginal (and the role of queer and other subcultural voices) in other societies may vary greatly, as may the manner in which these categories are understood. That said, the varied responses to *Harry Potter* as an international sensation would make for interesting study, in its own right, perhaps beginning with a comparison of the cover art and illustrations used in the different international editions. (For the record, Harry still looks like a young butch dyke on most of the covers, in my opinion.)
5. This essay does not analyze the movies, which, although largely faithful to the original plot, do not present the characters in as much depth as the book. The flat characters and thin emotion of the movies, especially the early ones, as countless reviewers have noted, render it difficult for viewers to identify with and become invested in Harry and his friends in the same way that readers do. Thus the appeal for the kind of queer appropriation I address throughout this essay is much diluted, although by no means completely absent, as some reviews of the movie in the gay press indicate. See, for example, Mersmann.
6. See, among others, Schafer.

7. Drawing from recent theorizing about queer temporalities (Edelman, Halberstam) and queer phenomenology (Ahmed), Kathryn Bond Stockton's excellent and provocative *The Queer Child: Or, Growing Sideways in the Twentieth Century* argues for the queerness, at least in some sense, of all children in ways that similarly press the boundaries of traditional theorizing, such as Bettelheim's, about childhood.

8. For example, see Croft.

9. A fair amount of scholarship analyzes representations of gender in *Harry Potter*, especially in the earlier novels. For arguments that Rowling reinscribes traditional gender roles, see, for instance, Heilman and Mayes-Elma. Representative examples of contrasting arguments for nonhegemonic gender in the book include Lerer and Wannamaker.

10. See "Homosexuality" p. 200. Also see MacDonald.

11. For thoughtful summaries of the various religious-based positions for and against Harry Potter, see Cockrell, Gish, and Wagner.

12. See Neal for more on this position.

13. The extent to which extreme Christian fundamentalism might be considered marginal is debatable, given its increasing popularity and growing links to those in political power in the united States. That point will not be explored here. Still, the position Christian fundamentalists occupy is far from center, and frequently they position themselves as an oppressed minority.

14. Actually, L. Frank Baum's *The Wonderful World of Oz* was attacked by religious groups when it was first published. However, there seems to be no objections to it or the movie version, *The Wizard of Oz*, now, and the title doesn't even come up in detractors' criticism about *Harry Potter* and magic in children's books.

15. For more on the Harry Potter Alliance, see Jasiewicz.

WORKS CITED

Abanes, Richard. *Harry Potter and the Bible: The Menace Behind the Magick.* Camp Hill, PA: Horizon, 2001. Print.

"About." *The Harry Potter Alliance: The Weapon We Have Is Love!* The Harry Potter Alliance, n.d. Web. 18 July 2010. <http://www.thehpalliance.org/>.

Ahmed, Sara. *Queer Phenomenology: Orientations, Objects, Others.* Durham: Duke UP, 2006. Print.

"All-Time Box Office: World-Wide." *The Internet Movie Database.* IMDb.com, 4 Aug. 2010. Web. 18 July 2010. <http://www.imdb.com/boxoffice/alltimegross?region=world-wide>.

Baum, L. Frank. *The Wonderful Wizard of Oz.* New York: Signet, 2006. Print.

Bechdel, Alison. "Booked, #343." *Dykes and Sundry Other Carbon-Based Life-Forms to Look Out For.* Los Angeles: Alyson, 2003. Print.

Bernstein, Richard. "The Reality of the Fantasy in the Harry Potter Stories." *The New York Times.* 30 Nov. 1999. Web. 8 Nov. 2001. <http://www.cesnur.org/recens/potter_09.htm>.

Bernstein, Robin. "'Too Realistic' and 'Too Distorted': The Attack on Louise Fitzhugh's *Harriet the Spy* and the Gaze of the Queer Child." *Critical Matrix* 12.1-2 (2001): 26–47. Print.

Booth, Jenny, and Agencies. "J.K. Rowling Publishes Harry Potter Spin-Off." *The Times Online*. Times Newspapers, 1 Nov. 2007. Web. 18 July 2010. <http://entertainment.timesonline.co.uk/tol/arts_and_entertainment/books/article2784397.ece>.

Bronski. Michael. "There's Something About Harry." *ThePhoenix.com*. The Boston Phoenix, 27 June–3 July 2003. Web. 12 July 2010.

Butler, Judith. *Bodies that Matter: On the Discursive Limits of "Sex."* New York: Routledge, 1993. Print.

————. "Doing Justice to Someone: Sex Reassignment and Allegories of Transsexuality." *GLQ: A Journal of Lesbian and Gay Studies* 7.4 (2001): 621–36. Print.

Chasin, Alexandra. *Selling Out: The Gay and Lesbian Movement Goes to Market*. New York: Palgrave, 2000. Print.

Chambers, Joseph. "The Harry Potter Series a Vision of the Antichrist." *Paw Creek Ministries: Pastor Joseph Chambers*. 8 Nov. 2001. Web. <www.pawcreek.org> 26 Oct. 2009.

The Chronicles of Narnia: The Lion, the Witch and the Wardrobe. Dir. Andrew Adamson. Disney, 2005. Film.

Cockrell, Amanda. "Harry Potter and the Witch Hunters: A Social Context for the Attacks on *Harry Potter*." *The Journal of American Culture* 29.1 (March 2006): 24–30. Print.

Croft, Jay. "Harry Potter and Me: If We Could Wave a Magic Wand." *The Atlanta Journal-Constitution*. 16 Nov. 2001. Web. 17 Jan. 2002. <http://www.accessatlanta.com/ajc/opinion/croft/potter.html>,

Dickens, Charles. *David Copperfield*. London: Penguin, 2004. Print.

Doty, Alexander. *Making Things Perfectly Queer: Interpreting Mass Culture*. Minneapolis: U of Minnesota P, 1993. Print.

Edelman, Lee. *No Future: Queer Theory and the Death Drive*. Durham: Duke UP, 2004. Print.

"Everything You Might Want to Know." *J.K. Rowling Official Site*. Warner Bros. n.d. Web. 18 July 2010. <www.jkrowling.com>.

Falconer, Rachel. *The Crossover Novel: Contemporary Children's Fiction and Its Adult Readership*. New York: Routledge, 2009. Print.

"Falwell Apologizes to Gays, Feminists, Lesbians." *CNN.com/U.S*. Cable News Network, 14 Sept. 2001. Web. 8 Nov. 2001. <http://www/CNN.com/2001/US09/14/Falwell.apology/index.html>.

Foucault, Michel. "What Is Critique?" *The Politics of Truth*. Ed. Sylvère Lotringer and Lysa Hochroth. New York: Semiotext(e), 1997. Print.

Garner, Dwight. "Ten Years Later, Harry Potter Vanishes from the Best-Seller List." *Paper Cuts: A Blog about Books*. NY Times, 1 May 2008. Web. 2 Aug. 2010. <http://papercuts.blogs.nytimes.com/2008/05/01/ten-years-later-harry-potter-vanishes-from-the-best-seller-list/>.

254   JILL R. EHNENN

Girard, Renè. "From Mimetic Desire to the Monstrous Double." *Violence and the Sacred*. Trans. Patrick Gregory. Baltimore: Johns Hopkins UP, 1977. 143–68. Print.

Gish, Kimbra Wilder. "Hunting Down Harry Potter: An Exploration of Religious Concerns about Children's Literature." *The Horn Book Magazine* 76.3 (May/June 2000): 262–71. Print.

Grove, Martin A. "Box Office Analysis: 'Harry Potter' Breaks Records." *Hollywood.com*. Hollywood.com, 18 Nov. 2001. Web. 4 Aug. 2010. <http://www.hollywood.com/news/Box_Office_Analysis_Harry_Potter_breaks_records/1097810>.

Halberstam, Judith. *In a Queer Time and Place: Transgender Bodies, Subcultural Lives.* New York: NYU P, 2005. Print.

Halperin, David M. *Saint=Foucault: Towards a Gay Hagiography.* New York: Oxford UP, 1995. Print.

Hari, Johann. "Is Harry Potter Gay?," *Johann Hari.* N.p. 26 Nov. 2003. Web. 12 July 2010. <http://www.johannhari.com/2003/11/27/is-harry-potter-gay>.

Harry Potter and the Sorcerer's Stone. Dir. Chris Columbus. Warner, 2001. Film.

Harry Potter: Witchcraft Repackaged. Dir. And Perf. Caryl Matrisciana and Robert S. McGee. Jeremiah Films, 2001. Film.

Harvey, Linda. "Christian Parents: Stop Trusting Harry Potter." *WorldNetDaily.* WorldNetDaily.com, 24 Oct. 2007. Web. 17 July 2010. <http://www.wnd.com/news/article.asp?ARTICLE_ID=58299>.

Hebdige, Dick. *Subculture: The Meaning of Style.* London: Methuen, 1979. Print.

Heilman, Elizabeth E. "Blue Wizards and Pink Witches: Representations of Gender Identity and Power." *Harry Potter's World: Multidisciplinary Critical Perspectives.* Ed. Elizabeth E. Heilman. New York: Routledge, 2003. 221–39. Print.

"The HP Alliance." *The Harry Potter Alliance: The Weapon We Have Is Love!* The Harry Potter Alliance, n.d. Web. 18 July 2010. <http://www.thehpalliance.org/>.

Hughes, Thomas. *Tom Brown's School Days.* New York: Oxford World Press, 1999. Print.

Jasiewicz, Isia. "How Crazy Are Harry Potter Fans?" *Newsweek.* Newsweek, 14 July 2009.Web. 18 July 2010. <http://www.newsweek.com/2009/07/13/how-crazy-are-harry-potter-fans.html>.

"JK Rowling Outs Dumbledore as Gay." *BBC News.* BBC, 20 Oct. 2007. Web. 18 July 2010. <http://news.bbc.co.uk/2/hi/7053982.stm>.

Kroll, Luisa. "The World's Richest Self-Made Women." *Forbes.com.* Forbes Digital, 14 June 2010. Web. 2 Aug. 2010. <http://www.forbes.com/2010/06/14/richest-women-entrepreneur-billionaire-whitman-oprah-rowling.html>.

Lerer, Seth. *Children's Literature: A Reader's History from Aesop to Harry Potter.* Chicago: U Chicago P, 2008. Print.

Lewis, C.S. *The Chronicles of Narnia.* New York: Harper, 2001. Print.

The Lord of the Rings: The Fellowship of the Ring. Dir. Peter Jackson. New Line, 2001. Film.

MacDonald, Marianne. "Harry Potter and the Fan Fiction Phenom." *Gay and Lesbian Review.* 13.1 (2006): 28–30. Print.

Mayes-Elma, Ruthann. *Females and Harry Potter: Not All That Empowering.* Lanham, MA: Rowman and Littlefield, 2006. Print.

Mersmann, Andrew. "Harry Potter is Such a Homo." 17 Jan. 2002. Web. 2 Aug. 2010. http://gaydarradio.com/UserPortal/Article/Detail.aspx?ID=7696&sid=66

Mudhar, Raju. "Outing Dumbledore Sparks Fierce Debate." *TheStar.com.* Toronto Star, 23 Oct. 2007. Web. 12 July 2010. <http://www.thestar.com/entertainment/Books/article/269449>.

Neal, Connie. *What's a Christian to Do with Harry Potter?* Colorado Springs: Waterbrook, 2001. Print.

Paulson, Michael. "Christian Conservatives Prefer Frodo to Harry." *Boston Globe.* Globe Newspaper Company, 27 Dec. 2001. Web. 17 Jan. 2002.

Pugh, Tison, and David L. Wallace. "Heteronormative Heroism and Queering the School Story in J.K. Rowling's Harry Potter Series." *Children's Literature Association Quarterly* 31.3 (2006): 260–81. Print.

Routledge, Christopher. "Harry Potter and the Mystery of Ordinary Life." *Mystery in Children's Literature: From the Rational to the Supernatural.* Ed. Adrienne E. Gavin and Christopher Routledge. New York: Palgrave, 2001. 202-09. Print.

Rowling, J.K. *Harry Potter and the Chamber of Secrets.* New York: Scholastic, 1999. Print.

———. *Harry Potter and the Deathly Hallows.* New York: Scholastic, 2007. Print.

———. *Harry Potter and the Goblet of Fire.* New York: Scholastic, 2000. Print.

———. *Harry Potter and the Prisoner of Azkaban.* New York: Scholastic, 1999. Print.

———. *Harry Potter and the Sorcerer's Stone.* New York: Scholastic, 1998. Print.

Rubin, Gayle. "Thinking Sex: Notes for a Radical Theory of the Politics of Sexuality." *The Lesbian and Gay Studies Reader.* Ed. Henry Abelove, Michèle Aina Barale, and David M. Halperin. New York: Routledge, 1993. 3–44. Print.

Schafer, Elizabeth D. *Exploring Harry Potter.* Osprey FL: Beacham, 2000. Print.

Stockton, Kathryn Bond. *The Queer Child: Or Growing Sideways in the Twentieth Century.* Durham: Duke UP, 2009. Print.

Tolkien, J.R.R. *The Lord of the Rings Trilogy.* New York: Ballantine, 1971. Print.

"Top 100 Banned/Challenged Books: 2000–2009." *American Library Association.* ALA, n.d. Web. 18 July 2010. <http://www.ala.org/ala/issuesadvocacy/banned/frequentlychallenged/challengedbydecade/2000_2009/index.cfm>.

Tosenberger, Catherine. "Homosexuality at the Online Hogwarts: Harry Potter Slash Fanfiction." *Children's Literature.* 36 (2008): 185–207. Print.

———. "Oh My God, the Fanfiction!" *Children's Literature Association Quarterly* 33.2 (2008): 200–06. Print.

Wagner, Rachel. "Bewitching the Box Office: Harry Potter and Religious Controversy." *Journal of Religion and Film* 7.2 (2003): n.d. Web. 11 Aug. 2010.

Wannamaker, Annette. "Men in Cloaks and High-heeled Boots, Men Wielding Pink Umbrellas: Witchy Masculinities in the Harry Potter Novels." *The Looking Glass: New Perspectives on Children's Literature* 10.1 (2006). Web. 2 May 2010.

Warner, Michael. *The Trouble with Normal: Sex, Politics and the Ethics of Queer Life.* New York: Free Press, 1999. Print.

Warren, Karen J. *Ecofeminist Philosophy: A Western Perspective on What It Is and Why It Matters*. Lanham: Rowman, 2000. Print.

Weiss, Jeffrey. " 'Rings,' 'Potter' Delve into Complexities of Morality, Power, and Life's Choices." *The Dallas Morning News*. Dallasnews.com, 8 Jan. 2002. Web. 8 Jan. 2002.

Westman, Karin E. "The Weapon We Have Is Love." *Children's Literature Association Quarterly* 33.2 (2008): 193–99.

The Wizard of Oz. Dir. Victor Fleming. MGM, 1939. Film.

Zipes, Jack. *Sticks and Stones: The Troublesome Success of Children's Literature from Slovenly Peter to Harry Potter*. New York: Routledge, 2002. Print.

INDEX